CHAPTER 1
SPREADSHEET BASICS

SS3
OVERVIEW

SS4
ELECTRONIC SPREADSHEETS

SS5
GETTING STARTED
Starting Windows
Starting Microsoft Excel

SS11
UNDERSTANDING MICROSOFT EXCEL
The Microsoft Excel Window
The Workbook Window: Columns, Rows, and Cells
The Formula Bar
The Help Feature

SS20
OPERATING MENUS
Using a Menu Bar
Menu Indicators
Using a Control Menu
Using a Shortcut Menu

SS24
OPERATING COMMAND BUTTONS
Resizing Buttons
Toolbars

SS27
A QUICK START: THE BASICS
Setting the Default Drive
Entering Data
Saving a Workbook
Closing a Workbook
Creating a New Workbook
Opening a Workbook
Exiting Excel and Windows

SS34
CREATING A WORKBOOK
Constant Values and Formulas
Entering Constant Values and Formulas
The Recalculation Feature
Mathematical Operators

SS43
THE RANGE CONCEPT
Typing a Range for a Function
Pointing to a Range for a Function
Selecting a Range for Toolbar or Menu Commands

SS48
PRINTING A WORKSHEET
Printing to the Screen
Printing to a Printer
Printing a Selected Range

SS51
EDITING A WORKSHEET
Replacing Cell Contents
Inserting and Deleting Rows or Columns

CHAPTER 2
ENHANCING SPREADSHEETS

SS69
OVERVIEW

SS70
USING RANGES IN COMMANDS
Aligning Data
Adjusting Number Format
Copying Cells
Moving Cells
Transposing Cells
Using Range Names

SS95
RESETTING WORKSHEET DEFAULTS
Format
Alignment
Column Width

SS100
ADJUSTING COLUMN WIDTH
Changing Individual Column Width
Changing Width in a Column Range
Hiding and Unhiding Columns

SS106
ENHANCING A WORKSHEET WITH FONTS, COLORS AND LINES
Changing a Font
Changing Color
Adding Lines
Providing Additional Emphasis

SS115
CELL REFERENCES
Relative and Absolute References
Mixed References
Fixing Circular References

SS120
FUNCTIONS
Function Structure
A Function Sampler
Using the Function Wizard

SS125
MANAGING LARGE SPREADSHEETS
Freezing Panes
Splitting

SS129
PRINTING TECHNIQUES
Page Breaks
Page Setup Options

CHAPTER 3
ADVANCED SPREADSHEETS

SS146
OVERVIEW

SS146
PREPARING FOR THIS CHAPTER

SS148
MODULE 1: CHARTS
Creating a Chart

Manipulating a Chart
Editing Chart Parts
Chart Types
"Exploding" Data
Printing a Chart

SS166
MODULE 2: CONDITIONAL FUNCTIONS
The IF Function
Table Lookups—VLOOKUP and HLOOKUP

SS171
MODULE 3: DATA MANAGEMENT
Module 3A: Generating a Sequence of Numbers
Module 3B: Sorting Data
Module 3C: Creating a Data Distribution
Module 3D: Information Revtrieval— Data Queries
Module 3E: Using Data Functions

SS192
MODULE 4: MACROS
Creating a Macro
Running a Macro
Assigning a Macro
Adding Another Macro
Editing a Macro

SS200
MODULE 5: USING MULTIPLE WORKBOOKS
Switching Between Windows
Arranging Windows
Resizing Windows
Manipulating Data Between Workbooks

SS211
MODULE 6: USING MULTIPLE SHEETS
Using Sheet Tabs
Manipulating Data Between Sheets

SS219
MODULE 7: PROTECTING THE SPREADSHEET
Setting the Unprotected Range
Activating the Protection Feature

SS222
MODULE 8: SHARING DATA AMONG APPLICATIONS
Exporting and Importing
Exporting Data from Excel
Exporting Data into Excel
Linking Data from other Office Applications

APPENDIX
MICROSOFT EXCEL VERSION 5.0 FEATURE AND OPERATION REFERENCE

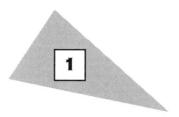

SPREADSHEETS WITH MICROSOFT EXCEL 5.0

SPREADSHEET BASICS: CREATING A WORKSHEET

OUTLINE

Overview

Electronic Spreadsheets

Getting Started
　Starting Windows
　Mouse and Keyboard
　　Operations
　Starting Microsoft Excel

Understand Microsoft Excel
　The Microsoft Excel Window
　The Workbook Window:
　　Columns, Rows, and
　　Cells
　The Formula Bar
　The Help Feature

Operating Menus
　Using a Menu Bar

　Menu Indicators
　Using a Control Menu
　Using a Shortcut Menu

Operating Command Buttons
　Resizing Buttons
　Toolbars

A Quick Start: The Basics
　Setting the Default Drive
　Entering Data
　Saving a Workbook
　Closing a Workbook
　Creating a New Workbook
　Opening a Workbook
　Exiting Microsoft Excel
　　Windows

Creating a Worksheet
　Constant Values and Formulas

Entering Constant Values and
　Formulas
The Recalculation Feature
Mathematical Operators

The Range Concept
　Typing a Range for a Function
　Pointing to a Range for a Function

Printing a Worksheet
　Printing to the Screen
　Printing to a Printer
　Printing a Selected Range

Editing a Worksheet
　Replacing Cell Contents
　Inserting and Deleting Rows or
　　Columns

OBJECTIVES

After completing this chapter you will be able to:

1. Explain the general capabilities of a spreadsheet program.
2. Describe the procedures to start and exit Microsoft Excel.
3. Explain the various components of the Microsoft Excel and workbook windows.
4. Explain the differences between a constant value and formula.
5. Enter data into a workbook, perform basic edits on the data, and save the workbook on a disk.
6. Insert and delete columns and rows.
7. Close a workbook, create a new workbook, open a file, and prepare a printed copy.

OVERVIEW

Chapter 1 introduces the concept of electronic spreadsheets by presenting the basic techniques for using Microsoft Excel, a well-known windows based spreadsheet package. First, you will learn how to start

Windows and Microsoft Excel, how to interpret the screen, and how to enter and save data. Once you have mastered these basics, you will examine constant values and formulas. Then, basic printing and editing will be introduced. Although this chapter is based on Microsoft Excel Version 5.0, many of the techniques discussed will work with earlier releases as well.

ELECTRONIC SPREADSHEETS

A computerized **spreadsheet** is the electronic equivalent of the multicolumned paper used by accountants. A spreadsheet, or **worksheet,** is used to display data in columnar (column and row) form. Spreadsheet programs are used to create balance sheets, payroll reports, income statements, and other financial documents. They allow users to enter, edit, and manipulate data in the form of words, numbers, and formulas. More important, spreadsheet programs include a recalculation feature, which automatically recalculates formulas when interdependent values are changed. This feature allows you to evaluate "What if?" questions by modifying values and seeing their mathematical consequences quickly and easily.

All modern spreadsheet programs are based on the original VisiCalc program created in the 1970s and thus are remarkably similar in features and layout. Today, Microsoft Excel is a widely used spreadsheet program. Microsoft Excel combines spreadsheet features with graphics and file management.

The instructions in this module pertain to Microsoft Excel Version 5.0. Microsoft Excel is a windows application based on a *graphical user interface,* or *GUI* (pronounced "gooey"), which uses symbols and menus instead of typewritten commands to help you communicate with the computer. It is similar to using a red traffic light to indicate "stop." Many GUI symbols and operations have become standard throughout the industry. This makes communicating with the computer more universal.

The GUI environment in which Microsoft Excel operates is called *Microsoft Windows.* In this environment, you work with rectangular boxes called windows and symbols (pictures) called icons.

Microsoft Excel is also a *What-You-See-Is-What-You-Get,* or *WYSIWYG* (pronounced "wizzy-wig"), electronic spreadsheet. This means that you work in a screen that resembles your final printed page. For example, if you create a column (bar) chart in your spreadsheet, the display on your screen will look like the chart that will appear on the final printed page.

Microsoft Excel's capabilities can be invoked by mouse or keyboard. This book will refer to mouse actions as the *Mouse Approach* and keystrokes as the *Keyboard Approach.* Note that only one method may be presented for some procedures.

Many keystrokes presented under the Keyboard Approach are *shortcut keys* (command keystrokes) common to most Windows applications. For example, pressing the Alt and F4 keys together will exit most Windows applications.

It is highly recommended that you use the Mouse Approach when operating Microsoft Excel for Windows. This approach is visually easier and sometimes quicker than the Keyboard Approach. In addition, this text will often refer to Microsoft Excel as simply "Excel."

CHAPTER 1   SPREADSHEET BASICS: CREATING A WORKSHEET   **SS5**

GETTING STARTED

Before you begin, be certain you have all the necessary tools: a hard disk or network that contains DOS, Windows, and Microsoft Excel for Windows, and a formatted diskette on which you will store the documents you create. It is assumed that you will be using Microsoft Excel on a hard-disk drive, although directions for networks are included.

STARTING WINDOWS

Before starting any Windows application, you must first start Windows. As mentioned earlier, in the Windows environment, you work in rectangular boxes called *windows*. A window that contains an application is called an *application window,* and a window that contains a document is called a *document window.* A window may also request or provide information to perform a task, in which case the window is called a dialog box.

USING A HARD-DISK DRIVE.   It is assumed that the Windows and Microsoft Excel programs are on your hard disk, which is identified as drive C. To start Windows, follow these steps:

1. **Boot the operating system**

If the Windows Program Manager appears, go to Step 5. If your system boots to a menu, go to Step 3 in the next section, "Using a Network." If a C:\> prompt appears on your screen,

2. **Type** ⌑WIN⌑ **and press** ↵

    Note: Throughout this manual, text or commands that you should type will be shown in a box, as in ⌑WIN⌑ **.**

    If the Windows Program Manager appears, go to Step 5. If it does not appear, first check your typing in Step 2 and repeat the procedure. If Windows still does not start, you may have to access Windows through its subdirectory. To do so,

3. **Type** ⌑CD\WINDOWS⌑ **and press** ↵

4. **Type** ⌑WIN⌑ **and press** ↵

5. **Insert your data disk into drive A**

USING A NETWORK.   Microsoft Excel may be available to you through a local area network (LAN). If so, Excel is kept on another computer's hard-disk drive that is shared by many users. To use Excel, you must access the program from your own microcomputer. So many network configurations are in use today that it is difficult to predict which one you will use. Check with your instructor for exact directions. In general, however, to start Excel you will follow these steps:

1. **Boot the network operating system (perhaps with your own disk)**

2. **Type any command needed to get the network menu**

3. Insert a data diskette into drive A

4. Select (or type) the appropriate command shown on your screen to access Windows

PROGRAM MANAGER. As Windows is loading, a copyright picture will briefly appear and then be replaced by Program Manager as in Figure SS1-1. (The actual size and contents of your Program Manager may differ.) This GUI menu system uses icons to represent applications or files (called *program-items*). These icons are organized into groups or submenus (called *program groups*) for easier visual access. Each program group may appear as a (document) window or icon. Soon you will start Microsoft Excel by using its program item icon.

If you need to enlarge Program Manager to a full-screen window,

Press Alt + Spacebar and then X

MOUSE AND KEYBOARD OPERATIONS

Skip this section if you are already familiar with using a mouse and keyboard.

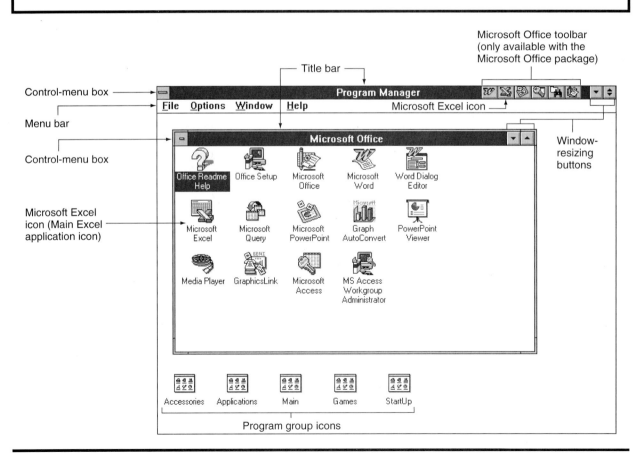

FIGURE SS1-1 ■ PROGRAM MANAGER AND THE MICROSOFT OFFICE WINDOWS

CHAPTER 1 SPREADSHEET BASICS: CREATING A WORKSHEET SS7

USING A MOUSE. A *mouse* is an input device that allows you to control a *mouse pointer* (graphical image) on your screen and select program features. As you move your mouse on a flat surface, the mouse pointer moves on your screen in a similar fashion. In Excel, the mouse pointer may appear in the forms displayed in Figure SS1-2a. Pointing means moving the mouse. To *point* (move) your mouse pointer:

1. **Slowly move your mouse on a flat surface or mouse pad (a small rubber pad) and notice the direction in which the mouse pointer moves on your screen**

FIGURE SS1-2 ■ **MOUSE SYMBOLS AND MOUSE ACTIONS**

(a) Common mouse symbols
(b) Common mouse actions

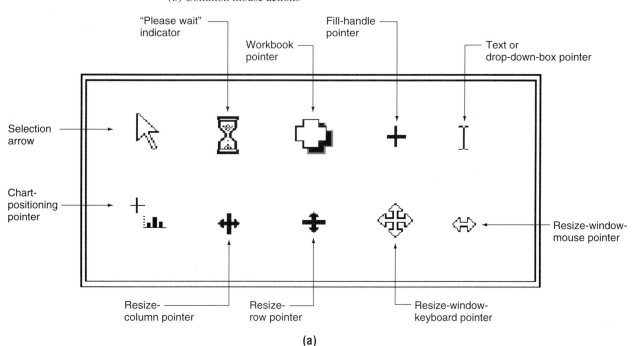

Mouse Actions	Explanations
Point	Move the mouse, and thus the mouse pointer, to the desired item.
Click	Press and quickly release the left mouse button.
Double-click	Rapidly press and release the left mouse button twice.
Drag	Press and hold the left mouse button, move the pointer to the desired location and release the button to select.

(b)

Note: If you run out of space, simply lift your mouse, place it in the original position, and start moving it again.

2. Point to the "P" in the title "Program Manager" (it should be near the top center of your screen)

3. Point to *Help* on the menu bar

Clicking involves quickly pressing and releasing the *left* mouse button. This action will normally select the item at which the mouse pointer is positioned. Try this:

4. Click *Help* for its pull-down menu

5. Point to and click *About Program Manager* to see its dialog box

Another basic mouse action, called *double-clicking,* involves quickly pressing and releasing the left mouse button twice. To practice double-clicking,

6. Point to the *control-menu* box—the small box with a bar at the upper left corner of the About Program Manager dialog box (see the icon in the left margin)

7. Double-click the About Program Manager dialog box's *control-menu* box

Note: If the dialog box does not disappear, you may not be clicking quickly enough. If a control menu appears, your system read your double-click as a single click. This menu can be used to resize, move, close the window, or switch to another window. In this case, either click *Close* to exit the dialog box, or press the Alt key and then try double-clicking again.

Many Windows applications also support a feature called *Drag and Drop.* This feature allows you to use a mouse to move an object from one place to another. This feature will be illustrated in later chapters.

Common mouse actions are summarized in Figure SS1-2b.

USING A KEYBOARD. A Windows application's features can also be accessed by keyboard. Keystrokes required to operate the Microsoft Excel menu system are discussed under the section "Operating Menus."

Most applications also provide special keystrokes, called *shortcut keys* that provide quick access to certain commands. Shortcut keys generally involve pressing a function key, either alone or in combination with the Ctrl, Alt, and/or Shift keys (a listing of shortcut keys can be found in the appendix). Function keys may be located at the extreme left of your keyboard (labeled F1 through F12) or across the top in one horizontal row (labeled F1 through F12). As an example, to open the Help window using its shortcut key,

1. Press `F1`

To close the Help window using shortcut keys,

2. Press `Alt` + `F4` (hold the Alt key while pressing the F4 key and then release both keys)

STARTING MICROSOFT EXCEL

The procedure to start Microsoft Excel is the same as that for starting any Windows application from Program Manager. Note that Microsoft Excel is usually part of the

CHAPTER 1   SPREADSHEET BASICS: CREATING A WORKSHEET   SS9

Microsoft Office or Microsoft Excel group in Program Manager. Figure SS1-1 displays the Microsoft Office group as a window. It contains program-item icons that represent the Microsoft Excel application and several other Microsoft applications. Remember, *program-item icons* are used to start an application.

> Note: Your Microsoft Excel icon may appear in another window. Check with your instructor for its location. Although the following procedures start Microsoft Excel from the Microsoft Office group, they can be applied to any group that contains the Microsoft Excel icon.

1. Locate the *Microsoft Office* window or icon in your Program Manager's workspace

If your Microsoft Office group is already a window, go to Step 4. If it appears as a group icon (see left margin of Step 2), do the following to enlarge it to a window:

MOUSE APPROACH	KEYBOARD APPROACH
2. Point to the *Microsoft Office* group icon Remember, to point with a mouse, slowly move the mouse on a flat surface to move the mouse pointer (arrow) on your screen to the Microsoft Office group icon 3. Double-click the *Microsoft Office* group icon to resize a window	2. If necessary, press `Ctrl` + `F6` (hold the Ctrl key and press the F6 key) until the highlight moves to the Microsoft Office group icon (see icon in left margin) 3. Press `↵` to resize the icon to a window

To start Microsoft Excel using its program-item icon,

MOUSE APPROACH	KEYBOARD APPROACH
4. Point to the *Microsoft Excel* icon 5. Double-click the *Microsoft Excel* icon	4. If ncessary, press the arrow keys to move the highlight to the Microsoft Excel icon 5. Press `↵` to start Microsoft Excel

A Microsoft Excel copyright screen may appear briefly but will quickly be replaced by the Microsoft Excel window as in Figure SS1-3a. Now, if needed,

6. Press `Alt` + `Spacebar` and then `X` to enlarge to full screen.

> Tip: If your system has Microsoft Office, you can also start Excel from within the Microsoft Office toolbar. When activate, this toolbar will appear at the top right of your screen as in Figure SS1-1. If it is not active, double-click the *Microsoft Office* icon in the Microsoft Office window. Now, to start Excel, click the *Excel* icon on the toolbar.

Excel provides transition features to help Lotus 1-2-3 users convert to Excel. When on, the features allow Excel to respond to some basic Lotus 1-2-3 keyboard commands. This module uses Microsoft Excel keystrokes, which require all transition features to be set off, as in Figure SS1-3b. Note that only the *Microsoft Excel Menu* option button is selected and that all transition check boxes are empty (set off). To check if these transition features are set off,

SS10 SPREADSHEETS WITH MICROSOFT EXCEL 5.0

FIGURE SS1-3 ■ THE MICROSOFT EXCEL WINDOW

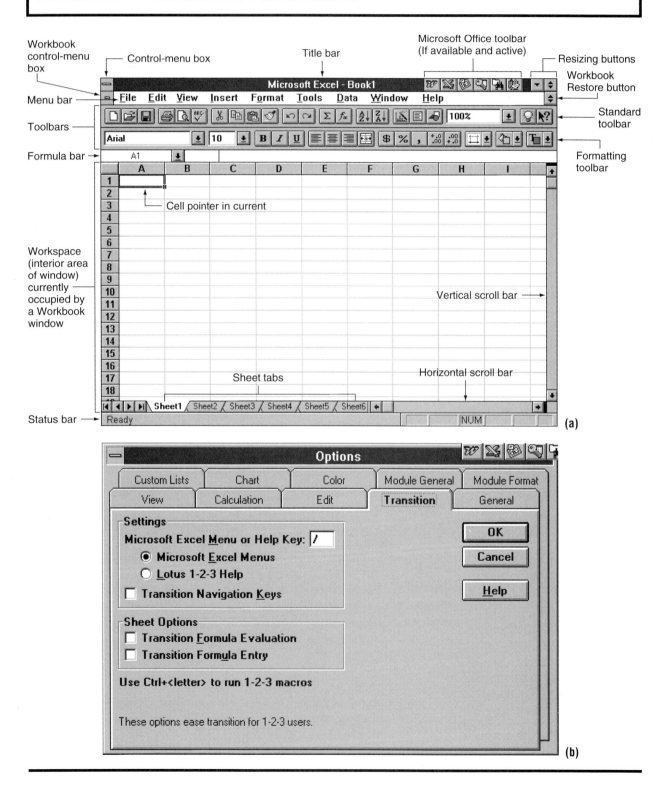

CHAPTER 1 SPREADSHEET BASICS: CREATING A WORKSHEET   **SS11**

MOUSE APPROACH

1. Click *Tools, Options* for its dialog box

2. Click *Transition* tab

3. If needed, click the *Microsoft Excel Menus* option button

KEYBOARD APPROACH

1. Press Alt + T , O for the Options dialog box

2. Press T for the Transition tab

3. If needed, press Alt + E to select the Microsoft Excel Menus option button

4. An "X" in a check box indicates that the feature is on. Examine the following check boxes to see if they are set off (blank) as in Figure SS1-3b.

- *Transition Navigation Keys*
- *Transition Formula Evaluation*
- *Transition Formula Entry*

If they are all blank, go to Step 6, otherwise, do Step 5.

MOUSE APPROACH

5. Click any check box to remove the "X"

6. Click *OK*

KEYBOARD APPROACH

5. Press ALT + the underlined letter of each check box that requires an "X" to be removed

6. Press ↵

If you are using your own computer system, this procedure only needs to be performed once. If you are using a network, repeat these steps right after you start Excel.

CHECKPOINT

✓ Describe how to start Windows.
✓ What is Program Manager?
✓ What is a mouse and mouse pointer?
✓ What are shortcut keys?
✓ Describe how to start Microsoft Excel from Program Manager.

UNDERSTANDING MICROSOFT EXCEL

The Microsoft Excel window, as shown in Figure SS1-3a, is the main application window that appears each time you start the program. Occupying its workspace (interior window space) is a new workbook that looks like a big grid. In Excel, a **workbook** is a document file whose contents are viewed through a *workbook window.* Workbooks are like binders with accounting paper (paper with columns and rows). Each page in a workbook is called a **sheet.** Sheets (there are 16 in the default workbook) may contain worksheets, charts, or other information. The content of a sheet can be very large; the portion of the sheet that appears in your workbook window represents only a small portion of the entire sheet.

There is only one Microsoft Excel window. However, depending on your computer memory, multiple workbooks may be opened in its workspace, each encased in its own workbook window.

THE MICROSOFT EXCEL WINDOW

Like all application windows, the Microsoft Excel window (Figure SS1-3a) has standard Windows and unique Excel features. Locate each feature on your screen as you read about its operation.

TITLE BAR. The *title bar* is generally at the top of a window. It is a standard Windows feature that identifies the window, in this case, "Microsoft Excel." It also has a control-menu box at its left end and two resizing button at its right end.

As discussed earlier, you can use the control-menu box to close a window by double-clicking with your mouse. It can also be used to open the window's control-menu by clicking it once. Control-menu operations are further discussed under "Using a Control-Menu."

A window can also be quickly resized by either double-clicking the title bar or clicking a resizing button with your mouse. Try this,

Note: If you do not have a mouse, just read this section.

1. Point anywhere within the Microsoft Excel *title bar* (except for the control-menu box or resizing buttons)

2. Double-click it (rapidly click your left mouse button twice)

The Excel window should now appear as a smaller window. Note also that the restore button (upward and downward triangles) in the right end the title bar has been replaced by a maximize button (upward triangle).

3. To return the window to a full screen (maximized), point to and click the *maximize* button

> Tip: Instead of clicking the *maximize* button in Step 3, you can also double-click the *title bar* again to resize the window to full screen.

MENU BAR. Excel's *menu bar* is located directly below its title bar. A *menu bar*, which is present only in application windows, provides mouse or keyboard access to an application's commands through pull-down menus. A **pull-down menu** provides a list of commands related to the menu bar item. For example, the menu bar item *File*, opens to a pull-down menu with file-management commands. Menu-bar operations are discussed under the "Operating Menus" section.

TOOLBARS. Just below the menu bar are two Excel toolbars: the Standard toolbar and the Format toolbar. Each **toolbar** contains *command buttons* and *drop-down boxes* that can be used to access Excel features by mouse. **Command buttons** are mouse shortcuts to a program's features. For example, clicking the *Print* button will start the printing process. A **drop-down box** first appears as a rectangular box with a ⬇ button at its right. Clicking the ⬇ button will open a drop-down list. For example, clicking the ⬇ button of the Font drop-down box (displaying "Arial") of the Formatting toolbar will open a drop-down list of available fonts. See the "Toolbars" section of this chapter for further discussions of toolbar operations.

FORMULA BAR. Beneath the toolbars is Excel's formula bar. The **formula bar** provides information about data entered into a worksheet. See "The Formula Bar" section of this chapter for a detailed discussion of its operation.

WORKSPACE AND WORKBOOK WINDOW.   Located between the formula bar and the status bar is the workspace. This is the large interior space of the window that is currently occupied by a workbook window. See the next section "The Workbook Window: Columns, Rows, and Cells" for further discussion on workbooks.

STATUS BAR.   At the bottom of the window is Excel's status bar. The **status bar** displays messages regarding the operation in progress or a selected command on its left side and toggle switch (on/off switch) indicators on its right side. Currently, your status bar's left side displays "Ready," indicating that Excel is ready for your next operation. Your status bar may also display "CAPS" (Caps Lock), "NUM" (Number Lock), and "SCRL" (Scroll Lock) on its right side when these toggle switches are set in the on position. Pressing a toggle key, for example, the Caps Lock key, turns the feature on or off.

THE WORKBOOK WINDOW: COLUMNS, ROWS, AND CELLS

Look at the workbook window on your screen and in Figure SS1-3a. It currently displays an electronic spreadsheet called a **worksheet.** Worksheets are divided into vertical *columns* and horizontal *rows.* The letters along the top border (A through I) designate columns, and the numbers in the left border (1 through 18) designate rows. Columns are lettered A through Z, then AA through AZ, BA through BZ, and so on. Rows are numbered consecutively starting with 1. The intersection of a column and a row forms a box called a **cell.** Each cell is identified by its column and row coordinates (**cell addresses**). For example, Cell A1 is formed by the intersection of Column A and Row 1 (the column letter is always listed first, followed by the row number).

New workbook windows always display the first 9 columns and 18 rows, but this changes as you adjust column widths or move the cell pointer. The worksheet itself can contain as many as 16,384 rows and 256 columns, depending on available computer memory.

THE CURRENT CELL.   The **current cell** is the one that will receive the next data you enter or be affected by the next command. The screen identifies the current cell in two ways. First, the cell is visually indicated in the worksheet area with a **cell pointer** or, simply, *pointer*—a rectangular box with dark borders that outlines one cell. Second, the cell address is listed in the left side of the formulas bar (fifth row from top). These two indicators in Figure SS1-3a show that the current cell is A1.

MOVING AROUND THE WORKSHEET.   You can move the cell pointer from cell to cell by using the mouse or the keyboard. With the mouse, simply point to a desired cell and click. With the keyboard, press the Up, Down, Left, or Right arrow key. Try this to move the cell pointer to cell 5:

MOUSE APPROACH	KEYBOARD APPROACH
1. Point to *Cell E5*	1. Press → until the pointer moves to *Cell E1*
2. Click *Cell E5*	2. Press ↓ until the pointer moves to *Cell E5*

Notice how the cell pointer's position and the cell address change.

SCROLLING BY KEYBOARD. If you move the pointer past the rightmost screen column (or below the bottom row), the worksheet in the workbook window will **scroll,** or reposition itself automatically to display the current cell. Because the commands to move the cell pointer beyond the current display area by mouse and keyboard are quite different, they are addressed separately. Try this keyboard exercise first:

1. **Move to Cell I5**

    As shown in Figure SS1-4a, Column A is still on the screen.

2. **Press → once**

As shown in Figure SS1-4b, Column J now appears, and Column A has disappeared. But remember that the screen is merely a window to a larger spreadsheet. Columns or rows may not be shown in the worksheet window's workspace, but they are still part of the spreadsheet.

3. **Move back to Cell A5**

Column A reappears. Figure SS1-5 lists the keys that relocate your pointer. You can move one cell at a time with an arrow key, or one screen at a time with Pg Up and Pg Dn. To examine the effect of these keys on the screen,

---

FIGURE SS1-4 ■ SCROLLING BY KEYBOARD

(a) The pointer is placed at the edge of the screen. (b) As the pointer is moved to the right by pressing the Right arrow key, Column J appears on the screen as Column A disappear at the left.

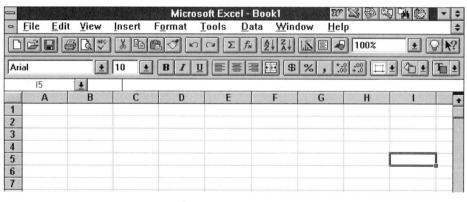

CHAPTER 1   SPREADSHEET BASICS: CREATING A WORKSHEET   SS15

4. **Press a few of the keys listed in Figure SS1-5**

Now, to move the cell pointer quickly to Cell A1—the *home cell,*

5. **Press Ctrl + Home**

SCROLLING BY MOUSE. Moving the cell pointer by mouse to a cell beyond the current display requires the use of a **scroll bar,** a common Windows tool that allows you to view the contents of a window that is not in the current viewing area. As shown in Figure SS1-3a, a workbook window has both a horizontal and a vertical scroll bar.

FIGURE SS1-5 ■ POINTER MOVEMENT KEYS

↑	Moves the pointer up one cell.
↓	Moves the pointer down one cell.
→	Moves the pointer right one cell.
←	Moves the pointer left one cell.
Pg Up	Moves the pointer up one screen.
Pg Dn	Moves the pointer down one screen.
Alt + **Pg Dn**	Moves the pointer right one screen.
Alt + **Pg Up**	Moves the pointer left one screen.
Home	Moves the pointer to the left end of a row.
End	Holding this key and pressing an arrow key moves the pointer to the edge of the worksheet that is in the direction of the arrow.
Scroll Lock	When pressed, the worksheet moves and the pointer remains stationary as an arrow key is pressed.
F5	Opens the GoTo dialog box to go to a cell. For example, pressing F5, typing the cell address A6 and then pressing the Enter key will cause the pointer to go to cell A6.
Ctrl + **End**	Moves the pointer to the last cell in the lower right corner of a worksheet.
Ctrl + **Home**	Moves the pointer to Cell A1.
Ctrl + ←	Moves the pointer left to the intersection of a blank and a nonblank cell.
Ctrl + →	Moves the pointer right to the intersection of a blank and a nonblank cell.
Ctrl + ↑	Moves the pointer up to the intersection of a blank and a nonblank cell.
Ctrl + ↓	Moves the pointer down to the intersection of a blank and a nonblank cell.

FIGURE SS1-6 ■ SCROLLING BY MOUSE

(a) Clicking the down arrow of the vertical scroll bar display Row 19. (b) Clicking Cell A19 moves the pointer there.

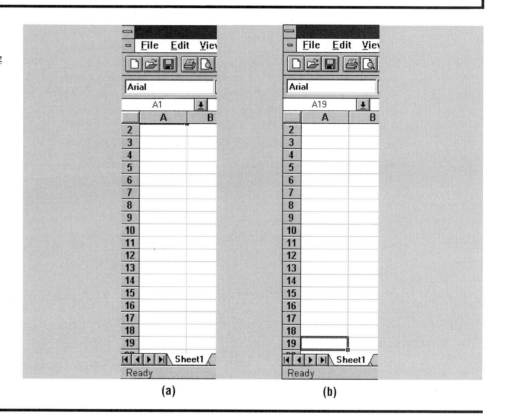

(a)   (b)

Scroll bars can be accessed only by mouse. They do not move the cell pointer, only the display area. Once a desired cell is in view, the mouse may be used to move the cell pointer by pointing to the desired cell and then clicking it.

Scroll bars have arrow buttons at each end. Clicking a scroll bar's arrow button will scroll (move) the spreadsheet one row or column in the direction of that arrow. Scroll bars also contain a scroll box. Dragging the scroll box along the scroll bar will quickly scroll through the spreadsheet. Try this exercise:

1. **Point to the** ↓ **button of the vertical scroll bar and click once**

As shown in Figure SS1-6a, Row 19 appears as Row 1 disappears. The cell pointer also disappears, because it is still in Cell A1. Now, try moving the Cell pointer to Cell A19.

2. **Point to and click** *Cell A19*

The cell pointer now appears in Cell A19 as shown in Figure SS1-6b.

3. **Press** Ctrl + Home **to move to Cell A1**

COMMON WINDOWS FEATURES. Like all document windows, workbook windows have a control-menu box, title bar, and resizing button (or buttons). The

CHAPTER 1   SPREADSHEET BASICS: CREATING A WORKSHEET   SS17

location of these features depends on the size of the window. For instance, whenever the workbook window on your screen is *maximized* (enlarged to maximum size), it shares its title bar with the *Microsoft Excel* window's title bar. As shown in Figure SS1-3a, the title bar's caption, "Book1," next to "Microsoft Excel" is the current workbook's name. "Book1" also indicates that you have not assigned a specific name to the workbook.

A maximized workbook's control-menu box and restore button (a window resizing button), as shown in Figure SS1-3a, occupy the left and right ends of the menu bar. Try the following steps to resize the workbook window to a smaller window in *Microsoft Excel* window's workspace.

MOUSE APPROACH

1. Point to the *restore* button (right end of the menu bar)
2. Click it

KEYBOARD APPROACH

1. Press Alt + − (Minus key) for worksheet window's control menu
2. Press R to restore

Tip: Instead of Steps 1 & 2, you can also press the Ctrl and F5 keys.

As shown in Figure SS1-7, the workbook window should now be a smaller window with its own title bar. Its control-menu box appears at the top left and two resizing buttons are at the top right.

FIGURE SS1-7 ■ **THE WORKBOOK WINDOW**

A less-than maximized workbook window has its own title bar. Its control menu box and resizing buttons occupy the right and left ends of its title bar, similar to Microsoft Excel's title bar.

UNIQUE EXCEL FEATURES. A workbook window, as shown in Figure SS1-7, has several unique Excel features, including sheet tabs, tab-scroll buttons, and tab, horizontal, and vertical split bars. *Sheet tabs* are used to identify sheets in a workbook and enable you to switch back and forth between them. Remember, a sheet is like a page in a book and may contain a worksheet, chart or other information. Although additional sheets can be added, 16 sheets are available in a new workbook. *Tab-scroll* buttons can be used to scroll through multiple sheets by clicking them with your mouse. Dragging a *split bar* with your mouse will split the workbook window into separate panes (parts). This allows you to view different areas of multiple sheets (tab split bar) or a single sheet (horizontal or vertical split bar) at the same time. Multiple sheet operations and workbook window splitting techniques are discussed in Chapter 3.

To enlarge your workbook window back to its maximum size:

MOUSE APPROACH	KEYBOARD APPROACH
1. Point to the *maximize* button (right end of title bar)	1. Press Alt + —
2. Click it	2. Press X for maximize

> Tip: You may also double-click a workbook window's title bar to resize the window or press the Ctrl + F10 keys.

THE FORMULA BAR

The *formula bar,* shown in Figure SS1-8a, is located below the toolbars. It provides information about the current cell address (location) and its content. The formula bar has three parts: named box (left side), entry area (right side) and command button(s).

THE NAME BOX. The **name box,** located on left side of the formula bar, provides information about the current cell address. Your name box should show "A1," which indicates that the cell pointer is in Cell A1.

The name box can also be used to move the cell pointer to different areas of the current workbook. Cell pointer movements using the name box are demonstrated later.

ENTRY AREA. The **entry area,** located on the right side of the formula bar, displays the content of the current cell. It can also be used to enter or edit data in the current cell.

COMMAND BUTTONS. Currently, the formula bar displays only the ▼ button of the name box. This button can be used to open a drop-down list of the workbook's named areas. Naming areas of a workbook are discussed later.

When data is entered into a cell, the formula bar becomes active and three other command buttons appear. Try this,

1. Move the cell pointer to Cell A1

2. Type SAMPLE (do not press enter)

Note: As you type "SAMPLE," it appears in both the entry area and the current cell. In addition, a vertical blinking line, called the *insertion point,* also moves to the right in the current cell as you type. The *insertion point* indicates where the next character you enter will appear.

CHAPTER 1   SPREADSHEET BASICS: CREATING A WORKSHEET   SS19

FIGURE SS1-8 ■ THE FORMULA BAR

(a) The formula bar is located below the Format toolbar. (b) The cancel box, enter box and Function Wizard buttons appear when data is entered into a cell. As data is entered, it appears in both the entry area and the cell.

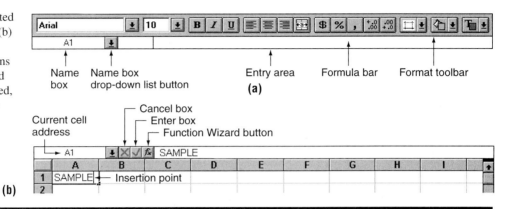

(a)

(b)

Your formula bar and Cell A1 content should appear as Figure SS1-8b. Note also that the cancel box (X), enter box ✓, and Function Wizard *fx* buttons appear to the left of "SAMPLE" on the formula bar. At this point you can edit the entry or accept it into Cell A1 by either clicking the enter-box button or pressing the Enter key. The Function Wizard button can be used to place a function (built-in formula) in the current cell. Functions are discussed later. For now, do the following to cancel the entry.

MOUSE APPROACH	KEYBOARD APPROACH
3. Click the *Cancel* (X) button	3. Press Esc

Note: The formula bar also becomes active when editing cell contents.

THE HELP FEATURE

Microsoft Excel's on-line *Help* feature includes general and specific *Help* windows, a *Search* feature, tutorials, and other related help tools. The on-line tutorials include an overall preview of Excel and examples and demos on specific topics. The help feature can also be accessed through most dialog boxes to assist you in its operations. To open the *Help Contents* window,

MOUSE APPROACH	KEYBOARD APPROACH
1. Click *Help* (on the menu bar) and then *Contents*	1. Press F1

To select an item from the *Help* window by mouse, simply point to it and click. With the keyboard, press the Tab key to move the highlight to the item and then press the Enter key. For now, exit the *Help* window using its menu bar:

MOUSE APPROACH	KEYBOARD APPROACH
2. Click *File* and then *Exit*	2. Press Alt + F and then X

You may continue working through the module or exit Excel and Windows now. To exit both in the same way:

MOUSE APPROACH

3. Click *File* and then *Exit* to exit Excel

4. If "Save Changes in 'Book1'?" appears, click *No*

5. Click *File* and then *Exit* to exit Program Manager

6. Click the *OK* button to exit Windows

KEYBOARD APPROACH

3. Press `Alt` + `F4` to exit Excel

4. If "Save Changes in 'Book1'?" appears, press `N`

5. Press `Alt` + `F4` to exit Program Manager

6. Press `↵` to exit Windows

Other exiting techniques will be demonstrated later.

CHECKPOINT

✓ Start Windows and Excel and then move to Cell J10. In what two ways can you tell that J10 is the current cell?
✓ Describe the key components of the Microsoft Excel windows.
✓ Describe the key components of workbook window.
✓ Describe how to access Excel's on-line help feature.

OPERATING MENUS

Like all Windows applications, Excel has a menu system that can be used to access its many features. The Excel menu system contains standard Windows menu features, such as a menu bar (main menu) with pull-down menus and a control menu with window manipulating features. Excel also offers *Shortcut,* which provides quick access to specific features.

1. Start Windows and then Microsoft Excel, if needed

2. Press `Alt` + `Spacebar` , and then `X` to maximize, if needed

USING A MENU BAR

Excel's menu bar gives you access to most of the program's features through pull-down menus. Each provides a list of commands related to its menu-bar item. When a menu-bar item is selected, a pull-down menu is opened. This module will refer to a pull-down menu simply as a menu.

Note: *Click = point to and click.*

OPENING AND CLOSING A MENU. Try this to open the *File* menu:

MOUSE APPROACH

1. Click *File*

KEYBOARD APPROACH

1. Press `Alt` + `F`

Tip: many of the commands listed under the Mouse Approach relate to menu-bar selections. If you want to access those selections by keyboard instead of by mouse, simply press the Alt key and the underlined letter of the menu-bar item to open the menu and then press the underlined letter fo the menu item.

CHAPTER 1   SPREADSHEET BASICS: CREATING A WORKSHEET   SS21

FIGURE SS1-9 ■ A SAMPLE OF A PULL-DOWN MENU

Clicking *File* from the menu bar opens its pull-down menu. This figure only displays the top portion of the file menu.

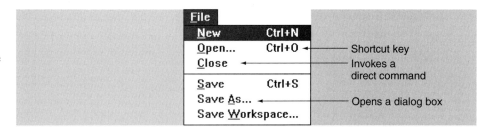

Now, do the following to close the menu:

MOUSE APPROACH	KEYBOARD APPROACH
2. Click any open space outside the menu	2. Press Alt once or Esc twice

IDENTIFYING A MENU ITEM'S FUNCTION. Moving the selection highlight to a menu item will display its function in the status bar. Try this:

MOUSE APPROACH	KEYBOARD APPROACH
1. Click *File* for the file menu again	1. Press Alt + F for the file menu again

The top of your file menu should appear as Figure SS1-9. Note that the selection highlight is on *New* and the message "Creates new document" appears in the status bar.

2. Press ↓ until the selection highlight is on *Save*

Now the message "Saves document" appears on the status bar.

3. Press Alt to close the file menu without selecting a command

SELECTING A MENU ITEM. Once a menu is open, simply click the desired menu item or press its underlined letter to select it. Try this to select *Exit* from the *File* menu to exit Excel:

MOUSE APPROACH	KEYBOARD APPROACH
1. Click *File* for the *File* menu	1. Press Alt + F (the underlined letter in *File*) for the *File* menu
2. Click *Exit*	2. Press X (the underlined letter of the menu item *Exit*)

You should now have exited Excel and returned to Program Manager. To restart Excel:

MOUSE APPROACH	KEYBOARD APPROACH
3. Double-click the *Microsoft Excel* icon	3. Press ↵

> Tip: Another way to open a menu and select a menu item by keyboard is to press the Alt key first to turn on the highlight. (The Alt key is a toggle (on/off) switch that activates or deactivates the highlight bar.) Once turned on, the highlight can be moved to a menu-bar item by pressing an arrow key and then the Enter key to open the menu. Next, press the Down arrow key to move the highlight to the desired menu item and press the Enter key to select the item.

MENU INDICATORS

Excel uses standard Windows menu indicators or conventions in its menu system. These conventions apply to all types of menus—pull-down menus, control menus and Shortcut menus. The *File* menu will be used as an example to help you understand these menu conventions.

MOUSE APPROACH

1. Click *File*

KEYBOARD APPROACH

1. Press Alt + F

The top portion of the *File* menu should appear again as shown in Figure SS1-9.

Menu items with *neither* a triangle pointer (▶) at their extreme right (not shown in Figure SS1-9) nor an ellipsis (. . .), such as *Close,* directly invoke a command. If shortcut keys can be used to invoke a menu item directly, they are displayed at the extreme right of the item. For example, the shortcut keys Ctrl + O are displayed to the right of *Open.*

FIGURE SS1-10 ■ MENU-BAR SELECTIONS

(a) Mouse and keyboard actions to select menu-bar and menu items. (b) Menu conventions.

Selecting a	Mouse Approach	Keyboard Approach
Menu-bar item letter	Point to and click the item	Press the Alt key and the item's underlined letter
Menu item	Point to and click the item	Press the item's underlined letter

(a)

Menu items with	Explanation
Ellipsis (. . .)	Opens to a dialog box or another window
▶ at far right	Opens to a cascading menu (submenu)
No notation	Invokes a command or other feature
Keys at far right	Shortcut key(s) to invoke the menu item using the keyboard
✓ to left of item	A toggle (on/off) feature that has been activated
Dimmed (or not visible) characters	A menu item not currently available

(b)

CHAPTER 1   SPREADSHEET BASICS: CREATING A WORKSHEET   **SS23**

FIGURE SS1-11 ■ CONTROL MENUS

(a) The control menu of Microsoft Excel can be used to resize or close the application or to switch to another running application.
(b) The control menu of a workbook (document) can be used to resize or close the workbook or to switch to another opened workbook.
(c) The control menu of a dialog box can be used to move or close the box.
(d) Selecting a control menu.

Restore		Restore	Ctrl+F5	
Move		Move	Ctrl+F7	
Size		Size	Ctrl+F8	
Minimize		Minimize	Ctrl+F9	
Maximize		Maximize	Ctrl+F10	
				Move
Close	Alt+F4	Close	Ctrl+F4	Close Alt+F4
Switch To... Ctrl+Esc		Next Window Ctrl+Tab		

(a)   (b)   (c)

Selecting a	Mouse Approach	Keyboard Approach
Control menu of an application window or dialog box	Click the application window's control-menu box	Press the Alt key and the spacebar
Control menu of a work-sheet (document) window	Click the worksheet window's control-menu box	Press the Alt and minus keys
Control menu of an application icon	Click the application icon	Press the Alt key and the spacebar
Control menu of a work-sheet (document) icon	Click the worksheet icon	Press the Alt and minus keys
Control-menu item	Click the item	Press the item's under-lined letter

(d)

Figure SS1-10a summarizes menu-bar mouse and keyboard actions required to open pull-down menus and select menu items. A list of standard windows menu indicators is displayed in Figure SS1-10b. To exit the File menu:

MOUSE APPROACH

2.   **Click on open space in the window**

KEYBOARD APPROACH

2.   **Press Alt once or Esc twice**

USING A CONTROL MENU

Like all windows, the Excel and workbook windows (and icons, when minimized) have a *control menu* that contains options to manipulate and close a window. Any dialog box also has a control menu. Figure SS1-11 displays examples of control menus and summarizes the mouse and keyboard actions required to open a control menu and make control-menu selections.

Note: A control-menu box (which opens to a control menu) is normally located in the upper-left corner of a window. However, the control-menu box of a maximized workbook window is at the left corner of the Microsoft Excel menu bar.

FIGURE SS1-12 ■ SHORTCUT MENU

Pointing to certain areas of an Excel window and clicking the right mouse button opens a Shortcut menu. This Shortcut menu appears when pointing to a cell in the workbook window and clicking the right mouse button.

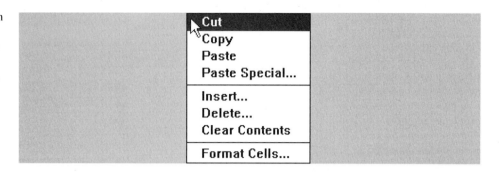

Control menus use the same menu indicators as the menu bar. Their operations are demonstrated throughout this module.

USING A SHORTCUT MENU

Shortcut Menus provide quick access to specific Excel features. A **Shortcut Menu** is opened by pointing to certain areas of Excel window and workbook and clicking the right mouse button. Try this:

1. **Point to an open space in the center of the workbook window**

2. **Click the right mouse button**

A Shortcut Menu should appear similar to Figure SS1-12. At this point you can select a Shortcut Menu item by clicking it.

3. **Point to and click (left button) outside of the Shortcut Menu to close it**

CHECKPOINT

✓ Describe the procedures to open and close a pull-down menu by mouse and keyboard.
✓ What do menu items followed by a triangle (▶) at their extreme right or an ellipsis (. . .) represent?
✓ Describe the actions required to open and select from a Shortcut Menu.
✓ Describe the actions to open a control-menu (Excel's and a workbook's).
✓ Describe how to close a window using its control-menu box.

OPERATING COMMAND BUTTONS

Many Microsoft Excel features can be quickly accessed by mouse by clicking, double-clicking, or dragging and dropping command buttons. (Remember, command buttons can be used to directly invoke certain commands.) For example, as demonstrated earlier, double-clicking a window's control-menu box closes the window.

Standard Windows command buttons include the control-menu box and resizing buttons. Unique Excel command buttons are available through toolbars. They are a series of pictures or symbols that appear below the menu bar. Clicking a toolbar will access the feature it represents. Excel also has a variety of other command buttons, for example, the Enter box button , which appears on the formula bar when entering data into a cell.

You will now learn more about the resizing buttons and toolbar buttons.

Note: Many buttons are only accessible by mouse. In this module, command buttons are displayed in the left margin of their related Mouse Approach commands, where available.

RESIZING BUTTONS

There are three types of resizing buttons: *minimize, restore,* and *maximize.* Resizing buttons generally appear at the right end of a window's title bar. A maximized workbook window's resizing button, however, appears at the right end of the menu bar. Each one is described briefly below.

- Clicking a *minimize button* reduces the window to an icon (also called a *minimized* window).
- Clicking a *restore button* reduces a maximized window to a smaller window. A maximized window is one that is enlarged to its largest size. The restore button appears only when a window is maximized.
- Clicking a *maximize button* resizes the window to a full screen (also called a *maximized* window). The maximize button appears only when a window is less than its largest size.

Resizing buttons are used as needed within this manual.

TOOLBARS

Excel opens with a Standard toolbar and a Format toolbar below its menu bar as in Figure SS1-13a. *Toolbars* provide mouse shortcuts to Excel's features through command buttons and drop-down boxes. The *Standard toolbar* can be used to access file management, editing, data manipulation, charting and a variety of other commonly used commands. The *Format toolbar* can be used to access worksheet formatting commands.

Excel also comes with a variety of other specialized toolbars that automatically appear when you invoke a command that relates to their operation. For example, the Chart toolbar will appear when you create a chart. These toolbars can also be manually turned on/off through the menu bar or a shortcut menu. All toolbars can be edited. In addition, Excel allows you to create your own custom toolbar. Specialized toolbar operations will be discussed as needed. See the appendix to create a custom toolbar.

IDENTIFYING A TOOLBAR BUTTON'S FUNCTION. Pointing to a toolbar button will display its function in a caption box below it and in the left side of the status bar. Try this:

1. **Point to the *Print* button on the Standard toolbar (do not click)**

FIGURE SS1-13 ■ STANDARD AND FORMAT TOOLBARS

(a) Excel opens with the Standard and Format toolbars below its menu bar. (b) Clicking the ▼ of a drop-down box opens its drop-down list.

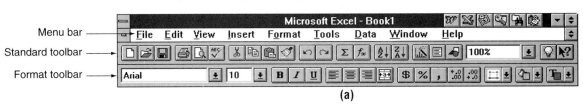

(a)

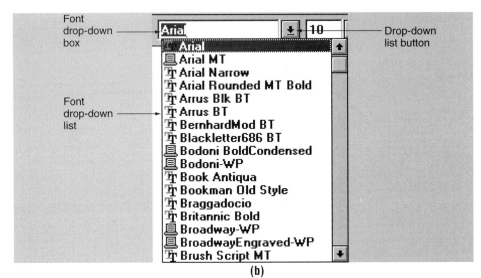

(b)

A caption box with the word "Print" will appear below the button and the message "Prints active document" will appear in the status bar.

2. **Point to another toolbar button and view its function**

USING TOOLBAR BUTTONS. Clicking a toolbar button normally invokes a command or opens a dialog box. Some toolbars contain drop-down boxes that appear as a box with a drop-down list ▼ button at its right. For example, the Font (type style) drop-down box at the left end of the Format toolbar opens to a drop-down list of available fonts (typefaces) similar to Figure SS1-13b. Try this:

1. Point to the ▼ button of the Font drop-down box
2. Click it

A Font drop-down list similar to Figure SS1-13b should now appear. (Note: Your font list may differ depending on the available fonts in your system.) To select from a drop-down list, simply click the desired item. For now, close the drop-down list without selecting a new font.

CHAPTER 1   SPREADSHEET BASICS: CREATING A WORKSHEET   SS27

MOUSE APPROACH	KEYBOARD APPROACH
3. Click an open space outside of the drop-down list	3. Press Esc

CHECKPOINT

✓ What is a command button?
✓ Identify and describe the three different types of resizing buttons.
✓ Where are toolbars located?
✓ What are toolbar buttons? How can you get a description of a toolbar button's functions?
✓ How do you open a drop-down box's list?

A QUICK START: THE BASICS

The following exercises demonstrate how to create, save, and open a spreadsheet. Use these techniques to save your work and return to it later. For clarity, keys are displayed in uppercase letters, but you need not type them this way: Excel recognizes *a5* as easily as *A5*.

SETTING THE DEFAULT DRIVE

Each time you begin Excel, you should confirm (and set if needed) the drive (for example, drive A) that Excel uses to hold your data disk. This is essential to ensure that your work will be saved on your data disk. Either the Save As or Open File dialog box can be used to verify and change (if needed) the default drive. The procedures are the same for both dialog boxes. Try this to use the Save As dialog box to check the default drive and change it to drive A (if needed):

MOUSE APPROACH	KEYBOARD APPROACH
1. Click *File* (on menu bar) for the File menu	1. Press Alt + F for the File menu
2. Click *Save As* for its dialog box	2. Press A for the Save As dialog box

Tip: Instead of steps 1 and 2, you can press the F12 key to open the Save As dialog box.

A Save As dialog box similar to Figure SS1-14a should appear. (Note: The content of your dialog box may differ depending on how Excel was programmed.)

The Save As dialog box has a variety of common Windows features as described in Figure SS1-14b. These features operate the same way in most dialog boxes. To select a feature by mouse, click the desired item. By keyboard, press the Alt key and the underlined letter of the option.

Now, examine your drives' drop-down box. If drive A appears, then just read Steps 1 and 2 and then do Step 3. If another drive appears, do the following to set it to drive A.

FIGURE SS1-14A ■ THE SAVE AS DIALOG BOX

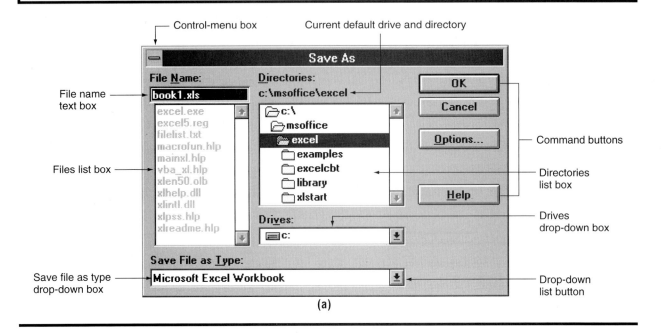

(a)

MOUSE APPROACH	KEYBOARD APPROACH
1. Click the ↓ button of the drives' drop-down box for its list	1. Press Alt + V for the drives' drop-down box
2. Click the *a:* drive icon	2. Press A and then ↵ to set the drive to A

At this point, you can either use the dialog box to save a file or exit the dialog box. To exit the dialog box with the new drive setting:

MOUSE APPROACH	KEYBOARD APPROACH
3. Click the *Cancel* button	3. Press Esc

The default drive will remain A until Excel is exited or the default is changed.

ENTERING DATA

The first step in the creation of a spreadsheet is to enter data in the desired cells. In this brief exercise, you will simply type your name and a number.

1. **Move to Cell A1 (Ctrl + Home) and type your first name**

Your name appears in the entry and in the cell. If you typed incorrectly, you can use the backspace key to erase the entry and then retype it.

2. **Move to Cell A3**

Note that as you moved the cell pointer, the previous entry stays in Cell A1.

CHAPTER 1   SPREADSHEET BASICS: CREATING A WORKSHEET   **SS29**

FIGURE SS1-14B ■ **COMMON DIALOG BOX FEATURES**

Feature	Description
Text Box	A box in which text can be entered (e.g., File Name text box).
List Box	A box that alphabetically lists options that are available for selection (e.g., Files list box, Directories list box).
Drop-down Box	An area that first appears as a rectangular box with a ⬇ button at its right side (e.g., Drives' drop-down box, Save File as Type drop-down box). Clicking this button opens a drop down list of available choices. The current selection is highlighted.
Command Buttons	Buttons that invoke a command or other option when selected (e.g., OK, Cancel, Options, and Help button).
Check Box	An option with a small square box on its left (not available in the Save As dialog box). Selecting an empty check box will place an "X" in it. This indicates that the feature is on. Several check boxes, if available, can be selected at once.
Option Button	An option with a small circle on its left (not available in the Save As dialog box). It operates similar to a check box, however, only one option button can be selected in a group of options.

---

3.   Type ⬚ 75 ⬚ and press ⏎

As you've seen here, an entry can be placed into a spreadsheet cell either by pressing the Enter key or by moving the cell pointer.

SAVING A WORKBOOK

A workbook can be saved using the Save or Save As command (File menu). Both commands will open the Save As dialog box if invoked on an unsaved workbook. (Remember, a document file in Excel is called a *workbook*.) Invoking the **Save** command on a previously saved workbook will quickly resave it under its original name. Invoking the **Save As** command on a previously saved workbook will allert you if a file with the same name exists on the disk. This command also allows you to save the file under a different name, thereby keeping the original workbook under its old name. This is useful when saving an updated workbook. Both commands are demonstrated here:

MOUSE APPROACH | **KEYBOARD APPROACH**

1.   Click *File* and then *Save* | 1.   Press **Ctrl** + **S**

The Save As dialog box should appear since this is the first time you are saving this workbook. As seen earlier, you can use this dialog to set the default drive. You can also use it to save a workbook in the Excel format (the default) or another program's format, change the default directory, assign a password to the workbook and a variety of other save options.

2.   Type ⬚ **SAMPLE**

MOUSE APPROACH	KEYBOARD APPROACH
3. Click the *OK* button for the Summary Info dialog box	3. Press ↵ for the Summary Info dialog box

The Summary Info dialog box can be used to label a file with information when the file is first saved. For now, to continue saving without placing additional information in this dialog box:

MOUSE APPROACH	KEYBOARD APPROACH
4. Click the OK button	4. Press ↵

The mouse pointer will briefly appear as an hourglass (indicating "please wait"). A row of "■■■" will also briefly appear in the status bar as your workbook is saved. Your workbook has been saved on the disk in the default drive with the name "SAMPLE.XLS." Excel automatically adds a ".XLS" filename extension to identify your file as an Excel workbook. The filename "SAMPLE.XLS" also appears in the title bar after it is saved.

> **Tip:** The ".XLS" filename extension also associates the file with Excel. Associated document files in the Window's environment allow you to open the file with its application at the same time through Window's File Manager or Program Manager. Refer to your Windows manual for detailed instructions on associated file operations.

Once you have saved a workbook, you can use either the Save As or Save command to resave it. Remember, the Save command resaves a file without confirmation. First try the Save As command to resave the workbook SAMPLE.

MOUSE APPROACH	KEYBOARD APPROACH
5. Click *File* and then *Save As* for its dialog box	5. Press F12 for the Save As dialog box

When the program prompts you for a filename, it displays the current name of the workbook, in this case, "SAMPLE.XLS" in the *File Name* text box.

MOUSE APPROACH	KEYBOARD APPROACH
6. Click the *OK* button to accept the current name	6. Press ↵ to accept the current name

Since a "SAMPLE.XLS" file already exists on your disk, Excel offers you a dialog box with the choices—*Yes* or *No*.

MOUSE APPROACH	KEYBOARD APPROACH
7. Click the *Yes* button to replace the old file	7. Press Y to replace the old file

The Yes button replaces the previous file on the disk with the new one. The No button returns you to the spreadsheet *without* saving.

Now, try the *Save* command to resave the file without confirmation. Try this:

MOUSE APPROACH	KEYBOARD APPROACH
8. Click *File* and then *Save*	8. Press Ctrl + S

Your file is now resaved under its previous name.

CHAPTER 1   SPREADSHEET BASICS: CREATING A WORKSHEET   SS31

CLOSING A WORKBOOK

Closing a workbook removes it (and its window) from Excel's workspace. Although you can open many workbooks in Excel's workspace, each additional workbook uses more system memory. Many opened workbooks may therefore affect the efficiency of your system. Unless otherwise needed, you should therefore close any workbook not in use. Multiple workbook operations are discussed in Chapter 3.

A workbook can be closed by using the Close command in the File menu or Control menu. It can also be closed by double-clicking its window's control-menu box or pressing the Ctrl + F4 keys. These closing techniques are presented throughout this text. Now, to close the active workbook by menu bar (remember, the active workbook is the one currently in use):

MOUSE APPROACH

1. Click *File* for its menu
2. Click *Close* to close the workbook

KEYBOARD APPROACH

1. Press Alt + F for the file menu
2. Press C to close the workbook

> Tip: If changes were made or the workbook was never saved, a dialog box will appear with the options *Yes*, *No*, and *Cancel*. Click *Yes* to save or resave the workbook and then close it.

Your Excel workspace should now be blank and the menu bar only displaying *File* and *Help* options.

CREATING A NEW WORKBOOK

At this point you can create a new workbook, open a saved workbook or exit Excel. The latter two options are discussed in the sections to follow. The **new** command (File menu) opens a new blank workbook in Excel's workspace.

MOUSE APPROACH

1. Click *File* and then *New* for a new workbook

KEYBOARD APPROACH

1. Press Ctrl + N for a new workbook

A new workbook with the title "BOOK2" will appear in its own window in Excel's workspace. Excel automatically labels new workbooks in sequence as you create them. For example, BOOK1, BOOK2, etc. As seen earlier, this workbook name can be changed upon saving the workbook. For now, use the workbook window's control menu to close it.

> Caution: In the next command, be sure to use the workbook's control menu box that is currently located to the left of *File* on the menu bar. *Do not* use Excel's control-menu box that is at the left end of its title bar.

MOUSE APPROACH

2. Click the workbook's *control-menu* box for its control menu
3. Click *Close*

KEYBOARD APPROACH

2. Press Alt + — for the workbook's control menu
3. Press C to close it

Excel's workspace is now empty again.

FIGURE SS1-15 ■ THE OPEN FILE DIALOG BOX

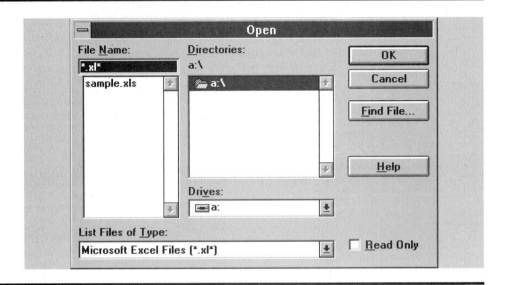

OPENING A WORKBOOK

The **open** command (File menu) retrieves a saved workbook into a workbook window. Excel offers two ways to open a saved workbook. You can type the name of the workbook or select it from a list.

TYPING A WORKBOOK'S NAME. If you know a workbook's name, the most direct way to open the worksheet is to type its name in the *File Name* text box of the *Open File* dialog box. Try this:

MOUSE APPROACH	KEYBOARD APPROACH
1. Click *File* and then *Open* for the Open File dialog box	1. Press Ctrl + O for the Open File dialog box

An Open File dialog box should appear as shown in Figure SS1-15. Notice that its components are similar to those of the *Save As* dialog box.

2. Type SAMPLE

Note: If you have just restarted Excel, make sure you set the default drive to A before opening (use the *drives* drop-down box).

MOUSE APPROACH	KEYBOARD APPROACH
1. Click the *OK* button to open the file	1. Press ↵ to open the file

SELECTING A WORKBOOK FROM A LIST. If you do not remember the name of a worksheet or its exact spelling, you can open a file by selecting from the *File* list of the *Open File* dialog box. Try this:

CHAPTER 1   SPREADSHEET BASICS: CREATING A WORKSHEET   SS33

MOUSE APPROACH	KEYBOARD APPROACH
1. Double-click the *control-menu* box of the workbook (located at the left end of the menu bar) to close the workbook	1. Press Ctrl + F4 to close the current workbook
2. Click *File* and then *Open*	2. Press Ctrl + O for the Open File dialog box
3. Click SAMPLE.XLS from the Files list	3. Press Tab to move the dotted highlight to the Files list box and then press Spacebar to change the highlight to a solid color (press ↓ , if needed, to move the highlight to SAMPLE.XLS)
4. Click the *OK* button	4. Press ↵ to open the file

Tip: If you are using a mouse, you can avoid Steps 3 and 4 by double-clicking SAMPLE.XLS in the *Files* list box.

EXITING MICROSOFT EXCEL AND WINDOWS

There are several ways to exit Excel and then Windows. You can use each window's control menu, use the menu bar, double-click each window's control-menu box, or press the Alt + F4 keys.

Since all Windows applications can be closed using the same techniques, the next exercise will close the Excel window using its control menu. Windows will then be exited using the Program Manager's menu bar. Other exiting techniques are demonstrated throughout this module.

MOUSE APPROACH	KEYBOARD APPROACH
1. Click the *control menu* box of the Microsoft Excel window (left side of Excel's title bar)	1. Press Alt + Spacebar for the Excel control menu (left side of Excel's title bar)
2. Click *Close*	2. Press C to close
3. Click *File* for Program Manager's File menu	3. Press Alt + F for Program Manager's File menu
4. Click *Exit* to exit Program Manager and for the Exit Windows dialog box	4. Press X to exit Program Manager and for the Exit Windows dialog box
5. Click the *OK* button	5. Press ↵ to exit Windows

Use these basic methods for saving and exiting as you work through the remainder of this chapter. You may stop at any point, remembering to save your work so that you can retrieve it later.

CHECKPOINT

✓ Describe the difference between the *Save As* and *Save* commands.
✓ Describe how to close a workbook.
✓ Type your name in Cell B5 and then close the workbook window without saving.
✓ Describe how to open a new workbook.
✓ Exit the Excel program using the menu bar.

CREATING A WORKSHEET

We will now examine some of the intricacies of creating and using spreadsheets. First prepare your program:

1. **Start Windows and then Excel**

2. **Maximize the Excel window, if needed (press** Alt + Spacebar **and then** X **)**

CONSTANT VALUES AND FORMULAS

The data you enter into a cell are classified as either *constant values* or *formulas*. Constant values are data directly entered into a cell, whereas, formulas are preceded by an equal (=) sign. Examples of constant values and formulas are in Figure SS1-16.

CONSTANT VALUES. A **constant value** may be text or a numeric value. Text—such as a report title or street address—can consist of any combination of alphabetic (A–Z), numeric (0–9), or special characters (?, *, etc.). A **numeric value**—such as 2 or 3.5—is simply a number without any alphabetic text. It can also include dates, times, currency, percentages, fractions, or scientific notation. Numeric values can be used in mathematical operations (as in formulas, which are discussed next) whereas, text cannot. A constant value will not change unless you edit it. Editing techniques are discussed later.

Numeric values generally start with a numeral, a decimal point, or a minus symbol (as in –2.3). Excel also reads numerals in brackets [()] as negative numbers.

In most cases, Excel recognizes data the way you entered it. An example of this is a social security number or address. There are times when you may want to restrict a numeric value from being available for use in a mathematical operation, for

FIGURE SS1-16 ■ **EXAMPLES OF CONSTANT VALUES AND FORMULAS**

Example	Description	Entered on the Keyboard As
Revenue	Text constant value	Revenue
.15	Numeric constant value	.15
$2,000,000	Numeric constant value	$2000000
.6*A5/100-B2	Formula	=.6*A5/100-B2
SUM(A1:A4)	Formula-function	=SUM(A1:A4)
C3-D2	Formula	=C3-D2
3rd Quarter	Text constant value	3rd Quarter

CHAPTER 1   SPREADSHEET BASICS: CREATING A WORKSHEET | SS35

example, an account number that contains only numeric values. In such cases, type an apostrophe (') before entering the number to instruct Excel to recognize it as text.

FORMULAS.   A **formula,** such as =A1*2, performs a mathematical operation on data in other cells. Formulas may include a sequence of constant values, cell addresses, operators (*/+−^) or functions. A **function,** such as =SUM(A1:A5), is a predetermined formula built into the spreadsheet. After you enter a formula into a cell, the entry appears in the *entry area of the formula bar,* but the numeric value resulting from the calculation appears in the *cell.* The value can in turn be used in other calculations. Also, the program will recalculate the value as values in related cells are altered. All formulas must start with an equal sign (=).

DISTINGUISHING CONSTANT VALUES FROM FORMULAS.   If you don't start with an equal sign when entering data, it will be recognized as a constant value. For example,

1.   **Move to Cell A1**

2.   **Type** | 718-555-1234 | **and press**   ↵

As shown in Figure SS1-17a, the entry *718-555-1234* appears as you enter it. In this case, the data has been entered as a text constant value and may be interpreted as a telephone number. Now, try this to enter the data as a formula:

3.   **Move to Cell A3**

FIGURE SS1-17 ■ CONFUSING CONSTANT VALUES AND FORMULAS

(a) Data entered without an equal sign (=) are recognized as constant values. (b) Data entered with an equal sign (=) are recognized as formulas. The result of a formula's calculation is displayed in the cell. (c) A mathematical operation that is entered without an equal sign (=) is mistaken for a constant value.

(a)

(b)

(c)

4. Press `=`

5. Type `718-555-1234` and press `↵`

> **Tip:** Remember, instead of pressing the Enter key in Steps 2 and 5, you can click the entry box (✓) on the formula bar to accept the entry.

As in Figure SS1-17b, your entry yields a *mathematical* result of −1071.

Similarly, formulas that begin with a cell reference (such as A1*5) will be mistaken for text constant value, since they begin with a letter. Try this:

6. Move to Cell C1

7. Type `A3*5` and press `↵`

As shown in Figure SS1-17c, the cell displays the data as it was typed, not its mathematical result. Such formulas should be typed with an initial equal symbol (=) to indicate that they are formulas.

8. Move to Cell C1, type `=A3*5` and press `↵`

The result of the formula (in this case, −5355) now appears in Cell C1. Now to close the workbook without saving by using its control-menu box or shortcut keys:

MOUSE APPROACH	KEYBOARD APPROACH
9. Double-click the worksheet's *control-menu* box (located at the left side of the menu bar)	9. Press `Ctrl` + `F4`
10. Click the *No* button to close the window without saving	10. Press `N` to close the window without saving

ENTERING CONSTANT VALUES AND FORMULAS

You are now ready to start a new workbook and enter data for the sales worksheet shown in Figure SS1-18. To do this, move to each cell using the arrow keys (or mouse), type the constant value or formula indicated, and then press the Enter key (or an arrow key).

1. Start Excel or close any open workbook

MOUSE APPROACH	KEYBOARD APPROACH
2. If needed, click *File* and then *New* for a new workbook	2. If needed, press `Ctrl` + `N` for a new workbook

3. Move the cell pointer to Cell A1

ENTERING TEXT CONSTANT VALUES. You will first practice entering text (in this case, column headings) into the spreadsheet.

1. Type your name and press `↵`

Your name is recognized as text because it begins with an equal sign (=). If your name exceeds the width of the cell, its letters will extend right and cover Cell B1 (this is fine for now).

CHAPTER 1   SPREADSHEET BASICS: CREATING A WORKSHEET   **SS37**

FIGURE SS1-18 ■ THE SALES WORKSHEET MODEL

Leave Cells D4 through D8
empty for now.

	A	B	C	D	E	F
1	Your Name				M/D/YY	
2						
3	Agent	Region A	Region B	Totals		
4	Michaels	500	200			
5	Martin	200	450			
6	Parker	300	325			
7	Williams	50	125			
8	Totals					
9						
10						
11						

---

2. **Move to Cell E1**

3. **Type today's date (Use M/D/YY format)**

4. **Press** ↵

> Tip: To retype or correct a cell entry, simply type over the original entry, which will be replaced when you press the Enter key. To erase an entry, move to the cell and click *Edit* and then *Clear*. With the keyboard, move to the cell and press the Delete key.

Using Figure SS1-18 as a guide,

5. **Enter the titles in Cells A3, B3, C3, and D3**

6. **Enter the names (or words) in Cells A4 through A8**

Notice that Excel automatically left-aligns the text.
   To save the workbook on your data disk as SHEET1:

Note: Skip Step 8 if your default drive is already A.

MOUSE APPROACH	**KEYBOARD APPROACH**
7. Click *File* and then *Save As* for its dialog box	7. Press F12 for the Save As dialog box
8. If needed, click the ⬇ button of the Drives' drop-down box, and the *a:* drive icon. Then double-click the *File Name* text box to change the default drive to A and move to the File Name text box	8. If needed, press Alt + V , A and then Alt + N to change the default drive to A and move to the File Name text box
9. Type SHEET1 in the File Name text box, click the *OK* button and then the next *OK* button to save the workbook	9. Type SHEET1 in the File Name text box and then press ↵ twice to save the workbook

You should save a spreadsheet often as you develop it. The few seconds it takes may prove valuable later if your work is lost or incorrectly modified.

ENTERING CONSTANT VALUES/NUMERIC VALUES. When you have finished entering the text, you are ready to enter the numeric values. Although data can be entered in any order, it is good practice to create row and column titles (text) before entering specific values.

1. Move to Cell B4

You can type numbers using the numeric keys on the top row of the regular keyboard or the keys on the numeric keypad after pressing the Num Lock key.

> **Tip: If your keyboard does not have separate arrow keys, remember to press the Num Lock key again before you attempt to use the numeric keypad to move the pointer.**

2. Type `500` **and press** ↓

Remember that pressing the arrow key also enters data. Notice, too, that the entry was recognized as a value because it starts with a number. It will be right-aligned in the cell.

3. Enter the remaining values in Cells B5 through B7

4. Enter the values in Cells C4 through C7

Your spreadsheet should resemble Figure SS1-18. Notice that there are no entries in Cells B8 or C8. These will come later.

5. Save again as *SHEET1* (*File*, *Save* or Ctrl+S)

ENTERING FORMULAS–MATHEMATICAL OPERATORS. You can now enter formulas using cell references (locations) and mathematical operators that will automatically compute totals and enter the results into the worksheet. A **mathematical operator** is a character used in a formula that tells the program to perform a certain calculation. Only the plus (+) operator is used in this section. Other mathematical operators are discussed under the "Mathematical Operators" section.

1. Move to Cell D4

Cell locations that are part of formulas can be typed or pointed to. In this example, you will type the first formula, but point to the second.

2. Type `=B4+C4` **and press** ↵

Remember that the initial equal symbol is needed to indicate that this entry is a formula. The formula will compute the total (700) for Cells B4 and C4, which contain all of Michaels' sales figures. Now, enter the next Column D formula—for Cell D5—using the pointing method:

3. Move to Cell D5 and press `=` **(equal)**

4. Press ← **twice to move to Cell B5**

Note that a light-color-dashed cell pointer appears and moves to Cell B5 as you press the ← key. In addition, Excel types the B5 cell address for you in the formula bar and Cell D5.

5. Press `+`

6. Move to Cell C5

CHAPTER 1   SPREADSHEET BASICS: CREATING A WORKSHEET   **SS39**

This address is also placed on the formula bar and Cell D5.

7. **Press** ⏎ **to accept the formula =B5+C5**

8. **Move back to Cell D5 for a moment**

Note that =B5+C5 appears in the formula bar while 650, the result of the formula appears in Cell D5 as in Figure SS1-19a.

Although this example shows typed formulas for clarity, you may use either method to enter formulas: either type the entire formula or type the math operators but *point* to the cells. Now, complete the Column D entries:

9. **In Cell D6, type** =B6+C6

FIGURE SS1-19 ■ **USING FORMULAS**

(a) Moving the cell pointer to a cell that contains a formula will display its formula in the formula bar. Note that only the result of the formula appears in the cell. (b) The sales worksheet with total formulas added is shown in Column D. (c) Adding the SUM function in Row 8 completes the worksheet.

D5	▼		=B5+C5 ◄—— Formula		
A	**B**	**C**	**D**	**E**	**F**
1 Your Name				M/D/YY	
2					
3 Agent	Region A	Region B	Totals		
4 Michaels	500	200	700		
5 Martin	200	450	650	◄—— Result of formula	
6 Parker	300	325			
7 Williams	50	125			

(a)

	A	**B**	**C**	**D**	**E**	**F**
1	Your Name				M/D/YY	
2						
3	Agent	Region A	Region B	Totals		
4	Michaels	500	200	700		
5	Martin	200	450	650		
6	Parker	300	325	625		
7	Williams	50	125	175		
8	Totals					
9						
10						
11						

(b)

	A	**B**	**C**	**D**	**E**	**F**
1	Your Name				M/D/YY	
2						
3	Agent	Region A	Region B	Totals		
4	Michaels	500	200	700		
5	Martin	200	450	650		
6	Parker	300	325	625		
7	Williams	50	125	175		
8	Totals	1050	1100	2150		
9						
10						
11						

(c)

10. In Cell D7, type =B7+C7 and press ↵

Your workbook should resemble Figure SS1-19b. If it does not, return to the cell that is incorrect, retype, and enter the correction.

11. Save the *SHEET1* workbook again

ENTERING FORMULAS—FUNCTIONS. Although you could enter formulas using cell references and mathematical operators to compute the totals in Row 8, an easier method uses one of Excel's many built-in functions. For example, the formulas =B4+B5+B6+B7 typed into Cell B8 would correctly compute the total of the sales figures in Row B, but it is cumbersome to use. Imagine having to total 100 cells—the typing would take forever. Instead, you can invoke a built-in SUM function as follows:

1. Move to Cell B8

2. Type =SUM(B4:B7) and press ↵

The SUM function instructs the program to compute the total for all the cell values listed in the range specified within the parentheses (more on range shortly). That is, the program will add all the cells between B4 and B7, which includes B4, B5, B6, and B7. If you wanted to add all cells from Z1 to Z1000, you would type the range as *(Z1:Z1000)*. As you can see, this is much easier than typing every cell address.

Enter the remaining functions as follows:

3. In Cell C8, type =SUM(C4:C7)

4. In Cell D8, type =SUM(D4:D7) and press ↵

Your screen should resemble Figure SS1-19c. If it does not, return to the cell that is incorrect, retype, and enter the correction.

5. Save the *SHEET1* workbook again and then close it

Note that Cell D8 contains the grand total, which can be computed many ways. The function *SUM(D4:D7)* summed the totals for each agent, but you could have also summed the totals for each region with =B8+C8, or totaled all the individual sales figures with *SUM(B4:C7)*. See the Appendix for a comprehensive list of functions.

> Tip: There are many ways to compute a result. Although you should be consistent and rational, as long as your math is correct it doesn't matter what formula or function you use.

THE RECALCULATION FEATURE

A powerful spreadsheet feature is **automatic recalculation,** which recalculates formulas whenever values in related cells are changed. This feature allows you to update or modify values and see their mathematical consequences immediately.

1. Start Excel or close any open workbook

2. Open the *SHEET1* spreadsheet (if needed, change the default drive before opening)

3. Move to Cell B4

4. Type 600 and press ↵

CHAPTER 1   SPREADSHEET BASICS: CREATING A WORKSHEET   SS41

FIGURE SS1-20 ■ THE RECALCULATION FEATURE

A change in Cell B4 causes
related cells (D4, B8 and D8)
to change as well.

	A	B	C	D	E	F
1	Your Name				M/D/YY	
2						
3	Agent	Region A	Region B	Totals		
4	Michaels	600	200	800		
5	Martin	200	450	650		
6	Parker	300	325	625		
7	Williams	50	125	175		
8	Totals	1150	1100	2250		
9						
10						
11						

These cells change
automatically to
show new results

This action changes Michaels' Region A sales from 500 to 600. As shown in SS1-20, not only did the value in Cell B4 change, but also, because of automatic recalculation, values changed in Cells B8, D4, and D8. Compare the results with the original spreadsheet in Figure SS1-19c. Every cell whose value depended on the value in Cell B4 has changed.

ANSWERING "WHAT IF?" QUESTIONS. The recalculation feature greatly expands the utility of electronic spreadsheets. Certainly, interrelating cells with formulas simplifies worksheet use, but it also allows easy modification and enhanced decision making. Most businesspeople go through an extensive series of "What if?" scenarios when making key decisions. For example, what if Region A totals are 10 percent lower? Or what if Williams increases Region A sales to 500?

The ultimate effect of a change often depends on dozens of interdependent figures. Consider all the values that must be recalculated to answer a simply stated financial question like, "What if some of my income is deferred into the next fiscal year?" How does this one action affect personal income-tax deductions, adjustments, and ultimately, tax liability? On the company's side, how are its payments for social security, withholding, pensions, and bonuses affected?

To examine how making changes affects column and row totals,

1. **Change a few values in Cells B4 through C7**

2. **Close the workbook without saving when you are finished**

Remember, to close a workbook without saving, double-click its control-menu box and then click the *No* button. With the keyboard, press the Ctrl + F4 keys and then the N key.

A FURTHER WORD ON FORMULAS AND CONSTANT VALUES. In the last exercise, you modified cells with numeric constant values, but not those with formulas. Remember that a workbook shows a formula's *result,* not the formula itself. Although a formula result of 200 and a numeric constant value of 200 may look identical in a cell, they are not interchangeable. Formulas are "flexible" in that they can be recalculated; constant numeric values are not. If you replace a formula with a value, even though the number appears to be the same, the result can no longer be recalculated. Therefore, if you erase a formula by mistake, do not simply type its current result back into the cell. Instead, retype the *formula* to ensure that future recalculations will be mathematically correct.

MATHEMATICAL OPERATORS

As discussed earlier, a **mathematical operator** is a character used in a formula that tells the program to perform a certain calculation. There are a number of operators that you can use:

^ (caret)	exponentiation
* (asterisk)	multiplication
/ (slash)	division
+ (plus)	addition
− (minus)	subtraction

As in normal mathematics, when these operators are used in combination, the *hierarchy of operations,* or order of precedence of the operators, is as follows: (1) exponentiation is performed first; (2) multiplication and division are performed next, in order reading from left to right; and (3) addition and subtraction are last, also performed in order from left to right.

When parentheses surround parts of a formula, however, the operation inside the parentheses takes precedence. More than one pair of parentheses are evaluated from innermost to outermost, and from left to right.

> **Tip: The sentence "Please Excuse My Dear Aunt Sally" (for Parentheses, Exponentiation, Multiplication, Division, Addition, Subtraction) is a helpful mnemonic device for remembering the hierarchy of operations.**

To see how the hierarchy works, consider the following formula:

$$=A1/A2-A3*A4\verb|^|2$$

This results in the following sequence of computations:

1. **The value in Cell A4 is raised to the second power**

2. **The value in Cell A1 is divided by the value in Cell A2**

3. **The value in Cell A3 is multiplied by the result of Step 1**

4. **Step 3's result is subtracted from the result of Step 2**

If A1 = 6, A2 = 4, A3 = 2, and A4 = 3, the result would be + 6/4 − 2*3^2, or −16.5.

Now consider the same formula with added parentheses:

$$=A1/(A2-A3)*A4\verb|^|2$$

CHAPTER 1　SPREADSHEET BASICS: CREATING A WORKSHEET　SS43

FIGURE SS1-21 ■ **SOME HIERARCHY EXAMPLES**

If A1 = 3, A2 = 4, A3 = 5, A4 = 6:

Mathematical Operation	Answer
=A1/A2 + A3*A4	30.75
=A1/(A2 + A3)*A4	2.0
=(A1/A2 + A3)*A4	34.5
=(A1^2 + A3)/(A2 + A4)	1.4
=A4 − A1/A2*A3	2.25
=(A4 − A1)/(A2*A3)	0.15

This formula produces a different sequence:

1. **Cell A3's value is subtracted from the value in Cell A2**

2. **The value in Cell A4 is raised to the second power**

3. **The value in Cell A1 is divided by the result of Step 1**

4. **The result of Step 3 is multiplied by the result of Step 2**

This formula, using the same cell values as before, yields a result of 27.

Figure SS1-21 provides further practice with evaluating the hierarchy of operations by listing a few illustrative formulas and their results.

CHECKPOINT

✓ On a new workbook, type in the number 1234 as a text constant value in Cell A1. Which character did you type before the number?
✓ What key must be entered to identify an entry as a formula?
✓ In Cell A3, enter a formula that will add 5 to a value in Cell A2.
✓ What is the result of the formula 6 + (3*2)^2–(12/2)*7?
✓ Describe the mathematical operators that can be used in an Excel formula.

THE RANGE CONCEPT

Although data can be manipulated cell by cell, much of a spreadsheet's power comes from its ability to affect a large group of cells at one time. Many of Excel's commands (formatting, copying, moving, printing, erasing, inserting, sorting, and

SS44 | SPREADSHEETS WITH MICROSOFT EXCEL 5.0

FIGURE SS1-22 ■ **EXAMPLES OF TYPICAL RANGES**

---

graphing, to name a few) rely on your ability to describe a *range* of spreadsheet cells. As shown in Figure SS1-22, a **range** is a rectangular grouping of one or more cells. Because of its shape, a range can easily be identified by indicating its diagonal corners. That is, to identify a range, specify the cell in its upper left corner, followed by a colon (for separation purposes), and then the cell in its lower right corner. Thus, the range E8:G19 indicates all 36 cells in the Cell E8 through Cell G19 (Columns E, F, and G; Rows 8 and 19). Ranges can contain a single cell, or many cells grouped in one or more rows or columns.

Excel also allows the selection of several ranges that may be separate, touching, or overlapping. This process is discussed in the appendix. The following exercise explores the fundamentals of specifying a single range.

1. **Start Excel or close any open workbook**

2. **If needed, open a new workbook (File, New or Ctrl + N)**

3. **Enter the data into eight cells as shown in Figure SS1-23a**

Assume you want to create two sums in Cells B7 and C7, which will total their respective columns. You can specify a range by typing its endpoints or pointing to them.

TYPING A RANGE FOR A FUNCTION

The most direct way to identify a range is to type it, as you did in the section on functions. Try one more here:

1. **Move to Cell B7**

2. **Type =SUM(B2:B5) **

3. **Press ↵ **

CHAPTER 1   SPREADSHEET BASICS: CREATING A WORKSHEET   **SS45**

FIGURE SS1-23   ■   **IDENTIFYING RANGES**

(a) Data for Cells B2 through C5. (b) Pointing to the first cell in a range places its cell address in the formula bar and cell. (c) Pressing and holding the Shift key while moving the pointer selects the range with a light dashed outline and types the cell address in the formula bar and cell. (d) The completed range has been entered.

	A	B	C	D
1				
2		10	7	
3		7	6	
4		81	78	
5		2	1	
6				
7				
8				
9				

(a)

C2   ↕ ✕ f_x =SUM(C2

	A	B	C	D
1				
2		10	7	
3		7	6	
4		81	78	
5		2	1	
6				
7		100	=SUM(C2	
8				
9				

(b)

C2   ↕ ✕ f_x =SUM(C2:C5

	A	B	C	D
1				
2		10	7	
3		7	6	
4		81	78	
5		2	1	
6				
7		100	=SUM(C2:C5	
8				
9				

(c)

	A	B	C	D
1				
2		10	7	
3		7	6	
4		81	78	
5		2	1	
6				
7		100	92	
8				
9				

(d)

The cells included within the parentheses of the SUM function identify a range whose upper left corner is Cell B2 and whose lower right corner is Cell B5. The function then computes the sum of this cell range.

POINTING TO A RANGE FOR A FUNCTION

You may prefer to point to cells to specify a range. Not only does this save typing, but the screen will also visually display the range as you define it. Try this:

1. Move to Cell C7

2. Type =SUM((but do *not* press the Enter key)

Tip: Clicking the Function Wizard (*fx*) button will open a dialog box with a list of functions.

Of course, you could type the range (C2:C5) as before, but try pointing instead, as follows:

MOUSE APPROACH	KEYBOARD APPROACH
3. Click *Cell C2*	3. Move the cell pointer to Cell C2

Notice how the program simultaneously types the cell address (C2) in the entry area of the formula bar and in Cell C7 as shown in Figure SS1-23b. A "Point" message also appears in the status bar.

MOUSE APPROACH	KEYBOARD APPROACH
4. Press and hold Shift while clicking *Cell C5*	4. Press and hold Shift while moving to Cell C5

Notice that the second cell address changes to show the current cell. Cell C5's address appears on the formula bar as shown in Figure SS1-23c. Notice, too, that a light dashed outline appears around the cell range C2 through C5—a helpful visual indication of the selected range. To complete the function,

5. Press ↵

Note that Excel automatically places a ")" at the end of the function. Your screen should now resemble Figure SS1-23d.

6. Save as *SAMPLE2* (Remember to change the default drive to A if needed)

For clarity, this module gives instructions that specify ranges by typing them, but you may point or type ranges as you prefer. Keep in mind, though, that you cannot mix techniques within one range specification. If you type the first cell in a range, you must type the second. If you point to the first, point to the second.

SELECTING A RANGE FOR TOOLBAR OR MENU COMMANDS

You can also set a range for use with many toolbar or menu commands using a mouse or the keyboard. Do the following to prepare for the next exercises:

1. Move to Cell C7

CHAPTER 1 SPREADSHEET BASICS: CREATING A WORKSHEET   SS47

MOUSE APPROACH	KEYBOARD APPROACH
2. Click *Edit, Clear* and then *All* to erase the sum	2. Press Delete to erase the sum
3. Move to Cell C2	

A few common techniques to set a range prior to clicking a toolbar button are discussed next.

SELECTING A RANGE USING THE SHIFT KEY. To select the range C2:C7 using the Shift key as part of the command,

MOUSE APPROACH	KEYBOARD APPROACH
4. Press and hold Shift while clicking Cell C7	4. Press and hold Shift while pressing ↓ five times

At this point, you can invoke a command to effect the range by using the menu bar or toolbar. Try this:

5. Point to and click the *Auto Sum* button

The sum will appear at the bottom cell of the range, which must be left empty. Now, to remove the range,

MOUSE APPROACH	KEYBOARD APPROACH
6. Click an open area	6. Move the pointer to any cell

SELECTING A RANGE BY DRAGGING. To set a range by dragging your mouse over the desired range:

7. Repeat Steps 1 through 3

8. Point to *Cell C2* and then press and hold the left mouse button

9. While holding the mouse button, point to *Cell C7*

10. Release the button

   The range *C2:C7* is highlighted

Now that your range has been selected, you can invoke a variety of commands by using Toolbar or Menu commands. Try this:

11. Point to and click the *Auto Sum* button

12. Remove the selection highlight

13. Close the workbook without saving

> Tip: These selection techniques can be used whenever a range is selected before invoking a command.

CHECKPOINT

✓ Using the pointing method, create a sum in Cell B7 that totals all cells from B2 to B5.

- ✓ Using the typing method, create a sum in Cell C7 that totals all cells from C2 to C5.
- ✓ Using either typing or pointing, create a sum in D7 that totals all cells from B2 to C5. Save as SAMPLE2.
- ✓ How do you delete a cell entry?
- ✓ Describe the procedures to use the Auto Sum toolbar button.

PRINTING A WORKSHEET

Most spreadsheets are ultimately printed on paper. To prepare for this exercise,

1. **Start Excel or close any open workbook**
2. **Open *SHEET1***

You are now ready to print the spreadsheet. In this exercise, you will print the entire worksheet, from Cell A1 to Cell E10. Excel allows you to print to your screen (using *Print Preview*) or to print to a printer. You may also print a selected range of a worksheet, multiple worksheets, specific pages of a worksheet, the entire workbook, or multiple copies. The exercises in this section will illustrate print previewing, printing a selected worksheet, and then printing a selected range of a worksheet.

PRINTING TO THE SCREEN

Excel's *Print Preview* feature allows you to view a worksheet or a selected range of a worksheet as it will appear on paper. Try this:

MOUSE APPROACH	KEYBOARD APPROACH
1. Click *File* and then *Print Preview* for its dialog box	1. Press Alt + F and then V for the Print Preview dialog box

The top of your *Print Preview* window should appear similar to Figure SS1-24a. To enlarge the view of the worksheet,

MOUSE APPROACH	KEYBOARD APPROACH
2. Click the *Zoom* button to enlarge the view	2. Press ↵ to enlarge the view

Your screen should resemble Figure SS1-24b. The *Print Preview* toolbar can also be used to invoke a variety of other commands. Now, to return to the workbook,

MOUSE APPROACH	KEYBOARD APPROACH
3. Click the *Close* button	3. Press Esc

PRINTING TO A PRINTER

To print the current worksheet to your printer,

1. **Turn on your printer**

CHAPTER 1   SPREADSHEET BASICS: CREATING A WORKSHEET   SS49

FIGURE SS1-24 ■ THE *PRINT PREVIEW* WINDOW

(a) The *Print Preview* window. (b) Zooming the view of a worksheet.

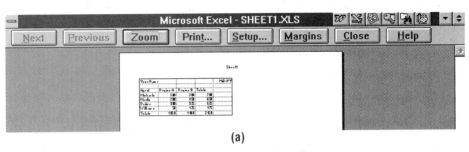

(a)

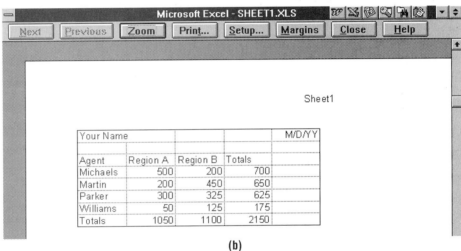

(b)

MOUSE APPROACH	KEYBOARD APPROACH
2. Click *File* and then *Print* for its dialog box	1. Press Ctrl + P for the Print dialog box

The *Print* dialog box should appear as in Figure SS1-25a. Note that its default setting is to print the current worksheet (selected sheet[s]). Other print options include printing a specific range of a worksheet (selection), the entire workbook, specified pages, and multiple copies. You can also access the *Print Preview* feature and make page setup changes using this dialog box. To print the entire worksheet,

MOUSE APPROACH	KEYBOARD APPROACH
3. Click the *OK* button	3. Press ↵

The contents of your printed worksheet should appear as in Figure SS1-25b. Note that the column and row identifiers do not appear on the printed spreadsheet, only in the worksheet cells themselves.

FIGURE SS1-25 ■ PRINTING THE CURRENT WORKSHEET

(a) The Print Dialog box.
(b) The printed worksheet. (Note that Excel automatically places the sheet tab name at the upper right corner of the page and a page number at the bottom center of the page.)

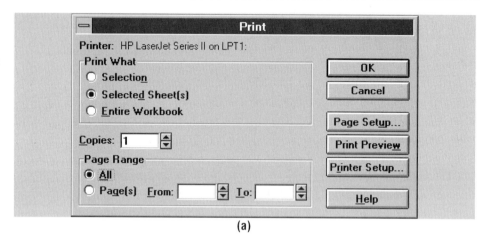

PRINTING A SELECTED RANGE

At times, you may want to print only a portion of a worksheet. To do so, you must first tell Excel your desired range. For example, to print only Columns A and B of "SHEET1," follow these steps:

1. Select the range A1:B8

MOUSE APPROACH	KEYBOARD APPROACH
2. Click *File* and then *Print* for its dialog box	2. Press Ctrl + P for the Print dialog box
3. Click *Selection*	3. Press Alt + N for Selection

To print the selected range:

MOUSE APPROACH	KEYBOARD APPROACH
4. Click the *OK* button to print	4. Press ↵ to print

Your printed copy should resemble Figure SS1-26. As before, column and row identifiers are not printed.

CHAPTER 1   SPREADSHEET BASICS: CREATING A WORKSHEET   **SS51**

FIGURE SS1-26 ■ PRINTING A SELECTED PRINT RANGE

Your Name	
Agent	Region A
Michaels	500
Martin	200
Parker	300
Williams	50
Totals	1050

---

5.   Close the workbook without saving

CHECKPOINT

✓   What does the Print Preview command do?
✓   What does the Zoom command do in the Print Preview window?
✓   Print out the cells in Column B only.
✓   Print out the cells in Columns B and C on a new page.
✓   Print both of these ranges on the *same page*.

EDITING A WORKSHEET

At some point, you may want to change cell data. Perhaps you want to correct a mistake or change a constant value or formula. To prepare for this exercise,

1.   Start Excel or close any open workbook

2.   Open *SHEET1*

It should resemble Figure SS1-19c.

REPLACING CELL CONTENTS

There are three basic ways to change the contents of a cell: (1) move to the cell and retype its contents, (2) use the *Edit* mode to insert or delete characters, or (3) erase a cell's contents through the command menu. The following exercises briefly present each technique.

RETYPING.   The most direct way to replace cell contents is to move to the cell and retype its data. For example,

1.   In Cell A4, type | Smith |

2.   In Cell C5, type | 575 | **and press** ↵

The previous contents (*Michaels* and *450*) have been replaced with the new entries. This technique works well when completely different data must be entered, but you must retype the entire entry even when minor changes are needed.

EDITING. A better method for minor adjustments is to use the *Edit* mode. This is particularly useful when you have created long formulas and do not want to reenter them. Any cell data can be edited with the following procedure:

1. Move to Cell B7

MOUSE APPROACH	KEYBOARD APPROACH
2. Double-click *Cell B7* to invoke *Edit*	2. Press F2 to invoke *Edit*

Note that "Edit" appears on the left side of the status bar. You can now use the arrow keys to move the insertion point and then type additional characters (or delete them) as needed.

3. If needed press the arrow keys to move the insertion point before the 5 in 50.

Your Cell B7 should resemble Figure SS1-27.

4. Type 1

The new character is inserted at the insertion-point location. Notice that the number now reads *150*.

5. Press ↵ to accept the change

Here's another example:

6. Move back to Cell B7

MOUSE APPROACH	KEYBOARD APPROACH
7. Double-click Cell B7	7. Press F2

Again, the cell contents appear on the entry line.

8. Move the insertion point before the *1* in *150*

9. Press Delete

The *150* has been changed back to *50*.

10. Press ↵ to accept the change

After double-clicking the cell or pressing F2, you may use the Home key to move quickly to the beginning of a long cell entry, or the End key to move to the end. Try this on your own. You may also want to experiment with the Insert key (which turns on the typeover feature) and the Backspace key.

FIGURE SS1-27 ■ EDITING A CELL

Double-clicking a cell or pressing the F2 key will invoke the Edit mode and activate the insertion point.

6	Parker	300
7	Williams	50
8	Totals	1050

Insertion point

ERASING CELLS. At times, you will simply want to erase cell contents. The *Edit* menu offers a *Clear* command for this purpose.

1. Move to Cell E1

MOUSE APPROACH	KEYBOARD APPROACH
2. Click *Edit, Clear,* and then *All*	2. Press Delete

The date is gone.

> Tip: When you use the *Edit* menu to invoke the *Clear* command, a *Clear* dialog box will appear with three options: Cell contents only (Default), Styles only, or both. Styles relates to text and graphic enhancement.

You can also erase a range of cells by specifying the range *before* pressing the Enter key as follows:

3. Move to Cell D3

MOUSE APPROACH	KEYBOARD APPROACH
4. Press and hold Shift while clicking Cell D8	4. Press Shift while pressing ↓ to expand the range to Cell D8
5. Click *Edit Clear* and then *All*	5. Press Delete to erase the range
6. Click *Cell D3* (or any cell) to remove the range selection highlight	6. Move to Cell D3 (or any cell) to remove the range selection highlight

All data in Cells D3:D8 have been deleted.

UNDOING AN ACTION. The **Undo** command (Edit menu) can be used to undo your last action. Try this:

MOUSE APPROACH	KEYBOARD APPROACH
1. Click *Edit* and then *Undo*	1. Press Ctrl + Z to undo

The last set of erased cells returns to the screen.

2. Remove the range selection
3. Close the workbook without saving

INSERTING AND DELETING ROWS OR COLUMNS

Rows or columns can be added to or removed from your worksheet using the *Rows* or *Columns* command (insert menu). The following exercise inserts rows before and after the list of names in "SHEET1," inserts a column between the region sales data, and then deletes it.

INSERTING A ROW. The basic technique for inserting a row is to position the pointer where you want the new row to appear, and then invoke the *Rows* command (insert menu). Try this:

1. Open SHEET1

2. Move to Cell A4 (any cell in Row 4 will do)

Your screen should resemble Figure SS1-28a.

MOUSE APPROACH	KEYBOARD APPROACH
3. Click _Insert_ and then _Rows_ to insert a row	**3. Press** `Alt` **+** `I` **and then** `R` **to insert a Row**

A new row appears in Row 4, as shown in Figure SS1-28b. All rows below the new one have been moved down one row and all formulas have been adjusted.

4. Move to Cell B9 and examine its contents in the formula bar

Note that the formula has been adjusted to reflect the added row. The formula range now reads *B5:B8* instead of *B4:B7*. The program automatically adjusts all formulas affected by adding rows (or columns).

A note of caution: Rows added *outside* a function's stated range will *not* be included in the adjusted function range. For a new row to be included, it must be added *within* the endpoints—upper left to lower right cell of the function's range. For

---

FIGURE SS1-28 ■ INSERTING A ROW

(a) The cell pointer is positioned in Row 4, where the new row will be inserted. (b) When the new row is inserted, all rows below it shift down one row.

	A	B	C	D	E	F
1	Your Name				M/D/YY	
2						
3	Agent	Region A	Region B	Totals		
4	Michaels	500	200	700		
5	Martin	200	450	650		
6	Parker	300	325	625		
7	Williams	50	125	175		
8	Totals	1050	1100	2150		
9						
10						
11						

(a)

	A	B	C	D	E	F
1	Your Name				M/D/YY	
2						
3	Agent	Region A	Region B	Totals		
4						
5	Michaels	500	200	700		
6	Martin	200	450	650		
7	Parker	300	325	625		
8	Williams	50	125	175		
9	Totals	1050	1100	2150		
10						
11						

(b)

example, you just added a row *above* the old Row 4, outside the range B4:B7. If you were to type data into this row, it would not be included in the column total (unless, of course, you edited the range yourself to include it). However, if you had added the row within the range endpoints—that is, between Row 4 and Row 7—the program would automatically extend the range to include it. Keep this in mind when adding rows or columns. Now, add one more row as follows:

5. **Stay in Cell B9 (any cell in Row 9 will do)**

MOUSE APPROACH	KEYBOARD APPROACH
6. Click *Insert* and then *Rows*	6. Press Alt + I and then R

7. **Save this spreadsheet as SHEET2 (*File*, Save *As* or F12)**

To insert more than one row, you must first select the desired range to be inserted.

8. **Move to Cell A2**

MOUSE APPROACH	KEYBOARD APPROACH
9. Press and hold Shift while clicking Cell A4 to select a range of three rows	9. Press and hold Shift while pressing ↓ twice to select a range of three rows ending with Cell A4

Three rows are now selected on the screen to be added. Note that the first cell of a selected range contains a dark border (the anchor cell). All subsequent cells of the range are highlighted.

MOUSE APPROACH	KEYBOARD APPROACH
10. Press and hold Shift while clicking Cell A3	10. Press and hold Shift while pressing ↑ once

Now only two rows are selected (including Cell A2). You can adjust the number of rows to be added before invoking the insertion feature.

MOUSE APPROACH	KEYBOARD APPROACH
11. Click *Insert* and then *Rows* to insert the two rows	11. Press Alt + I and then R to insert the two rows

Two rows have now been added to your worksheet.

INSERTING A COLUMN. You can insert a column (in this case, between Columns B and C) by following the same procedure, but choose *Columns* instead of *Rows* from the Insert menu.

1. **Move to Cell C6 (any cell in Column C will do)**

MOUSE APPROACH	KEYBOARD APPROACH
2. Click *Insert* and then *Columns* to insert a column	2. Press Alt + I and then C to insert a column

A new column has been inserted at Column C, and all columns that follow have been moved to the right.

3. **Move to Cell E7 and examine this cell's contents**

The formula now reads =*B7+D7,* reflecting that Column C is now Column D.

4. Save this spreadsheet as *SHEET3*

> Tip: Formulas do not include the inserted row or column in their calculations, but simply adjust their current cell references to their new locations. Only ranges can expand automatically to reflect inserted rows or columns.

DELETING A ROW OR COLUMN. You can delete rows and columns with a similar technique—move to the row or column to be deleted, and use the *Delete* dialog box of the *Edit* menu.

1. Open *SHEET3* (if needed)
2. Move to Cell C7 (any cell in Column C will do)

MOUSE APPROACH	KEYBOARD APPROACH
3. Press *Edit* and then *Delete* for the Delete dialog box	3. Press Alt + E and then D for the Delete dialog box
4. Click *Entire Column* and then the *OK* button	4. Press C and then ↵

The column is gone. All columns to its right are shifted left, and all formulas are readjusted to reflect the change.

More than one row or column can be deleted by selecting its range, as before.

5. Move to Cell C2 (any cell in Row 2 is fine)

MOUSE APPROACH	KEYBOARD APPROACH
6. Press and hold Shift while clicking Cell C3 to highlight two rows of cells	6. Press and hold Shift while pressing ↓ once to highlight two rows of cells
7. Click *Edit* and then *Delete* for the Delete dialog box	7. Press Alt + E and then D for the Delete dialog box
8. Click the *Entire Row* and then the *OK* button	8. Press R and then ↵

Column D and Row 10 should now display the totals. If they do not, use *Undo* or open "SHEET3," and repeat the *Delete* procedure. To exit Excel without saving the worksheet,

MOUSE APPROACH	KEYBOARD APPROACH
9. Double-click Excel's *control-menu* box and then the *No* button	9. Press Alt + F4 and then N

10. Exit windows

CHECKPOINT

✓ Open SHEET1. With typeover, change *Williams* in Cell A7 to *West* and *200* in C4 to *375*. Use the Edit mode to remove the *s* in *Totals* in Cells D1 and A8.
✓ Insert a row at Row 6. Fill in the four new cells with *Burstein, 100, 150,* and the formula =*B6+C6*. Print the worksheet.

CHAPTER 1   SPREADSHEET BASICS: CREATING A WORKSHEET   **SS57**

✓   Insert a column at Column A, save as SHEET3a, and exit Excel and Windows.

✓   Describe how to delete a row.

✓   Describe how to delete a column.

SUMMARY

■   A spreadsheet, or worksheet, displays data in columnar form. It is composed of cells formed by vertical columns and horizontal rows.

■   The Excel window has a title bar, menu bar, toolbars, formula bar, workspace, and status bar.

■   The workbook window occupies Excel window's workspace and displays only a portion of the entire spreadsheet, identifying columns with letters and rows with numbers. Each cell is identified by a cell address, which displays the cell's column and row coordinates.

■   The current cell will receive data or be affected by the next command. The current cell is indicated by a cell pointer that resembles a dark bordered rectangle in the workbook window and a cell address in the name box of the formula bar.

■   When the cell pointer is moved off the workbook window's display area by keyboard, the worksheet will scroll, or reposition itself, to display the current cell.

■   Excel features can be accessed by mouse or keyboard through its menu bar. Each menu-bar item opens to a pull-down menu. Selecting by mouse involves clicking the menu-bar item and then the menu item. With the keyboard, pressing the Alt key and the underlined letter of the menu-bar item opens its menu. Pressing the underlined letter of the menu item selects the item.

■   Toolbars contain a series of command buttons and drop-down boxes that provide quick access to the program's features by mouse. Shortcut keys are also available for many commands to provide fast keyboard access to Excel features.

■   The status bar, the bottom row of the Excel window, displays the mode indicator (which shows what the program is doing), description of a selected command, caps lock, number lock, and scroll lock indicators.

■   Constant values are data directly entered into a cell. Data may include text or numeric values. Text includes any combination of alphabetic (A–Z), numeric (0–9), or special characters (?, *, etc.). Numeric values are numbers without any alphabetic text that can be used in mathematical operations. A constant value will not change unless you edit it.

■   Formulas must start with an equal sign (=). They perform mathematical operations on data in other cells. They may include a sequence of constant values, cell addresses, operators (*/+ −^), and functions.

■   A function is a predetermined formula built into the spreadsheet.

■   Formulas follow the hierarchy of operations: parentheses, exponentiation (^), multiplication (*) or division (/), and addition (+) or subtraction (−).

■   The recalculation feature automatically recalculates formulas when values in related cells are changed. This feature allows "What if?" questions to be investigated.

■   A range is a rectangular grouping of cells. It is identified by specifying diagonal corners—its upper-left cell and lower-right cell (or lower-left and upper-right cells)—separated by a period. Ranges can be designated by typing, pointing or dragging.

■   The chapter presented the following commands:

SPREADSHEETS WITH MICROSOFT EXCEL 5.0

Command	Mouse Approach	Keyboard Approach
Menu-bar item	Menu-bar item	**Alt** + underlined letter
Save As dialog box	*File, Save As*	**F12**
Save	*File, Save*	**Ctrl** + **S**
Open	*File, Open*	**Ctrl** + **O**
Erase	*Edit, Clear, All*	**Delete**
Exit	*File, Exit*	**Alt** + **F4**
Undo	*Edit, Undo*	**Alt** + **Z**
Help	*Help, Content*	**F1**
Edit a cell	Double-click it	**F2**
Close workbook	*File, Close*	**Ctrl** + **F4**
Insert a row/column	*Insert, Row or Column*	**Alt** + **I** , **R**
Delete a row/column	*Edit, Delete, Entire Row,* or Entire *Column, OK*	**Alt** + **E** , **D** , **R** or **C** **↵**
Print	*File, Print*	**Ctrl** + **P**

KEY TERMS

Shown in parentheses are the page numbers on which key terms are boldfaced.

Automatic recalculation (SS40)
Cell (SS13)
Cell address (SS13)
Cell pointer (SS13)
Closing (SS31)
Command buttons (SS12)
Constant value (SS34)
Current cell (SS13)
Drop-down box (SS12)
Entry area (SS18)
Formula (SS35)

Formula bar (SS12)
Function (SS35)
Mathematical operator (SS38)
Name box (SS18)
New (SS31)
Numeric value (SS34)
Open (SS32)
Pull-down menu (SS12)
Range (SS44)
Save (SS29)
Save As (SS29)

Scroll (SS14)
Scroll bar (SS15)
Sheet (SS11)
Shortcut menu (SS24)
Spreadsheet (SS4)
Status bar (SS13)
Toolbar (SS12)
Undo (SS53)
Workbook (SS11)
Worksheet (SS4)

QUIZ

TRUE/FALSE

1. A workbook may contain only a worksheet.
2. Columns are identified by letters.

CHAPTER 1   SPREADSHEET BASICS: CREATING A WORKSHEET   **SS59**

3. The current cell is visually identified by the cell pointer.
4. Pressing the Home key moves the cell pointer to the center of the worksheet.
5. The current cell address is normally displayed in the formula bar.
6. The menu-bar pull down menu can be opened by pressing the Ctrl key and the underlined letter of the item.
7. Pressing the Esc key while in a menu or dialog box will back you up one command step.
8. Formulas must start with an apostrophe to be recognized by the program.
9. Excel functions must begin with an = symbol.
10. Excel treats the typed entry *E1 + E2* as a constant value.

MULTIPLE CHOICE

11. Which of these is *not* part of the Excel window?
    a. Menu bar
    b. DOS prompt
    c. Workspace
    d. Status bar
12. The _ displays the column and row coordinates of a cell.
    a. formula bar
    b. cell pointer
    c. status bar
    d. window
13. _ refers to automatically repositioning the worksheet area window to show the current cell.
    a. Windowing
    b. Addressing
    c. Pointing
    d. Scrolling
14. Which of these is *never* displayed in the formula bar?
    a. Entry area
    b. Cell address
    c. Date and time
    d. Command button(s)
15. The _ displays a one-word message that shows what the spreadsheet is currently doing.
    a. status bar
    b. toolbar
    c. menu bar
    d. cell pointer
16. Which key invokes the pull-down menu?
    a. The Alt key
    b. The Alt key and the underlined letter of a menu-bar item
    c. The Esc key
    d. The underlined letter of a menu-bar item
17. Which one of these cell entries is *not* a formula?
    a. =35+C7
    b. =A5*B6
    c. =SUM(B7:B23)
    d. 52

18. A phone-number entry typed as *718-555-1212* will be treated as a _ by Excel.
    a. function
    b. formula
    c. constant value-number
    d. constant value-text
19. The range "rectangle" is normally specified from
    a. Upper left to lower right
    b. Upper left to upper right
    c. Upper right to lower right
    d. Lower left to lower right
20. How would =SUM(B2:B5) change after a column is inserted with the cell pointer in Cell B3?
    a. =SUM(B3:B6)
    b. =SUM(C2:C5)
    c. =SUM(B2:B6)
    d. =SUM(C2:C6)

MATCHING

Select the lettered item from the figure that best matches each phrase below:

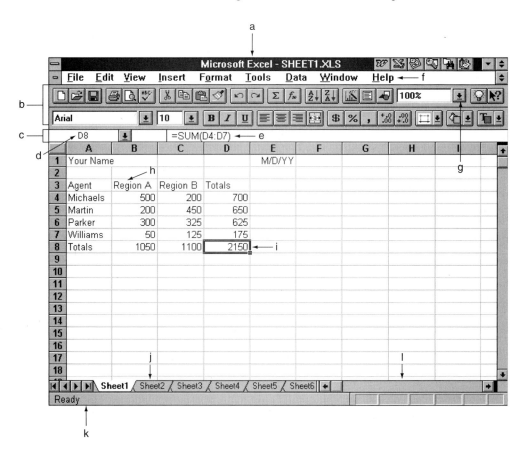

21. A series of command buttons that can be used to access Excel features quickly.
22. Displays a window's name.

CHAPTER 1   SPREADSHEET BASICS: CREATING A WORKSHEET   SS61

23. The Excel cell pointer.
24. A standard Windows feature that opens to pull-down menus containing commands related to the application.
25. The function command in Cell D8.
26. The area of the Excel window called the formula bar.
27. Clicking this button opens a drop-down list.
28. The name box.
29. The area of the window that indicates what the spreadsheet is currently doing.
30. A constant value.

ANSWERS

True/False: 1. F; 2. T; 3. T; 4. F; 5. T; 6. F; 7. T; 8. F; 9. T; 10. T
Multiple Choice: 11. b; 12. a; 13. d; 14. c; 15. a; 16. b; 17. d; 18. d; 19. a; 20. b
Matching: 21. b; 22. a; 23. i; 24. f; 25. e; 26. c; 27. g; 28. d; 29. k; 30. h

---

EXERCISES

I. OPERATIONS

Provide the Excel Mouse Approach and Keyboard Approach actions (as appropriate) required to do each of the following operations. For each operation, assume a hard-disk system with a data diskette in drive A. Further assume that the data diskette contains files named "JULY.XLS" and "OCTOBER.XLS."

1. Start Windows and then the Excel program.
2. Set the default drive to A as you open "OCTOBER.XLS."
3. Erase the contents of Cell E7.
4. Insert a row at Row 9.
5. Delete Column C.
6. Display a total of Cells B5 through B22 in Cell B24.
7. Print the worksheet so that it includes all cells up to Row 5 and Column F.
8. Save the workbook with its same name—OCTOBER.
9. Save the workbook with a new name—NOVEMBER.
10. Close the workbook.
11. Exit the program and then Windows.

II. COMMANDS

Describe fully, using as few words as possible, what command is initiated, or what is accomplished, in Excel by the actions described below. Assume that each exercise part is independent of any previous parts.

1. Pressing the **Ctrl** + **Home** key
2. Clicking the restore button of a workbook window
3. Double-clicking the workbook window's control-menu box
4. Typing =C5*C6 and then pressing →
5. Pressing the **Alt** + **F4** keys

6. Pressing the `F1` key
7. Double-clicking the Excel window's control-menu box
8. Pressing the `Ctrl` + `P` keys
9. Pressing the `Ctrl` + `F4` keys
10. Pressing the `PgDn` key
11. Pressing the `Ctrl` + `Z` keys
12. Pressing the `Ctrl` + `S` keys
13. Typing `'165`

III. APPLICATIONS

Perform the following operations and briefly tell how you accomplished each operation and describe its results. Note: Of the six applications, each pair relates to school, home, and business, respectively.

APPLICATION 1: CLUB BUDGET

Save the workbook as "CLUB1" after each operation is completed so that you can continue this exercise later. (Remember to set the default drive to A before saving the workbook.)

1. Start Excel
2. Create the following spreadsheet. Enter your name in Cell A1 and the current date in Cell A2 as shown. Complete the rest of your spreadsheet to match the example.

	A	B	C	D	E	F
1	Your Name					
2	Date					
3						
4	ART CLUB BUDGET					
5						
6			JAN	FEB	MAR	TOTAL
7						
8	Meeting Expenses		50	60	70	
9	Art Supplies		75	50	80	
10	Guest Speakers		50	100	50	
11	Field Trips		150	125	100	
12	Art Exhibitions		300	350	400	
13						
14	Total Funds Needed					
15						
16						

3. Enter a formula in Cell F8 that will total the three months Meeting Expenses.
4. Enter similar formulas in Cells F9 through F12 to accomplish the same result on each respective row.
5. Enter a SUM function in Cell F14 to total all the expenses that appear in Column F.
6. Save this workbook as "CLUB1." (Be sure to set the default drive to A if you haven't already done so.)
7. Type `1st QUARTER` in Cell D1. Print the spreadsheet.

8. Change the amount in Cell C9 to 65 and Cell E11 to 140.
9. Insert a Row 11 (between *Guest Speakers* and *Field Trips*). Type Awards in Cell A11, 75 in Cell C11, 100 in Cell D11, and 125 in Cell E11. Type a formula in Cell F11 to compute the total as before.
10. Type REVISED in Cell D2. Print the entire spreadsheet.
11. Delete Row 10 to remove *Guest Speakers*.
12. Print part of the spreadsheet that includes all cells from Cells A6 through Cell C12.
13. Place a SUM function in Cell C14 through Cell E14 to total each month's expenses.
14. Save the workbook as "CLUB1," print the entire worksheet, and then exit the program.

APPLICATION 2: GPA

Save the workbook in this exercise as "GPA1" after each operation is completed so that you can continue this exercise later. (Remember to set the default drive to A before you save the workbook.)

1. Start Excel.
2. Create the following spreadsheet. Enter your name in Cell A1 and the current date in Cell A2 as shown. Complete the rest of your spreadsheet to match the example. For now, all text should be left-aligned in the cells, except the entries in Column B. They are to be entered as right-aligned text.

	A	B	C	D	E	F
1	Your Name					
2	Date					
3						
4	GRADES					
5						
6	COURSE	TERM	GRADE	CREDITS	POINTS	TOT.PTS.
7						
8	MUS101	9203	A	2	4	
9	ART102	9203	B	3	3	
10	BUS101	9203	A	3	4	
11	BUS105	9201	B	3	3	
12	HIS104	9301	B	3	3	
13						
14						

3. Enter a formula in Cell F8 that will multiply the credits in Cell D8 by the points in Cell E8.
4. Enter similar formulas in Cells F9 through F12 to accomplish the same result on each respective row.
5. Enter a SUM function in Cell F14 to total the five courses that appear in Column F.
6. Save this worksheet as "GPA1." (Remember to set the default drive to A, if you haven't already done so.)
7. Type SPRING-93 in Cell F1. Print the entire spreadsheet.
8. Change the grade in Cell C9 to *A* and the points in Cell E9 to *4*.

9. Insert a row at Row 11 (between *BUS101* and *BUS105*). Type ENG103 in Cell A11, "9203" in Cell B11, B in Cell C11, 4 in Cell D11, and 3 in Cell E11. Type a formula in Cell F11 to compute the value as before.
10. Type UPDATED in Cell F1. Print the entire spreadsheet.
11. Delete Row 12 to remove *BUS105*.
12. Print the part of the spreadsheet that includes all cells from Cell A6 through Cell F12.
13. Place a SUM function in Cell D14 that totals the credits column.
14. Save the workbook as "GPA1," print the entire worksheet, and then exit the program.

APPLICATION 3: CHECKBOOK

Save the workbook as "CHECKING" after each operation is completed so that you can continue this exercise later. (Remember to set the default drive to A before saving the workbook.)

1. Start Excel.
2. Create the following spreadsheet. Enter your name in Cell A1 and the current date in Cell A2 as shown. Complete the rest of your spreadsheet to match the example.

	A	B	C	D	E	F	G
1	Your Name						
2	Date						
3							
4	CHECKING ACCOUNT						
5							
6	DATE	CHECK#	PAYEE		PMT	DEPOSIT	BALANCE
7							
8	1-Jan		Deposit pay check			1200	
9	4-Jan	106	R. Landlord		600		
10	10-Jan	107	Telephone Co.		65		
11	15-Jan		Deposit pay check			1200	
12	28-Jan	109	Electric Co.		80		
13							
14							

3. Enter a formula in Cell G8 that substracts Cell E8 (PMT) from Cell F8 (Deposit) the starting balance.
4. Enter a formula in Cell G9 that starts with Cell G8, adds Cell F9 and then subtracts Cell E9 to calculate the balance.
5. Enter similar formulas in Cells G10 through G12 to accomplish the same result.
6. Save this workbook as "CHECK1." (Remember to set the default drive to A if you haven't already done so.)
7. Type JANUARY 19XX in Cell E1. Print the spreadsheet.
8. Change the amount in Cell E9 to **700** and Cell F11 to **1400.**
9. Insert a Row 11 (between *10-Jan* and *15-Jan*). Type 12-Jan in Cell A11, 106 in Cell B11, Water Co. in Cell C11, and 45 in Cell E11. Type a formula in Cell G11 to compute the balance as before.

CHAPTER 1 SPREADSHEET BASICS: CREATING A WORKSHEET   SS65

10. Type [CORRECTED] in Cell D2. Print the entire spreadsheet.
11. Delete Row 12 to remove *28-Jan*.
12. Print part of the spreadsheet that includes all cells from Cells A6 through Cell C12.
13. Place a SUM function in Cell E14 and Cell F14 to total the payments and deposits column.
14. Save the workbook as "CHECK1," print the entire worksheet, and then exit the program.

APPLICATION 4: INVESTMENTS

Save the workbook as "INVEST1" after each operation is completed so that you can continue this exercise later. (Remember to set the default drive to A before saving the workbook.)

1. Start Excel.
2. Create the following spreadsheet. Enter your name in Cell A1 and the current date in Cell A2 as shown. Complete the rest of your spreadsheet to match the example.

	A	B	C	D	E	F
1	Your Name					
2	Date					
3						
4	INVESTMENTS					
5						
6	TYPE		DATE	PRICE	QUANTITY	TOTAL
7						
8	CDs		2/5/XX	1000	7	
9	TEDDY CORP.		3/15/XX	10.75	200	
10	SAVINGS BONDS		4/20/XX	50	5	
11	BLASTER CORP.		7/2/XX	5.25	300	
12	ACE MUSIC CORP.		10/20/XX	20.5	100	
13						
14						

3. Enter a formula in Cell F8 that will multiply the price in Cell D8 by the quantity in Cell E8.
4. Enter similar formulas in Cells F9 through F12 to accomplish the same result on each respective row.
5. Enter a SUM function in Cell F14 to total the five investments that appear in Column F.
6. Save this workbook as "INVEST1." (Remember to set the default drive to A if you haven't already done so.)
7. Type [YEAR ENDED 12/31/XX] in Cell E1. Print the spreadsheet.
8. Change the amount in Cell E10 to **100** and Cell D12 to **10.25.**
9. Insert a row at Row 5 and then type [PURCH] in Cell D6.
10. Insert a column at Column D (between *DATE* and *PRICE*). Type [SELLING] in Cell D6, [PRICE] in Cell D7, [1030] in Cell D9, [12] in Cell D10, [100] in Cell D11, [6] in Cell D12, and [15.75] in Cell D13.

11. Insert a column at Column G (between *QUANTITY* and *PURCH*). Type [TOTAL] in Cells G6 and H6, [SALES] in Cell G7, [PURCH] in Cell H7, and [PROFIT/] in Cell I6 and [(LOSS)] in Cell I7.
12. Enter formulas in Cells G9 through G13 that will multiply the selling price in Column D by the quantity in Column F.
13. Enter formulas in Cells I9 through I13 that will subtract the TOTAL PURCHASES (Column H) from TOTAL SALES (Column G).
14. Place a SUM function in Cell G15 and Cell I15 to total overall sales, purchases and profit/(losses).
15. Save the workbook as "INVEST1," print the entire worksheet, and then exit the program.

APPLICATION 5: INVENTORY

Save the workbook as "STOCK1" after each operation is completed so that you can continue this exercise later. (Remember to set the default drive to A the first time you save the worksheet.)

1. Start Excel.
2. Create the following spreadsheet. Enter your name in Cell A1 and the current date in Cell A2 as shown. Complete the rest of your spreadsheet to match the example.

	A	B	C	D	E
1	Your Name				
2	Date				
3					
4	INVENTORY				
5					
6	ITEM	COST	QUANTITY	VALUE	
7					
8	Disk	0.75	115		
9	Paper	5.25	21		
10	Ribbon	3.15	7		
11	Labels	10.65	11		
12					
13	TOTAL				
14					
15					

3. Enter a formula in Cell D8 that will multiply the disk cost in Cell B8 by the quantity in Cell C8.
4. Enter similar formulas in Cells D9 through D11 to accomplish the same result on each respective row.
5. Enter a SUM function in Cell D13 to total the four values that appear in Column D.
6. Save this worksheet as "STOCK1." (Remember to set the default drive to A if you haven't already done so.)
7. Type [EX1-7] in Cell D1. Print the entire spreadsheet.
8. Change the cost in Cell B8 to *1.25* and the quantity in Cell C10 to *9*.
9. Insert a row at Row 9 (between *Disk* and *Paper*). Type [Disk Box] in Cell A9, [3.25] in Cell B9, and [1] in Cell C9. Type a formula in Cell D9 to compute the value as before.

10. Type `EX-10` in Cell D1. Print the entire spreadsheet. Save as "STOCK."
11. Delete Row 7. Do *not* save again.
12. Erase Cell D1 and type `EX-12` in Cell C1. Print the part of the spreadsheet that includes all cells from Cell A1 to C11. Do *not* save.
13. Exit the spreadsheet program.

APPLICATION 6: TICKETS

Save the workbook in this exercise as "TICKET1" after each operation is completed so that you can continue this exercise later. (Remember to set the default drive to A the first time you save the worksheet.)

1. Start Excel.
2. Create the following spreadsheet. Enter your name in Cell A1 and the current date in Cell A2 as shown. Complete the rest of your spreadsheet to match the example. For now, all labels should be left-aligned in the cells.

	A	B	C	D	E
1	Your Name				
2	Date				
3					
4	TICKETS				
5					
6	SEAT	PRICE	QUANTITY	SOLD	VALUE
7					
8	Orchestra	60	500	245	
9	Lodge	50	300	123	
10	Mezzanine	30	200	87	
11	Balcony	15	250	168	
12					
13					

3. Enter a formula in Cell E8 that will multiply the ticket price in Cell B8 by the amount sold in Cell D8.
4. Enter similar formulas in Cells E9 through E11 to accomplish the same result on each respective row.
5. Enter a SUM function in Cell E13 to total the four receipts that appear in Column E.
6. Save this workbook as "TICKET1." (Remember to set the default drive to A, if you haven't done so already.)
7. Type `Matinee` in Cell E1. Print the entire spreadsheet.
8. Change the price in Cell B8 to *65* and the quantity in Cell C10 to *175*.
9. Insert a row at Row 9 (between *Orchestra* and *Loge*). Type `Box Seat` in Cell A9, `65` in Cell B9, `20` in Cell C9, and `15` in Cell D9. Type a formula in Cell E9 to compute the value as before.
10. Type `EVENING` in Cell E1. Print the entire spreadsheet.
11. Delete Row 7 and insert a column at Column E.
12. Type `EMPTY` in Cell E6. Create a formula in Cell E7 that subtracts the contents of Cell D7 from Cell C7. Enter similar formulas in Cells E8 through E11. Print the part of the spreadsheet that includes all cells from Cell A1 to Cell F11.
13. Place a SUM function in Cell E13 that totals the column.
14. Save the workbook as "TICKET1," print the entire worksheet, and then exit the program.

MASTERY CASES

The following Mastery Cases allow you to demonstrate how much you have learned about this software. Each case describes a fictitious problem or need that can be solved using the skills you have learned in this chapter. While minimum acceptable outcomes are specified, you are expected and encouraged to design your response (files, data, lists) in ways that display your personal mastery of the software. Feel free to show off your skills. Use "real" data from your own experience in your solution, although you may also fabricate data if needed.

These Mastery Cases allow you to display your ability to:

- Start the program
- Enter data into a worksheet
- Save the worksheet on disk
- Use ranges and formulas
- Print the worksheet
- Edit the worksheet

CASE 1. TRACKING YOUR EXAM GRADES: You would like to keep track of all your exam grades by course. Prepare a spreadsheet listing each course that you have taken. Next, list all exam grades that you earned across from each course. Make up courses and exam grades if needed. Be sure to head each column, for example, COURSE, EXAM 1 and so on. Create a column titled AVERAGE to the right of the last exam grade and calculate the average exam grade for each course. Save and print the worksheet.

CASE 2. CREATING A HOLIDAY-SHOPPING BUDGET: You would like to keep track of your holiday shopping. Prepare a spreadsheet with columns for the PERSON, GIFT, BUDGET (amount you want to spend), ACTUAL and DIFFERENCE. Enter a list of persons that you desire to buy a gift for and the type of gift. Make up a budget price for each gift and enter it into the BUDGET column. Now, make up an actual price (different from the budget price) for each gift and place it in the ACTUAL column. Calculate the difference between actual and budget in the DIFFERENCE column and then the overall total of each column. Save and print the budget.

CASE 3. CREATING A SALES REPORT: You have your own computer business and have completed your first year of operation. Create a simple sales report listing several of your products and displaying the units sold and their prices. Be sure to identify your company name, report title (Sales Report) and year-end date. Include columns for PRODUCT, UNITS SOLD, UNIT PRICE, and TOTAL. Calculate the sales dollars for each product in the TOTAL column. Also calculate overall totals for the UNITS SOLD and TOTAL columns. Save and print your sales report.

MICROSOFT EXCEL
VERSION 5.0

ENHANCING SPREADSHEETS:
RANGE AND DEFAULT CHANGES, FORMATS AND FUNCTIONS

OUTLINE

OVERVIEW

USING RANGES IN COMMANDS
  Aligning Data
  Adjusting Number Format
  Copying Cells
  Moving Cells
  Transposing Cells
  Using Range Names

RESETTING WORKSHEET DEFAULTS
  Format
  Alignment
  Column Width

ADJUSTING COLUMN WIDTH
  Changing Individual Column Width
  Changing Width in a Column Range
  Hiding and Unhiding Columns

ENHANCING A WORKSHEET WITH FONTS, COLORS AND LINES
  Changing a Font
  Changing Color
  Adding Lines
  Providing Additional Emphasis

CELLS REFERENCES
  Relative and Absolute References

Mixed References
Fixing Circular References

FUNCTIONS
  Function Structure
  A Function Sampler
  Using the Function Wizard

MANAGING LARGE SPREADSHEETS
  Freezing
  Splitting

PRINTING TECHNIQUES
  Page Breaks
  Page Setup Options

OBJECTIVES

After completing this chapter you will be able to

1. Explain how to align and format data.

2. Describe the procedures to copy and move cell contents.

3. Explain the effects of worksheet default changes.

4. Describe and differentiate among the three ways to change column widths: resetting the default, individually, and column-range.

5. Enhance a worksheet with different fonts, colors and lines.

6. Differentiate between relative and absolute references.

7. Examine functions and describe how to select them using the Function Wizard.

8. Describe techniques for handling large spreadsheets.

9. Demonstrate advanced printing techniques such as compressing page data and displaying column and row titles, column and row indicators, and grid lines.

OVERVIEW

Building on the skills developed in the previous chapter, this chapter examines commands that enhance your ability to create or modify spreadsheets efficiently, and commands that enhance the appearance of the

SS69

SS70 SPREADSHEETS WITH MICROSOFT EXCEL 5.0

spreadsheet itself. First, range and default changes that alter the appearance of spreadsheet cells are presented.

You will learn how to adjust data alignment, format numeric values and formula results and adjust column widths to better present your data. This chapter then explores the use of different type faces (called **fonts**), colors and lines to enhance the look of your worksheet. Next, methods to overcome cell-reference problems are discussed, followed by a closer look at using functions. Finally, techniques are presented for managing large spreadsheets, both on the screen and on the printer.

USING RANGES IN COMMANDS

Unlike *Default changes* that can affect the entire worksheet (as you will soon see), commands that use ranges change only specified cells. Some of the more useful commands control data alignment, numeric value and formula result, formatting, copying, and moving. To prepare for these exercises, first create the spreadsheet in Figure SS2-1 as follows:

1. **Start with a blank workbook on your screen**

    Note: Exercises in this chapter require your computer to be on and Excel to be active.

2. **Enter the data shown in Figure SS2-1**

Note that *Chapter Exercises* is typed completely in Cell A1, *Employee* in Cell A5, *Hours* in Cell B5, and so on.

3. **Save the workbook as *SS2-1a* (remember to set the default drive to A when saving)**

    This manual presents Excel commands to perform various operations. Be sure

---

FIGURE SS2-1 ■ THE INITIAL WORKSHEET

Note that column headings in Columns B through D do not line up neatly over their column values.

	A	B	C	D	E
1	Chapter Exercises				
2	Your Name				
3	Date				
4					
5	Employee	Hours	Pay	Gross	
6	Burstein	40	5.65		
7	Laudon	35	4		
8	Martin	38	5.75		
9	Parker	25	6.75		
10	Williams	32	3.5		
11					
12					

CHAPTER 2 ENHANCING SPREADSHEETS: RANGE AND DEFAULT CHANGES, FORMATS AND FUNCTIONS — SS71

that the Lotus 1-2-3 transition settings in Transition tab of the Options dialog box (Tools menu) are *off* before you begin. These transition features help Lotus 1-2-3 users to convert to Excel. They set the program to respond to some basic Lotus 1-2-3 keyboard commands. If you know Lotus 1-2-3, you may want to experiment with these features on your own. To check these settings:

MOUSE APPROACH	**KEYBOARD APPROACH**
1. Click *Tools, Options*	1. Press Alt + T, O
2. Click *Transition* tab	2. Press T for the Transition tab

Examine the settings. Only the *Microsoft Excel Menus* option button should be selected with a black dot (•) as in Figure SS2-2. All other options should be blank.

MOUSE APPROACH	**KEYBOARD APPROACH**
3. If settings are correct, click *OK* to return to the worksheet and skip Steps 4 through 6	3. If settings are correct, press Esc to return to the worksheet and skip Steps 4 through 6
4. If needed, click the *Microsoft Excel Menus* option button to select it	4. If needed, press Alt + E to select the *Microsoft Excel Menus* option button

Skip Step 5 if an "X" *does not* appear in any of the following check boxes: *Transition Navigation Keys, Transition Formula Evaluation,* or *Transition Formula Entry* as in Fugure SS2-2.

FIGURE SS2-2 ■ **THE TRANSITION TAB**

Since this manual uses only Excel commands, only the Microsoft Excel Menus option button should be selected in the Transition tab. All other options should be blank (off).

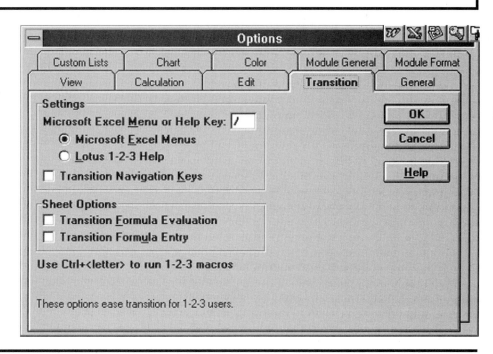

MOUSE APPROACH

5. Click each check box to remove the "X"
6. Click OK

KEYBOARD APPROACH

5. To remove the "X" from the check box—Transition Navigation Keys, press Alt + K ; Transition Formula Evaluation, press Alt + F ; Transition Formula Entry, press Alt + U
6. Press ↵

Note: Once set in your own system, Transition options remain the same until they are changed again, even if you exit Excel. If you are using a network, you may have to check the transition setting each time you begin your Excel session.

ALIGNING DATA

A quick look at the worksheet reveals a frequent irritant—some column headings may not line up neatly over their respective numeric values. In Figure SS2-1, for example, it is difficult to determine whether "Pay" refers to Column B or C. This is because of **alignment**—the position of data in a cell. Text is left-aligned in cells by default (whereas numeric values and formula results are always positioned on the right). The alignment of data in a cell can be changed using the Format Cells dialog box or Format toolbar buttons. This process involves first selecting the range to be changed and then invoking the desired command.

FIGURE SS2-3 ■ THE FORMAT CELLS DIALOG BOX

The Format Cells dialog box can be used to change the alignment of a range of data, multiple ranges, or a table.

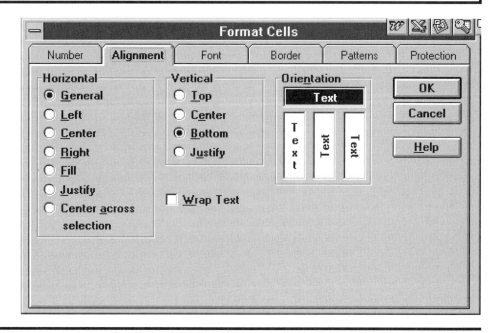

CHAPTER 2   ENHANCING SPREADSHEETS: RANGE AND DEFAULT CHANGES, FORMATS AND FUNCTIONS   SS73

ALIGN DATA WITHIN A CELL. The following exercise changes the data alignment in Cells B5 through D5:

1. Move to Cell B5—the left corner of the desired range

MOUSE APPROACH	KEYBOARD APPROACH
2. Press and hold `Shift` while clicking *Cell D5* to select the range B5:D5	2. Press and hold `Shift` while pressing `→` two times to select the range B5:D5
3. Click *Format, Cells*, and then the *Alignment* tab for the Alignment section of the Format Cells dialog box	3. Press `Ctrl` + `1` and then `A` for the Alignment section of the Format Cells dialog box

The Format Cells dialog box, shown in Figure SS2-3, can be used to make alignment changes on a range of data, multiple ranges, or a table (discussed later). Although only text-alignment changes are demonstrated here, the procedures for other alignment changes are the same.

MOUSE APPROACH	KEYBOARD APPROACH
4. Click *Right* to select right horizontal alignment	4. Press `Alt` + `R` to select right horizontal alignment
5. Click the *OK* button	5. Press `↵`
6. Move to Cell D6	

The text is now right-aligned, as shown in Figure SS2-4.

> Tip: Instead of Steps 3 and 4 above, you can simply click the *right-align* toolbar button. Other alignment toolbar buttons include a left-align, center-align and center-across columns button.

Now complete the worksheet by adding formulas for *Gross* as follows:

7. In Cell D6, type `=B6*C6`

FIGURE SS2-4 ■ ALIGNING DATA

The data in Row 5 have been right-aligned over their respective values.

	A	B	C	D	E
1	Chapter Exercises				
2	Your Name				
3	Date				
4					
5	Employee	Hours	Pay	Gross	
6	Burstein	40	5.65		
7	Laudon	35	4		
8	Martin	38	5.75		
9	Parker	25	6.75		

SS74 **SPREADSHEETS WITH MICROSOFT EXCEL 5.0**

FIGURE SS2-5 ■ USING FORMULAS

Formulas that calculate the gross pay have been added in Column D.

	A	B	C	D	E
1	Chapter Exercises				
2	Your Name				
3	Date				
4					
5	Employee	Hours	Pay	Gross	
6	Burstein	40	5.65	226	← The default format makes
7	Laudon	35	4	140	it difficult to compare
8	Martin	38	5.75	218.5	numbers.
9	Parker	25	6.75	168.75	
10	Williams	32	3.5	112	
11					
12					

---

8. In Cell D7, type =B7*C7

9. Complete similar entries for Cells D8, D9, and D10

Your worksheet should now resemble Figure SS2-5. If it does not, repeat Steps 7 though 9.

10. Save this worksheet again as *SS2-1A*

Try changing Column A data to the right, center, and then left. You can readjust data alignments of any range at any time. However, text that exceeds the width of a column (as in Cell A1 in this example) will always appear left-aligned. Numeric values and formula results that exceed a column's width may appear in scientific notation (for example, $1.12E+15$).

If your worksheet does not resemble Figure SS2-5 when you are finished,

11. Close the current workbook without saving and then open the *SS2-1A* workbook again before continuing.

> Tip: The alignment dialog box can also be used to change the alignment of a range of values.

CENTER-ALIGNING DATA ACROSS COLUMNS. When creating a title that applies to more than one column, the center-across columns option of the Format Cells dialog box is very helpful. Try this to center align the title "WEEKLY PAYROLL" across Cells A through D.

1. Move to Cell A5

2. Insert a Row *(Insert, Rows)*

3. Type WEEKLY PAYROLL and press ↵

4. Move back to Cell A5 and select the Range A5:D5

CHAPTER 2   ENHANCING SPREADSHEETS: RANGE AND DEFAULT CHANGES, FORMATS AND FUNCTIONS   SS75

	MOUSE APPROACH	**KEYBOARD APPROACH**

5. Click *Format, Cells, Alignment* tab, *Center across selection, OK* to center the title

5. Press Ctrl + 1, A, Alt + A, ↵ to center the title

6. **Move to Cell A1**

Your worksheet should appear as Figure SS2-6.

7. **Resave the workbook as SS2-1a and then close it**

ADJUSTING NUMBER FORMAT

As you have learned, numeric data may contain only numerals, decimal points, or math expressions. By default, these data appear in cells without commas, dollar signs, or trailing zeros after the decimal point. This is true whether data are entered as numeric constants (as in Columns B and C in Figure SS2-5), or are the result of a formula (as in Column D). Although this may be satisfactory for some spreadsheets, it is usually desirable to adjust a number's **format**—the way a number is displayed in a cell—from its default state to a more useful style. Changing a format can add commas or dollar signs to a range of numeric data. It can also standardize the number of decimal places shown in each cell, or even hide a cell's contents. Excel comes with 36 built-in number formats (codes) that can have up to four sections separated by semicolons: three for numbers and a fourth for text. Figure SS2-7a displays a sample of an Excel format code. Format codes are also grouped by category. A list of Excel format codes with samples and their respective categories are in Figure SS2-7b. Refer to these figures as you make the following format changes. The following exercises examine the most popular of these options, but all are invoked with similar techniques.

FIGURE SS2-6 ■ CENTER-ALIGNING DATA ACROSS COLUMNS

The title "WEEKLY PAYROLL" has been centered across cells A5 through D5.

	A	B	C	D	E
1	Chapter Exercises				
2	Your Name				
3	Date				
4					
5		WEEKLY PAYROLL			
6	Employee	Hours	Pay	Gross	
7	Burstein	40	5.65	226	
8	Laudon	35	4	140	
9	Martin	38	5.75	218.5	
10	Parker	25	6.75	168.75	
11	Williams	32	3.5	112	
12					
13					

FIGURE SS2-7 ■ FORMAT CODES

(a) A sample of format codes. (b) A summary of Excel's built-in format codes.

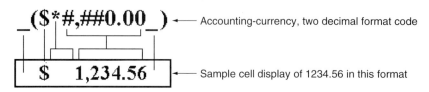

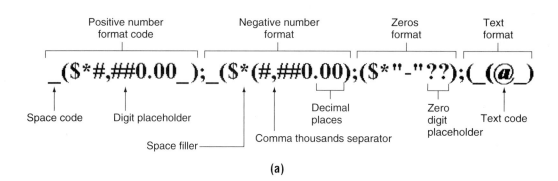

(a)

GENERAL NUMBER FORMAT. The *General format* is the default format for all new worksheets. As in Figure SS2-6, the General format displays a number as an integer (as in Cell B7-40), decimal fraction (as in Cell C7-5.65) or scientific notation (not displayed—1.4E+7).

When entering data into a General formatted cell, Excel automatically selects the correct format for that data, as in Figure SS2-8. For example, try the following:

1. Close any open workbook (*File, Close* or Ctrl + F4)
2. Open a new workbook (*File, New* or Ctrl + N)
3. Type the titles in Cells A1, C1, and E1 from Figure SS2-8
4. Move to Cell A3 and type *DATA*

Note that Excel automatically places a comma after the "1," as in _ _ $1,000.

5. In Cell A4, type $1000 (be sure to place a $ before typing 1000) and press ↵
6. In Cell A5, type 1,000 (be sure to place a comma after the 1) and press ↵
7. In Cell A6, type 10% and press ↵
8. In Cell A7, type the data 1/1/96 and press ↵
9. Type the text in Cells C3 through C7 as in Figure SS2-8
10. Type the data in Cells E3 through E7 as in Figure SS2-8

FIGURE SS2-7 ■ *(continued)*

	Format Code				Category	Samples			
	Positive	Negative	Zero	Text		Positive	Negative	Zero	Text
1	General				All	1234.56	-1234.56		
2	0				Number	1235	-1235		
3	0.00				Number	1234.56	-1234.56		
4	#,##0				Number	1,235	-1,235		
5	#,##0.00				Number	1,234.56	-1,234.56		
6	#,##0_)	(#,##0)			Number	1,235	(1,235)		
7	#,##0_)	[Red](#,##0)			Number	1,235	(1,235)		
8	#,##0.00_)	(#,##0.00)			Number	1,234.56	(1,234.56)		
9	#,##0.00_)	[Red](#,##0.00)			Number	1,234.56	(1,234.56)		
10	$#,##0_)	($#,##0)			Currency	$1,235	($1,235)		
11	$#,##0_)	[Red]($#,##0)			Currency	$1,235	($1,235)		
12	$#,##0.00_)	($#,##0.00)			Currency	$1,234.56	($1,234.56)		
13	$#,##0.00_)	[Red]($#,##0.00)			Currency	$1,234.56	($1,234.56)		
14	_($* #,##0_)	_($* (#,##0)	_($* "-"_)	_(@_)	Accounting	$ 1,235	$ (1,235)	$ -	1234.56
15	_(* #,##0_)	_(* (#,##0)	_(* "-"_)	_(@_)	Accounting	1,235	(1,235)	-	1234.56
16	_($* #,##0.00_)	_($* (#,##0.00)	_($* "-"??_)	_(@_)	Accounting	$ 1,234.56	$ (1,234.56)	$ -	1234.56
17	_(* #,##0.00_)	_(* (#,##0.00)	_(* "-"??_)	_(@_)	Accounting	1,234.56	(1,234.56)	-	1234.56
18	0%				Percentage	123456%	-123456%		
19	0.00%				Percentage	123456.00%	-123456.00%		
20	0.00E+00				Scientific	1.23E+03	-1.23E+03		
21	##0.0E+0				Scientific	1.2E+3	-1.2E+3		
22	# ?/?				Fraction	1234 5/9	-1234 5/9		
23	# ??/??				Fraction	1234 14/25	-1234 14/25		
24	m/d/yy				Date	1/1/95			
25	d-mmm-yy				Date	1-Jan-95			
26	d-mmm				Date	1-Jan			
27	mmm-yy				Date	Jan-95			
28	m/d/yy h:mm				Date/Time	1/1/95 1:50			
29	h:mm AM/PM				Time	1:50 AM			
30	h:mm:ss AM/PM				Time	1:50:24 PM			
31	h:mm				Time	1:50			
32	h:mm:ss				Time	1:50:24			
33	mm:ss				Time	50:24			
34	mm:ss.0				Time	50:24.0			
35	[h]:mm:ss				Time	1:50:24			
36	@				Text	1234.56	-1234.56		

(b)

Your worksheet should resemble Figure SS2-8 on page 78. Note that Excel automatically selected the correct number format for each entry. Also note that the alignment may differ slightly from one number format to another as in Cells A4 and A5.

11. Save this workbook as *FORMATS* and then close it

ACCOUNTING NUMBER FORMAT. The Accounting Number Format is a very useful format for presenting financial information. It includes four built-in number formats that display dollar signs against the left margin of a cell, negative numbers in brackets, and zero values as hyphens (-).

> **Tip:** When making format changes, it is highly advisable to use toolbar buttons where available. For example, the $ toolbar button will format data in the accounting style—currency, two decimal places, as in $ 1,000.00 (note that the $ sign is left aligned, whereas the number is right-aligned. The , button will format data in the accounting style—comma, two decimal places, as in 1,000.00.

Although the quicker method to make format changes is to use a toolbar button,

SS78 SPREADSHEETS WITH MICROSOFT EXCEL 5.0

FIGURE SS2-8 ■ AUTOMATIC-NUMBER FORMATTING

Excel automatically selects the correct format for data entered into a cell that is initially in General format (Excel's default setting).

	A	B	C	D	E	F	G
1	SAMPLE		CATEGORY		FORMAT CODES		
2							
3	DATA		ALL		GENERAL		
4	$1,000		CURRENCY		($#,##0_);[Red]($#,##0)		
5	1,000		NUMBER		#,##0		
6	10%		PERCENTAGE		0%		
7	1/1/96		DATE		m/d/yy		
8							
9							

---

the Number tab of the Format Cells dialog box is used next to show you the different available format codes. Try this,

1. Close any open workbook
2. Open the SS2-1a workbook
3. Move to Cell C7

MOUSE APPROACH	KEYBOARD APPROACH
4. Press and hold **Shift** while clicking *Cell C11* to select the range C7:D11	4. Press and hold **Shift** while pressing **↓** four times to select the range C7:D11
5. Click *Format, Cells, Number* tab, *Accounting* category (in the Category list box)	5. Press **Ctrl** + **1**, **N**, **Alt** + **C**, **↓** three times to Accounting in the Category box
6. In the Format Codes box, click the third format code down, which starts with _($*#,##0.00_);_($*(#,##0.00);	6. Press **Alt** + **F** and then press **↓** twice to select the Format Code starting with _($*#,##0.00_);_($*(#,##0.00);

  Tip: To quickly invoke the accounting-currency, two-decimal format, click the currency (**$**) toolbar button in place of Steps 5 and 6 above.

Your Number tab content (Format Cells dialog box) should appear as Figure SS2-9. Note that the Sample indicator at the bottom left of the dialog box displays $5.65. This is the number format that will appear in the selected range after you perform the next step.

Tip: The active cell must contain data for the Sample indicator of the Number tab (Format Cells dialog box) to display a sample.

MOUSE APPROACH	KEYBOARD APPROACH
7. Click *OK* button	7. Press **↵**

CHAPTER 2 ENHANCING SPREADSHEETS: RANGE AND DEFAULT CHANGES, FORMATS AND FUNCTIONS   SS79

FIGURE SS2-9 ■ THE FORMAT CELLS DIALOG BOX—NUMBER TAB

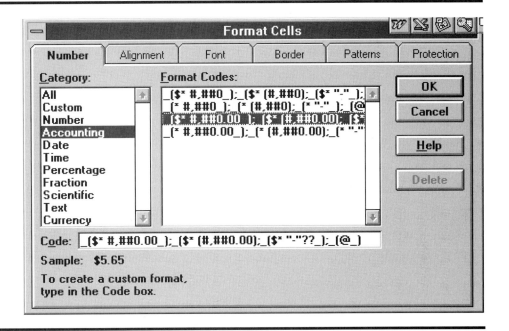

8. **Move to Cell A1**

Your worksheet should now resemble Figure SS2-10a. Note that all data in the range C7:D11 has been formatted to the currency, two-decimal accounting format. Now to format the data in the range C8:D11 in the comma, two-decimal accounting format,

9. **Select the range *C8:D11***

MOUSE APPROACH	KEYBOARD APPROACH
 10. Click the , button on the toolbar	10. Press Ctrl + 1 , Alt + F , ↓ , ↵

11. **Move to Cell A1**

As in Figure SS2-10b, the data in Cells C8 through D11 have now been changed to the accounting-comma, two-decimal format.

12. **Save the workbook as SS2-1b**

Cells may also be formatted before entering data. To do so, select the desired range and invoke the format command. Try this,

13. **Move to Cell D13**

14. **Format Cell D13 for Accounting-Currency, two-decimal format**

15. **In Cell D13, enter** =SUM(D7:D11)

16. **In Cell A13, type** TOTAL **and then press** ↵

SS80 SPREADSHEETS WITH MICROSOFT EXCEL 5.0

FIGURE SS2-10 ■ CHANGING NUMBER FORMATS

(a) All numbers in the range C7:D11 have been formatted to currency, two decimals-accounting style. (b) All numbers in the range C8:D11 have been reformatted to comma, two decimals-accounting style. (c) Cell D13 has been formatted to currency, two decimals-accounting style, after which a SUM function has been entered to total the range D7:D11.

	A	B	C	D	E
1	Chapter Exercises				
2	Your Name				
3	Date				
4					
5		WEEKLY PAYROLL			
6	Employee	Hours	Pay	Gross	
7	Burstein	40	$ 5.65	$ 226.00	
8	Laudon	35	$ 4.00	$ 140.00	
9	Martin	38	$ 5.75	$ 218.50	
10	Parker	25	$ 6.75	$ 168.75	
11	Williams	32	$ 3.50	$ 112.00	
12					

(a)

	A	B	C	D	E
1	Chapter Exercises				
2	Your Name				
3	Date				
4					
5		WEEKLY PAYROLL			
6	Employee	Hours	Pay	Gross	
7	Burstein	40	$ 5.65	$ 226.00	
8	Laudon	35	4.00	140.00	
9	Martin	38	5.75	218.50	
10	Parker	25	6.75	168.75	
11	Williams	32	3.50	112.00	
12					
13					

(b)

	A	B	C	D	E
1	Chapter Exercises				
2	Your Name				
3	Date				
4					
5		WEEKLY PAYROLL			
6	Employee	Hours	Pay	Gross	
7	Burstein	40	$ 5.65	$ 226.00	
8	Laudon	35	4.00	140.00	
9	Martin	38	5.75	218.50	
10	Parker	25	6.75	168.75	
11	Williams	32	3.50	112.00	
12					
13	TOTAL			$ 865.25	
14					
15					
16					

(c)

CHAPTER 2   ENHANCING SPREADSHEETS: RANGE AND DEFAULT CHANGES, FORMATS AND FUNCTIONS   SS81

Your worksheet should now resemble Figure SS2-10c. If it does not, repeat Steps 13 through 16.

17. Save the workbook as *SS2-1C* and then close it

CHANGING DECIMAL PLACES.   Clicking the *Increase Decimal* or *Decrease Decimal* toolbar button with your mouse is a quick way to change the decimal places. Try this,

1. Create a new workbook (*File, New* or Ctrl + N)

2. Type .7 into Cells C3 through C7

3. Type .7 into Cells E3 through E7

4. Place a SUM function in Cells C9 and E9 to total the columns

Your worksheet should appear as SS2-11a. Note that Excel automatically formats the cells for the required decimal places. To increase the decimal place display,

5. Select the range C3:C7

FIGURE SS2-11 ■ DISPLAY VERSUS CONTENTS

Formatting cells with two few decimal places may display incorrect results because the display is changed, not the number itself.

B	C	D	E	F	G
	0.7		0.7		
	0.7		0.7		
	0.7		0.7		
	0.7		0.7		
	0.7		0.7		
	3.5		3.5		

(a)

B	C	D	E	F	G
	0.7		1		
	0.7		1		
	0.7		1		
	0.7		1		
	0.7		1		
	3.5		4		

(b)

6. Click the *Increase Decimal* button once

Two decimal places now appear in the selected range.

7. Click the *Increase Decimal* button five more times

The cells in the selected range now display ######## indicating that the cell values contain more characters than the cell's width. At this point, you can change the column width (discussed later) or reduce the number of decimal places. Now, to reduce the decimal place back to one

8. Click the *Decrease Decimal* button six times (or as needed)

Your worksheet should resemble Figure SS2-11a again.

DISPLAY VERSUS CONTENTS. Formatting alters the display, or *appearance* of a cell, but does not change the actual cell contents. This can lead to some peculiar results. For example, format the numbers in Cells E3 through E9 to no decimal places,

1. Select the range E3:E9

2. Click the *Decrease Decimal* button

3. Move to Cell E10

The worksheet should now appear as Figure SS2-11b. Note that the numbers and total in Column C correctly shows that .7 added five times totals 3.5. Now, look at Column E where these cells have been reformatted as whole numbers (using the *Decrease Decimal* button). This column now shows 1+1+1+1+1=4! This occurs because each cell has been formatted to display a whole number, but the values in the cells remain as .7 and 3.5. Keep in mind that values may appear rounded to conform to formatting settings but are used unchanged in other spreadsheet formulas.

4. Close the workbook without saving

OTHER FORMAT CHANGES. The Number tab (Format Cells dialog box) offers a variety of built-in number format codes as listed in Figure SS2-7b. These codes, as seen earlier, are categorized into groups such as Accounting, Date, Percentage, etc. The steps to selecting a different number format code from the Number tab are the same as those described in the previous sections. To create custom number format codes, see the appendix.

COPYING CELLS

Although data can be *typed* into individual cells, it is much more efficient to *copy* data from one cell to another as needed. Any data can be copied. Constant values copy exactly; formulas including functions (unless the program is told otherwise) will have their cell references automatically adjusted to reflect their new location. For example, the formula =B7*C7 in Cell D7 (see Figure SS2-10c) multiplies hours (in B7) by pay (in C7). The formula =B8*C8 in Cell D8 does exactly the same thing for the corresponding cells in *its* row. Every formula in Column D is identical except its cell references, which must be relative to the row the formula is on. You created these formulas by typing each one—a lot of wasted effort. You can save time and reduce typing errors by *copying* one cell into others. **Copying** replicates the contents

CHAPTER 2   ENHANCING SPREADSHEETS: RANGE AND DEFAULT CHANGES, FORMATS AND FUNCTIONS   SS83

of a cell in other cells, automatically adjusting relative references to reflect the new cell address. It also copies any formatting or alignment that you have previously set.

The following exercises demonstrate the importance of the *Copy* command. To prepare for this exercise.

1. **Open the *SS2-1C* workbook (if needed)**

2. **Select the cell range D8:D11 (the source range)**

3. **Press Delete to erase cells D8:D11**

4. **Move to Cell D8**

Your worksheet should resemble Figure SS2-12. If it does not, repeat these steps before continuing.

The copy procedure has four parts: (1) selecting the **source range** to be copied, (2) invoking the *Copy* command (*Edit* menu), (3) selecting the **destination range** to which the selection will be copied, and (4) pressing the Enter Key or invoking the *Paste* command (*Edit* menu).

> **Tip: When you copy a cell's content, you copy all format and alignment settings of that cell.**

COPYING ONE CELL.   Assume that you have just finished entering the formula in Cell D7 and want to copy it into the rest of a column (or row) of cells. For example, the following exercise shows how to copy Cell D7 to several cells in Column D (D8:D11).

1. **Move to Cell D7 (the cell you want to copy)**

FIGURE SS2-12 ■ PREPARING TO COPY

Cells D8 through D11 have been erased to show the results of the copy procedure.

	A	B	C	D	E
1	Chapter Exercises				
2	Your Name				
3	Date				
4					
5		WEEKLY PAYROLL			
6	Employee	Hours	Pay	Gross	
7	Burstein	40	$ 5.65	$ 226.00	
8	Laudon	35	4.00		
9	Martin	38	5.75		
10	Parker	25	6.75		
11	Williams	32	3.50		
12					
13	TOTAL			$ 226.00	
14					
15					
16					

FIGURE SS2-13 ■ COPYING AND PASTING

(a) The message "Select destination and press Enter or choose Paste" appears in the title bar when the copy command is invoked.

	A	B	C	D	E	F
1	Chapter Exercises					
2	Your Name					
3	Date					
4						
5		WEEKLY PAYROLL				
6	Employee	Hours	Pay	Gross		
7	Burstein	40	$ 5.65	$ 226.00		
8	Laudon	35	4.00			
9	Martin	38	5.75			
10	Parker	25	6.75			
11	Williams	32	3.50			
12						
13	TOTAL			$ 226.00		
14						
15						
16						
17						
18						

Sheet1 / Sheet2 / Sheet3 / Sheet4 / Sheet5 / Sheet6
Select destination and press ENTER or choose Paste

(a)

MOUSE APPROACH

2. Click *Edit, Copy*

KEYBOARD APPROACH

2. Press [Ctrl] + [C] to copy

The Excel status bar now displays the message "Select destination and press Enter or choose Paste," as shown in Figure SS2-13a. Like all Windows applications, the *Copy* command first copies the selection to Windows *Clipboard*, a holding application. This process allows for the possibility of copying and moving data among multiple applications. Multiple application copying and moving techniques are discussed in the appendix.

> **Tip:** If the desired range to be copied is greater than one cell, select the range before invoking the copy command in Step 2.

The destination is the desired location in which the selection will be duplicated. This location can be a cell or a range of cells. To select the destination range D8:D11,

3. Move to Cell D8

MOUSE APPROACH

4. Press and hold [Shift] while clicking Cell D11

KEYBOARD APPROACH

4. Press and hold [Shift] while pressing ↓ three times to move to Cell D11

The destination range D8:D11 should now be highlighted as in Figure SS2-13b.

CHAPTER 2 ENHANCING SPREADSHEETS: RANGE AND DEFAULT CHANGES, FORMATS AND FUNCTIONS | SS85

FIGURE SS2-13 ■ (continued)

(b) Once a desired range has been copied to the Clipboard, the destination range is selected. (c) This is the completed copy.

	A	B	C	D	E	F
1	Chapter Exercises					
2	Your Name					
3	Date					
4						
5		WEEKLY PAYROLL				
6	Employee	Hours	Pay	Gross		
7	Burstein	40	$ 5.65	$ 226.00		
8	Laudon	35	4.00			
9	Martin	38	5.75			
10	Parker	25	6.75			
11	Williams	32	3.50			
12						
13	TOTAL			$ 226.00		
14						

(b)

	A	B	C	D	E	F
1	Chapter Exercises					
2	Your Name					
3	Date					
4						
5		WEEKLY PAYROLL				
6	Employee	Hours	Pay	Gross		
7	Burstein	40	$ 5.65	$ 226.00		
8	Laudon	35	4.00	$ 140.00		
9	Martin	38	5.75	$ 218.50		
10	Parker	25	6.75	$ 168.75		
11	Williams	32	3.50	$ 112.00		
12						
13	TOTAL			$ 865.25		
14						

(c)

To **paste** (transfer the copied selection from the Clipboard) to the destination range,

MOUSE APPROACH

5. Click *Edit, Paste*
6. Move to Cell D8

KEYBOARD APPROACH

5. Press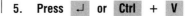

If you had wanted to copy the formula into one cell only (such as D8), you would have skipped Step 4 altogether. It was needed only to specify a destination range greater than one cell.

Your screen should resemble Figure SS2-13c. If it does not, repeat Steps 1 through 6. Examine the contents of the newly created cells. Note that the formula-cell addresses have been copied *relative* to each row, and that the formatting matches the copied cell.

To match your original worksheet in Figure SS2-10c, change the comma two-decimal accounting format in these cells as follows:

7. Select the range D8:D11

MOUSE APPROACH	KEYBOARD APPROACH
8. Click the `,` toolbar button	8. Press `Ctrl` + `1`, `Alt` + `F`, `↓` to select the Accounting Format code that starts with _(*#,##0.00_);_(*(#,##0.00);_("-"); and then press `↵`

9. Move to Cell A1
10. Close the workbook without saving

A few words of caution: if the *Copy* and *Paste* commands do not work as expected, you can retrieve the saved worksheet. You can also use the *Undo* feature immediately after copying to negate the *Copy* command.

COPYING A RANGE OF CELLS. You can copy a range of cells almost as easily as copying one cell. For example, suppose you wanted to copy all the data and formulas in Rows 7 through 10 starting at Row 12. This exercise demonstrates the technique.

1. Open the *SS2-1C* workbook
2. Select the range A7:D11

Note that the range is highlighted as shown in Figure SS2-14a.

MOUSE APPROACH	KEYBOARD APPROACH
3. Click *Edit*, *Copy* to the range to the Clipboard	3. Press `Ctrl` + `C` to copy the range to the Clipboard

The title bar now displays the message "Select destination and choose Edit Paste." When copying a range of cells, you need to specify only the *upper-left cell* where you want the copy to begin. The program knows exactly where to put the rest.

4. Move to Cell A12

MOUSE APPROACH	KEYBOARD APPROACH
5. Click *Edit*, *Paste*	1. Press `↵` or `Ctrl` + `V` to paste

6. Move to Cell A12

The copying is completed, and the spreadsheet should now resemble Figure SS2-14b. If it does not, repeat Steps 1 through 6. Examine your worksheet carefully. Note that constant values were copied exactly, whereas formulas were copied relative to their locations. In addition, all alignments and formatting were duplicated in the copied cells.

Practice copying one cell to another, one cell to a range of cells, and ranges of

CHAPTER 2 ENHANCING SPREADSHEETS: RANGE AND DEFAULT CHANGES, FORMATS AND FUNCTIONS | SS87

FIGURE SS2-14 ■ **COPYING A RANGE OF CELLS**

(a) Selecting the copy range.
(b) The range has been copied starting at Row 12.

	A	B	C	D	E
1	Chapter Exercises				
2	Your Name				
3	Date				
4					
5		WEEKLY PAYROLL			
6	Employee	Hours	Pay	Gross	
7	Burstein	40	$ 5.65	$ 226.00	
8	Laudon	35	4.00	140.00	
9	Martin	38	5.75	218.50	
10	Parker	25	6.75	168.75	
11	Williams	32	3.50	112.00	
12					
13	TOTAL			$ 865.25	
14					
15					

(a)

	A	B	C	D	E
1	Chapter Exercises				
2	Your Name				
3	Date				
4					
5		WEEKLY PAYROLL			
6	Employee	Hours	Pay	Gross	
7	Burstein	40	$ 5.65	$ 226.00	
8	Laudon	35	4.00	140.00	
9	Martin	38	5.75	218.50	
10	Parker	25	6.75	168.75	
11	Williams	32	3.50	112.00	
12	Burstein	40	$ 5.65	$ 226.00	
13	Laudon	35	4.00	140.00	
14	Martin	38	5.75	218.50	
15	Parker	25	6.75	168.75	
16	Williams	32	3.50	112.00	
17					
18					

(b)

cells, and ranges of cells to other ranges. Use cells in both rows and columns until you are satisfied with the effect of each procedure.

7. **Close the workbook without saving**

MOVING CELLS

Cell contents can be moved from one location to another using the *Cut* and *Paste* commands. The *Cut* and *Paste* commands (*Edit* menu) relocate the contents of a cell (or range of cells) *without* changing the cell references. For example, the formula =*A1*A2* stays constant no matter where it is moved. In addition, unlike the *Copy* command, the *Cut* command *erases* the contents of the Source range and places it in the Windows Clipboard for future pasting.

A warning about moving: A formula (function) does not change when its cell is moved, but *other* formulas that refer to the cell do! They adjust to reflect the new location of the moved cell. This is useful, unless the moved cell is a range endpoint. For example, if Cell A1 is moved to Cell B10, the formula =*SUM(A1:A5)* will now read =*SUM(B10:A5)*—yielding incorrect results. Use care when moving cells—save workbooks before moving cells, or be prepared to invoke the *Undo* command.

The following exercises demonstrate the *Cut* and *Paste* commands. First, move the date in Cell A3 to D1:

1. **Open the *SS2-1C* workbook**

2. **Move to Cell A3**

MOUSE APPROACH	KEYBOARD APPROACH
3. **Click *Edit, Cut* to move the selection to the Clipboard**	3. **Press Ctrl + X to move the selection to the Clipboard**

In the Windows environment, moving involves a *cut-and-paste* process. The **Cut** command moves the selection from its current position to the Clipboard, and the *Paste* command copies the selection from the Clipboard to the desired new location. Now to move the selection to Cell D1,

4. **Move to Cell D1**

FIGURE SS2-15 ■ CUTTING AND PASTING

The Cut and Paste commands (Edit menu) can reposition one or more cells without retyping or erasing.

	A	B	C	D	E
1	Chapter Exercises			Date	
2	Your Name				
3					
4		WEEKLY PAYROLL			
5	Employee	Hours	Pay	Gross	
6					
7	Burstein	40	$ 5.65	$ 226.00	
8	Laudon	35	4.00	140.00	
9	Martin	38	5.75	218.50	
10	Parker	25	6.75	168.75	
11	Williams	32	3.50	112.00	
12					
13	TOTAL			$ 865.25	
14					
15					

CHAPTER 2   ENHANCING SPREADSHEETS: RANGE AND DEFAULT CHANGES, FORMATS AND FUNCTIONS   SS89

MOUSE APPROACH	KEYBOARD APPROACH
5. Click *Edit, Paste*	5. Press ↵ or Ctrl + V

Now, try moving the column headings from Rows 5 and 6 to Cell A4.

6. Move to Cell A5

7. Select the range A5:D6

MOUSE APPROACH	KEYBOARD APPROACH
8. Click *Edit, Cut*	8. Press Ctrl + X to cut
9. Move to Cell A4	9. Move to Cell A4
10. Click *Edit, Paste*	10. Press Ctrl + V to paste
11. Move to Cell A1	

Your spreadsheet should now resemble Figure SS2-15. If it does not, repeat Steps 1 through 10.

12. Save this workbook as *SS2-1D* and then close it

TRANSPOSING CELLS

Copying replicates cells in other spreadsheet locations by maintaining their row or column orientation. That is, a *row* of cells must be copied to another *row*; a *column* of cells to another *column*. However, what if you need to shift a column of cells to form a row, or vice versa? Of course, you could move a row of data cell by cell to form a column, but this is tedious and will not work for formulas or functions. To remedy this situation, Excel offers a Paste Special command option called *Transpose* that allows you to copy cells while switching columns and rows in the process. **Transpose** copies cell contents while exchanging the orientation of columns and rows automatically.

For example, this exercise converts the column of cells in Figure SS2-14a to a row orientation (as shown in Figure SS2-16b).

1. Create a new workbook

2. Enter text in Cells B2 through B6 as in Figure SS2-16a

3. Select the range B2:B6

MOUSE APPROACH	KEYBOARD APPROACH
4. Click *Edit, Copy*	4. Press Ctrl + C to copy the range
5. Click *Cell D2*	5. Move to Cell D2
6. Click *Edit, Paste Special* for its dialog box	6. Press Alt + E, S for the Paste Special dialog box
7. Click the *Transpose* check box, *OK*	7. Press Alt + E to select the Transpose check box and then press ↵
8. Move to Cell D2	

Your worksheet should resemble Figure SS2-16b.

Once a range has been transposed, you can delete or erase unneeded cells.

SS90 | **SPREADSHEETS WITH MICROSOFT EXCEL 5.0**

FIGURE SS2-16 ■ **TRANSPOSING CELLS**

(a) The original column of cells. (b) Tranposing has moved Column B to Row 2.

	A	B	C	D	E	F	G	H	I	
1										
2		Hours								
3		40								
4		35								
5		38								
6		25								
7										
8										

(a)

	A	B	C	D	E	F	G	H	I	
1										
2		Hours		Hours	40	35	38	25		
3		40								
4		35								
5		38								
6		25								
7										
8										

(b)

---

9. **Move to Cell B2**

10. **Select the range B2:B6**

11. **Press** `Delete`

12. **Move to Cell A1**

Experiment with this command on your own—create another row or column of cells (or both) and transpose them.

13. **Close the workbook without saving**

USING RANGE NAMES

A **range name** can be used in a formula, function, or command, in place of actual cell addresses. For example, if the name PAY is assigned to the range C6:C10, then PAY can be used in any operation that refers to these cells—*=SUM(PAY)* totals the range.

Using range names is simpler than specifying cell addresses. Range names take less time to select and are easier to remember. The following exercises illustrate the creation, use, modification, and deletion of range names.

CHAPTER 2 ENHANCING SPREADSHEETS: RANGE AND DEFAULT CHANGES, FORMATS AND FUNCTIONS SS91

CREATING NAMES. Any valid range can be given a name. For this exercise, you will create two ranges—NAMES for the range A4:A10, and TIME for the range B6:B10. In general, range names should begin with alphabetic characters not with any symbols that might be misinterpreted as formulas or cell addresses by Excel.

1. **Open the *SS2-1D* workbook**

If you plan to point to the range,

2. **Position the pointer in Cell A5**

3. **Select the range A5:A11**

MOUSE APPROACH	KEYBOARD APPROACH
4. Click *Insert, Name, Define* for its dialog box	4. Press Alt + I , N , D for the Define Name dialog box
5. Type NAMES and click *OK*	5. Type NAMES and press ↵

For the second range name,

6. **Select the range B7:B11**

MOUSE APPROACH	KEYBOARD APPROACH
7. Click *Insert, Name, Define* for its dialog box	7. Press Alt + I , N , D for the Define Name dialog box
8. Type TIME and click *OK*	8. Type TIME and press ↵

9. **Move to Cell A1 and resave the *SS2-1d* worksheet**

> Tip: When you save the worksheet, range names are saved with it. If you do not save the worksheet, the range names will *not* be there when the worksheet is opened. Range names can also be created using the Name box (left side of the formula bar). To do so, select the desired range, click the Name box, type the name, and press Enter .

REVIEWING OR MODIFYING NAMES. You have created two range names. You can easily review (or modify) them by following this procedure:

MOUSE APPROACH	KEYBOARD APPROACH
1. Click *Edit, Go To* for its dialog box	1. Press F5 for the Go To dialog box

The Go To dialog box appears as in Figure SS2-17a. Note that all current range names are displayed in the Go To list box.

MOUSE APPROACH	KEYBOARD APPROACH
2. Double-click *TIME* in the Go To list box (or click *TIME, OK*)	2. Press Alt + G , ↓ twice, ↵ to select the TIME range

The range is selected. Its cell addresses are displayed in the Name box (formula bar) and on the worksheet screen as shown in Figure SS2-17b. At this point, you could simply look at the range address or modify it by typing a new one. When you have finished examining the screen,

3. **Move to Cell A1**

FIGURE SS2-17 ■ NAME RANGES

(a) The Go To dialog box displays current names defined in the worksheet.
(b) The selected range is identified in the formula bar and highlighted on the screen.

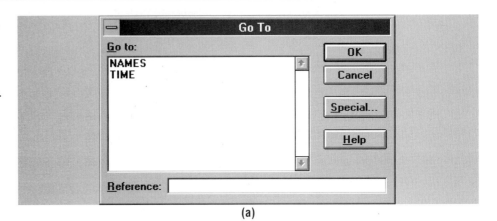

> **Tip:** You can also select a name from the Name drop-down list by clicking the ↓ button of the Name box (formula bar), and then clicking the desired name.

USING NAMES. Once range names are created, they can replace their corresponding cell addresses in any Excel procedure. These exercises illustrate how range names can be used in *Print* and *Print Preview* commands, and in a function.

MOUSE APPROACH

1. Click *Edit, Go To*
2. Double-click *NAMES*

KEYBOARD APPROACH

1. Press F5
2. Press Alt + G , use the arrow keys to move to NAMES, and then press ↵

CHAPTER 2   ENHANCING SPREADSHEETS: RANGE AND DEFAULT CHANGES, FORMATS AND FUNCTIONS   SS93

FIGURE SS2-18 ■ PRINT PREVIEWING AND PRINTING BY RANGE NAME

The Print Preview window has been set to display only the selected range.

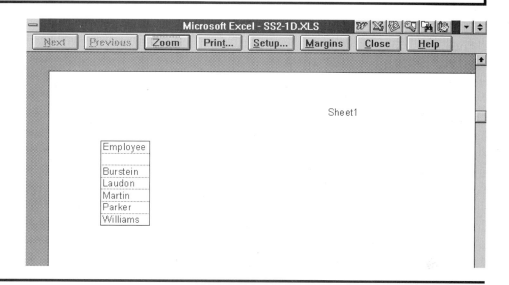

3. Click *File*, *Print*
4. Click *Selection*
5. Click *Print Preview*, *Zoom* to print the NAMES range to the screen

3. Press `Ctrl` + `P`
4. Press `Alt` + `N` to select Selection
5. Press `Alt` + `W`, `↵` to preview

The print range A5:A11 defined under the range name NAMES now appears in the print-preview screen as in Figure SS2-18. To print this range instead of print previewing, turn on your printer and replace Step 5 with clicking the *OK* button (or pressing the Enter key).

6. Press `Esc` to return to the Excel window

For an example of range name use in a function,

7. Move to Cell B13
8. Type `=SUM(TIME)` and press `↵`
9. Move to Cell B13

As shown in Figure SS2-19a, the =SUM function has correctly totaled the indicated range.

DELETING NAMES. When there is no longer any need for a range name, it can be deleted without harming the range itself or any formulas that refer to it.

MOUSE APPROACH

1. Click *Insert*, *Name*, *Define* for its dialog box

KEYBOARD APPROACH

1. Press `Alt` + `I`, `N`, `D` for the Define Name dialog box

SS94 SPREADSHEETS WITH MICROSOFT EXCEL 5.0

FIGURE SS2-19 ■ USING RANGE NAMES

(a) Range names can also be used in formulas.
(b) Deleting a name that is used in a formula invokes the message "#NAME?" in the cell that it is used.

Range name

| B13 | ▼ | =SUM(TIME) |

	A	B	C	D	E
1	Chapter Exercises			Date	
2	Your Name				
3					
4		WEEKLY PAYROLL			
5	Employee	Hours	Pay	Gross	
6					
7	Burstein	40	$ 5.65	$ 226.00	
8	Laudon	35	4.00	140.00	
9	Martin	38	5.75	218.50	
10	Parker	25	6.75	168.75	
11	Williams	32	3.50	112.00	
12					
13	TOTAL	170		$ 865.25	
14					
15					

(a)

| B13 | ▼ | =SUM(TIME) |

	A	B	C	D	E
1	Chapter Exercises			Date	
2	Your Name				
3					
4		WEEKLY PAYROLL			
5	Employee	Hours	Pay	Gross	
6					
7	Burstein	40	$ 5.65	$ 226.00	
8	Laudon	35	4.00	140.00	
9	Martin	38	5.75	218.50	
10	Parker	25	6.75	168.75	
11	Williams	32	3.50	112.00	
12					
13	TOTAL	#NAME?		$ 865.25	
14					
15		Contains a range name			
16		that has been deleted			

(b)

---

2. **Click *TIME***

3. **Click *Delete*, OK**

2. **Press Tab and then use the arrow keys to select TIME**

3. **Press Alt + D , ↵**

The range name TIME has been deleted. As shown in Figure SS2-19b, all cells remain undisturbed except for Cell B13. Since TIME no longer exists, the message "#NAME?" appears in Cell B13.

CHAPTER 2   ENHANCING SPREADSHEETS: RANGE AND DEFAULT CHANGES, FORMATS AND FUNCTIONS   SS95

4. Move to Cell B13 and press Delete

5. Close the workbook without saving

CHECKPOINT

✓ Open the SS2-1D workbook. Format the cells.
✓ Right-align all employee names and center-align hours in the Pay column to accounting-currency, two decimals format.
✓ Copy the formula in D7 to E7; then copy E7 into all cells from E8 to E11. Transpose the names in Cells A7:A11 to Row 16.
✓ Name the cell range A5:A11 PEOPLE.
✓ Use the range name PEOPLE to move this range to Column F, starting in F5. Save as "PAYROLL."

RESETTING WORKSHEET DEFAULTS

Excel has many default settings. Some default settings affect the view of the window; others, the behavior of the program (for example, the default number format) or the worksheet. This section focuses on worksheet default settings and will refer to them simply as *default changes*.

Whereas range changes adjust only a part of the spreadsheet, default changes are designed to affect the spreadsheet as a whole. **Default changes** change default settings that determine spreadsheet appearance. In general, default changes affect all the cells in a worksheet *except* those cells whose appearance (format, alignment, or column width) is set individually or by a range change. Although default changes can be used at any time, they are typically performed before data are entered into individual cells, so that the general appearance of all worksheet cells can be established. The following exercises demonstrate how default changes can affect the worksheet. First, prepare a demonstration worksheet as follows:

1. Close any open workbook and then open a new workbook

2. In Cell A1, type   LEFT

3. In Cell A2, type   RIGHT

4. In Cell A3, type   1234.5

5. In Cell A4, type   5678.9

6. Press ↵

7. Change Cell A2's alignment to right horizontal

8. Format Cell A4 to comma, one decimal

9. Move to Cell A1

Your spreadsheet should match Figure SS2-20. If it does not, fix the appropriate cells before continuing.

10. Save this workbook as *SS2-2A*

| FIGURE SS2-20 ■ DEMONSTRATION WORKSHEET FOR DEFAULT CHANGES |

	A	B
1	LEFT	
2	RIGHT	
3	1234.5	
4	5,678.9	
5		
6		

Notice that Cell A1 (which was typed without alignment or format changes has been automatically assigned the current default setting of *left-align*. Cell A3 (which has no range format adjustment) uses the current default format of general. You are now ready to explore changing default settings.

Note: Before invoking a default change, the cell pointer must be in a cell whose default changes have not been changed.

FORMAT

Default formats are identical to the range formats you have already learned, but default formats will affect all the cells in the spreadsheet that use the default setting.

1. **Open the *SS2-2A* workbook and move to Cell A1 if needed**

| FIGURE SS2-21 ■ THE STYLE DIALOG BOX |

This dialog box allows you to change the default style settings of the worksheet.

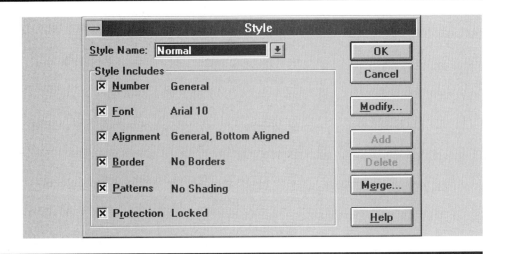

CHAPTER 2   ENHANCING SPREADSHEETS: RANGE AND DEFAULT CHANGES, FORMATS AND FUNCTIONS   **SS97**

MOUSE APPROACH	**KEYBOARD APPROACH**
2. Click *Format, Style* for its dialog box	2. Press **Alt** + **O** , **S** for the style dialog box

The style dialog box should appear as shown in Figure SS2-21. This dialog box displays the current style default settings and can be used to change these settings. Note the number style is currently set to General.

MOUSE APPROACH	**KEYBOARD APPROACH**
3. Click *Modify, Number* tab	3. Press **Alt** + **M** , **N**
4. Click *#,##0* (comma, 0 decimal) in the Format Codes list box	4. Press **Alt** + **F** and then use the arrow keys to select #,##0 (comma, 0 decimal)
5. Click *OK, OK*	5. Press ↵ , **Tab** four times to move to *OK,* ↵

Examine the worksheet on your screen and in Figure SS2-22. Notice that Cell A3 now uses the new default format, but Cell A4 does not. This is because default changes do not affect cells that have been formatted by range changes. This is true whether the range change was invoked before or after a default change.

Range changes always override worksheet default changes. Only cells with no specific format will reflect the new style default settings. If you want a formatted cell to use the default setting, you must remove its format. This can be done by the *Clear, Formats* command (Edit menu). The following exercise examines this further.

6.   Type   2468.1   in Cell B3 and press   ↵

Notice that the cell, which displays *2,468*, automatically uses the default format setting.

7.   Move to Cell B3 again

MOUSE APPROACH	**KEYBOARD APPROACH**
8. Click *Format, Cells, Number* tab, *#,##0.00* (comma, 2 decimal), *OK*	8. Press **Ctrl** + **1** , **N** , **Alt** + **F** , use arrow keys to select *#.##0.00* (comma, 2 decimal), ↵

FIGURE SS2-22 ■ RANGE VERSUS WORKSHEET DEFAULT CHANGES

	A	B
1	LEFT	
2	RIGHT	
3	1,235	
4	5,678.9	← Formatted cell remains unchanged
5		
6		

SS98 SPREADSHEETS WITH MICROSOFT EXCEL 5.0

Note that now the cell displays *2468.10*—the range format just added *overrides* the global default setting. To remove the cell's range format,

MOUSE APPROACH	KEYBOARD APPROACH
9. Click *Edit, Clear, Formats* to delete range formats	9. Press `Alt` + `E`, `A`, `F` to delete range formats

Note that the cell's display returns to the worksheet default setting.

10. Save this workbook as *SS2-2B*

ALIGNMENT

As you have seen, data alignment within a cell can be changed at any time by a range change.

The *Default* changes do *not* affect data aligned by a range change already on the worksheet. It simply changes how new data will be aligned. As always, you can still change the alignment with a range change. This exercise changes the default alignment from General (automatic) to Center-align.

1. Open the *SS2-2B* workbook if needed

2. Move to Cell A1

MOUSE APPROACH	KEYBOARD APPROACH
3. Click *Format, Style, Modify, Alignment* tab	3. Press `Alt` + `O`, `S`, `Alt` + `M`, `A` for the Alignment tab
4. Click *Center* for center horizontal alignment and then click *OK, OK*	4. Press `Alt` + `C` for center horizontal alignment, press `↵`, `Tab` four times to *OK* and then `↵`

FIGURE SS2-23 ■ **ENTERING NEW DATA**

(a) This illustrates changing the Default alignment to center-horizontal align. (b) New data entries are aligned with the default setting unless the cell was formatted with a range command.

	A	B	C
1	LEFT		
2	RIGHT		
3	1,235	2,468	
4	5,678.9		
5			
6			

(a)

	A	B	C
1	LEFT	TEST1	◄— Data typed with no range change
2	RIGHT	TEST2	◄— Data with a left-aligned range change
3	1,235	2,468	
4	5,678.9		
5			
6			

(b)

CHAPTER 2   ENHANCING SPREADSHEETS: RANGE AND DEFAULT CHANGES, FORMATS AND FUNCTIONS   SS99

Examine the worksheet on your screen and in Figure SS2-23a. Notice that only the data in Cell A1, A3, B1 and B3, whose alignment was not changed by a range command, is centered.

5.   In Cell B1, type   TEST1

6.   In Cell B2, type   TEST2   and press   ↵

7.   Move to Cell B2 and left-align the data

In examining your changes and Figure SS2-23b, note that the data in Cell B1, *TEST1*, was automatically assigned the default alignment—center. *TEST2* in Cell B2 remained left-aligned because it was aligned by a range change. Any data entered into a new cell or one that was not formatted with a range change will appear center-aligned.

8.   Save this workbook again as *SS2-2B*

COLUMN WIDTH

The worksheet default changes for column width allow you to change the width of all columns in the spreadsheet *except* those whose widths have been set individually or as a range (you will learn these commands shortly). The following exercise adjusts the default column width.

1.   Open the *SS2-2B* workbook if needed

2.   Move to Cell A1

MOUSE APPROACH	**KEYBOARD APPROACH**
3. Click *Format, Column, Standard Width* for its dialog	3. Press Alt + O , C , S for the Standard Width dialog box

Note that the default column width displayed in the Standard Width dialog box is 8.43.

4.   Type   12   in the Standard Column Width text box

MOUSE APPROACH	**KEYBOARD APPROACH**
5. Click *OK* to set the default column width to 12	5. Press ↵ to set the default column width to 12

Examine the worksheet on your screen and in Figure SS2-24a. Notice that all columns are now 12 characters wide. Because they are wider, fewer columns (only A through G) can be displayed on the worksheet screen. Try one more change:

MOUSE APPROACH	**KEYBOARD APPROACH**
6. Click *Format, Column, Standard Width*	6. Press Alt + O , C , S
7. Type 4 in the Standard Column Width text box and click *OK*	7. Type 4 in the Standard Column Width text box and press ↵

As shown in Figure SS2-24b, the columns are now four characters wide, allowing many more columns to be displayed at one time. A number of other notable changes are caused by the column-width adjustment. First, regardless of alignment, text that exceeds the new cell width (such as in Cells B1 and B2) are displayed at the left edge of the cell. In addition, the right side of some labels may be hidden by cell entries to their right (as in Cell A2). Finally, values may appear as number symbols (####)

| SS100 | **SPREADSHEETS WITH MICROSOFT EXCEL 5.0** |

FIGURE SS2-24 ■ CHANGING THE DEFAULT COLUMN WIDTH

(a) Column widths have been changed to 12 characters using the Standard Width dialog box. (b) Setting the column widths too narrow can overlap labels and obscure values.

	A	B	C	D	E	F	G
1	LEFT	TEST1					
2	RIGHT	TEST2					
3	1,235	2,468					
4	5,678.9						
5							
6							

(a)

	A	B	C	D	E	F	G	H	I	J	K	L	M	N	O	P	Q	R
1	LEFT	EST1																
2	IGHT	TEST2																
3	####	####																
4	###																	
5																		
6																		

(b)

---

filling a specific cell. Number symbols (#) such as the ones in Cells A3 and A4 indicate that the value in the cell cannot be displayed in its entirety. The value is still in the cell but it cannot be seen. There are two ways to remedy the situation—either change the cell's format to one that occupies less space or make the column wider.

8. **Change the default width back to 8.43**

9. **Close the workbook without saving**

CHECKPOINT

✓ What is the difference between a range change and a default change?
✓ Open the SS2-1D worksheet. Change the default number format to "comma, zero decimals."
✓ Which cells changed? Why?
✓ Change the default alignment to center.
✓ Change the default column width to 15. Save as "DEFAULT."

ADJUSTING COLUMN WIDTH

Although default column widths can be reset, you may also want to change the width of one or more individual columns. You can widen columns to accommodate longer text or value formats, or shorten columns to fit more columns on a page. The following exercises demonstrate the use of *Column* cascading menus (Format menu) which allow you to change column width, reset column default settings, and even hide columns from view.

CHANGING INDIVIDUAL COLUMN WIDTH

Column widths can be adjusted by using the *Column Width* dialog box or by dragging and dropping the border to the right of the column letter. Assume you want to change the widths of Columns B and D. The following exercises demonstrate both techniques.

THE *COLUMN WIDTH* DIALOG BOX. A single column width or a range of column widths can be set by using the *Column Width* dialog box. Try the following:

1. Open the *SS2-1D* workbook

2. Move to Cell B6 (any cell in Column B is fine)

FIGURE SS2-25 ■ **CHANGING INDIVIDUAL COLUMN WIDTH**

(a) The initial worksheet columns are set to a default of 8.43 characters. (b) This illustrates the *Column Width* dialog box.

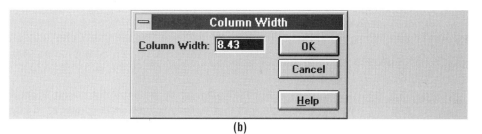

(continued)

FIGURE SS2-25 ■ *(continued)*

(c) Column B's width has been changed to 6.

	A	B	C	D	E
1	Chapter Exercises			Date	
2	Your Name				
3					
4		WEEKLY PAYROLL			
5	Employee	Hours	Pay	Gross	
6					
7	Burstein	40	$ 5.65	$ 226.00	
8	Laudon	35	4.00	140.00	
9	Martin	38	5.75	218.50	
10	Parker	25	6.75	168.75	
11	Williams	32	3.50	112.00	
12					
13	TOTAL			$ 865.25	
14					
15					
16					

(c)

Your worksheet should resemble Figure SS2-25a.

MOUSE APPROACH

3. Click *Format, Column, Width* for its dialog box

KEYBOARD APPROACH

3. Press **Alt** + **O**, **C**, **W** for the *Column Width* dialog box

The current width (8.43) appears in the column width text box of the *Column Width* dialog box as shown in Figure SS2-25b. Assume you want to change the width of this column to 6.

4. Type **6** in the Column Width text box to set the width to six characters

MOUSE APPROACH

5. Click *OK* to set new column width

KEYBOARD APPROACH

5. Press ↵ to set new column width

As shown in Figure SS2-25c, the width of Column B has changed.

DRAGGING AND DROPPING A COLUMN WIDTH. A column's width can also be changed by dragging and dropping the border to the right of a column letter. As you try the next exercise, examine the Cell Address area (left side) of the edit line for character-width messages. (If you do not have a mouse, use the column-width dialog box to change Column D's width to 12 characters.)

1. Slowly move your mouse pointer to the border to the right of the Column letter *D* until it changes to a resizing column-width pointer as in Figure SS2-26a

2. Press and hold the left mouse button while moving the mouse and border (drag) to the

CHAPTER 2   ENHANCING SPREADSHEETS: RANGE AND DEFAULT CHANGES, FORMATS AND FUNCTIONS   SS103

FIGURE SS2-26 ■ **DRAGGING AND DROPPING A COLUMN WIDTH**

(a) Slowly moving your mouse pointer to the border to the right of a column letter changes it to a Resizing column-width pointer.
(b) As you drag the Resizing column-width pointer, the column's new character width appears in the name box (formula bar). A horizontal line indicating where the new column border will appear is displayed below the pointer until the mouse is released.
(c) Column D has been resized to 12 characters.

	A	B	C	D	E	F	G	H
1	Chapter Exercises			Date				
2	Your Name							
3								

Resizing column-width pointer

(a)

Current position of resizing column-width pointer

Width: 7.00

	A	B	C	D	E	F	G	H
1	Chapter Exercises			Date				
2	Your Name							
3								

(b)

	A	B	C	D	E	F	G	H
1	Chapter Exercises			Date				
2	Your Name							
3								

(c)

---

left until the message "Width:7:00" appears in the name box (formula bar) area as in Figure SS2-26b

3.   **Release the mouse**

Column D is now narrowed by one character. Using the same technique, change Column D's width to six characters:

4.   **Again, move your mouse pointer to the border to the right of the Column letter** *D*

5.   **Drag the border to the left until "Width:6.0" appears in the selection indicator area**

6.   **Release the mouse**

Note that the column is now too narrow to show certain numeric data. Instead, number signs (####) fill the cell. Now use the same technique to increase the column width to 12 characters:

7.   **Point to the border to the right of the Column letter** *D*

8.   **Drag the border to the right until "Width:12.0" appears in the Cell Address area**

9.   **Release the mouse**

As shown in Figure SS2-26c, Column D is now 12 characters wide.

RESETTING TO THE DEFAULT WIDTH. Once column widths have been set individually, they do not respond to default changes. However, you can cancel the individual width and return the column to the default setting with a similar command sequence.

1. **Move to Cell D6 (any cell in Column D is fine)**

MOUSE APPROACH	KEYBOARD APPROACH
2. Click *Format, Column, Standard Width* for its dialog box	2. Press `Alt` + `C`, `S` for the Standard Width dialog box
3. Click the *OK* button	3. Press `↵`

Column D returns to the default width.

4. **Reset Column B's width to the default**

5. **Close the workbook without saving**

CHANGING WIDTH IN A COLUMN RANGE

The column-width dialog box can also be used to change the width of a range of columns. For this exercise, assume that you want to change Columns B, C, and D to 15 characters.

1. **Open the *SS2-1D* worksheet**

2. **Move to Cell B6 (or any cell in Column B)**

3. **Select the range B6:D6**

MOUSE APPROACH	KEYBOARD APPROACH
4. Click *Format, Column, Width* for its dialog box	4. Press `Alt` + `O`, `C`, `W` for the Column Width dialog box
5. Type `15` in the Column Width text box	5. Type `15` in the Column Width text box
6. Click *OK*	6. Press `↵`
7. Move to Cell B6	
8. Close the workbook without saving	

All three column widths have been changed to 15. You may also reset columns to the default by selecting *Standard Width* instead of *Width* in Step 4.

HIDING AND UNHIDING COLUMNS

At times, you may want to hide a column from view without harming its data or formulas (which continue to work correctly). This is especially useful when you want to eliminate specific columns from a printed copy of a spreadsheet.

HIDING COLUMNS. Assume that you want to hide Columns B and C from the *SS2-1D* worksheet as shown in Figure SS2-27.

1. **Open the *SS2-1D* workbook**

2. **Move to Cell B6 (or any cell in Column B)**

CHAPTER 2   ENHANCING SPREADSHEETS: RANGE AND DEFAULT CHANGES, FORMATS AND FUNCTIONS   SS105

FIGURE SS2-27 ■ HIDING COLUMNS

Columns B and C are hidden
in this worksheet.

	A	D	E	F	
1	Chapter E	Date			
2	Your Name				
3					
4	WEEKLY PAYROLL				
5	Employee	Gross			
6					
7	Burstein	$ 226.00			
8	Laudon	140.00			
9	Martin	218.50			
10	Parker	168.75			
11	Williams	112.00			
12					
13	TOTAL	$ 865.25			
14					
15					

---

3.   **Select the range B6:C6**

MOUSE APPROACH

4.   **Click** *Format, Column, Hide* **to hide Columns B and C**

KEYBOARD APPROACH

4.   **Press** `Alt` + `O` , `C` , `H` **to hide Columns B and C**

The columns are hidden. Notice (as in Figure SS2-27) that the border highlight displays Column A followed by Column D—a clear indication that some columns are missing. Note, too, that the *Gross* values still reflect the data from the hidden columns. You could now continue to use, save, or print the worksheet.

There may be some text overlap problems, as in Row 1. These can be left alone or fixed as needed. For example, remove the date in Cell D1 as follows:

5.   **In Cell D1, press** `Delete`

UNHIDING COLUMNS.   The procedure to "show," or redisplay, hidden columns is almost identical to the Hide command sequence:

1.   **Move to Cell A1 (or any cell in Column A)**

2.   **Select the range A1:D1**

MOUSE APPROACH

3.   **Click** *Format, Column, Unhide*

KEYBOARD APPROACH

3.   **Press** `Alt` + `O` , `C` , `U` **to unhide**

4.   **Move to Cell A1**

The hidden columns are redisplayed.

5.   **Close the workbook without saving**

SS106 SPREADSHEETS WITH MICROSOFT EXCEL 5.0

CHECKPOINT

✓ Open the SS2-1D worksheet. Use the *Column Width* dialog box to change Column A's width to four.

✓ Change Column B's width to six by the drag-and-drop technique.

✓ Reset the width in Columns A and B to the default setting.

✓ Hide Column C, print the worksheet, and then redisplay the column.

✓ Change the default width to 15. Do *not* save this spreadsheet.

ENHANCING A WORKSHEET WITH FONTS, COLORS AND LINES

Excel contains commands that enhance the appearance of your worksheet. As shown in Figure SS2-28, you can change the type styles or size of data for more professional-looking print; add lines and borders for better clarity; and emphasize data with color, highlighting, or shading. The following exercises introduce you to these enhancement features by modifying the "WEEKLY PAYROLL" worksheet in workbook SS2-1D to create the final worksheet as in Figure SS2-28.

Do the following to prepare for the exercises in this section.

1. **Open the *SS2-1D* workbook**

2. **Move to Cell A1**

3. **Delete Rows 1, 2 and 3 (Select the range A1:A3, *Edit*, *Delete*, Entire *Row*, *OK*)**

4. **Move to Cell A3 and delete Row 3**

5. **Move to Cell A8 and delete Row 8**

FIGURE SS2-28 ■ A WORKSHEET WITH FONT, COLOR, LINE, AND OTHER ENHANCEMENTS

	A	B	C	D	E
1	WEEKLY PAYROLL				
2	Employee	Hours	Pay	Gross	
3	Burstein	40	$ 5.65	$ 226.00	
4	Laudon	35	4.00	140.00	
5	Martin	38	5.75	218.50	
6	Parker	25	6.75	168.75	
7	Williams	32	3.50	112.00	
8	TOTAL			$ 865.25	
9					
10					

CHAPTER 2 ENHANCING SPREADSHEETS: RANGE AND DEFAULT CHANGES, FORMATS AND FUNCTIONS **SS107**

FIGURE SS2-29 ■ THE ADJUSTED WORKSHEET

Extra rows have been deleted in preparation for the worksheet enhancements in this section.

	A	B	C	D
1		WEEKLY PAYROLL		
2	Employee	Hours	Pay	Gross
3	Burstein	40	$ 5.65	$ 226.00
4	Laudon	35	4.00	140.00
5	Martin	38	5.75	218.50
6	Parker	25	6.75	168.75
7	Williams	32	3.50	112.00
8	TOTAL			$ 865.25
9				
10				

---

6. Move to Cell A1

Your worksheet should appear as Figure SS2-29. If not, close the workbook without saving and then repeat the previous Steps 1 through 6.

7. Save this workbook as SS2-1E

Commands for font, color and line enhancements under the Mouse Approach use the toolbar buttons where available. This method is the more efficient way to invoke such commands. The Keyboard Approach uses menu commands to make these enhancement changes where available. Remember, menu commands can be accessed by mouse or keyboard.

Font commands used in the following exercise can be invoked on a single cell, a range of cells, or before entering data.

CHANGING A FONT

A **font** is a typeface. Excel and Windows offer a number of basic font faces, sizes, and styles (bold, italic) from which to choose. Your system may also have other fonts available.

Assume that you want to emphasize the title "WEEKLY PAYROLL" by selecting a different font face, font size, and font style as in Figure SS2-28. As you will soon see, these changes can be done through the format toolbar or the Font tab of the Format Cells dialog box.

CHANGING A FONT FACE. The default *font face* used by Excel is *Arial*. This is the typeface that currently appears on your screen. To change it to another font face:

1. Move to Cell A1, if needed

The text "WEEKLY PAYROLL," which is aligned to fit across Columns A through D, should appear in the entry area of your Formula bar.

FIGURE SS2-30 ■ **CHANGE A FONT FACE**

(a) This is the Font drop-down list (Format toolbar).
(b) This shows the Font tab (Format Cells dialog box).

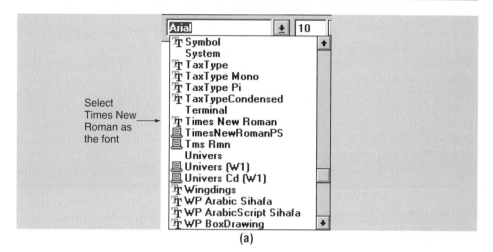

(a)

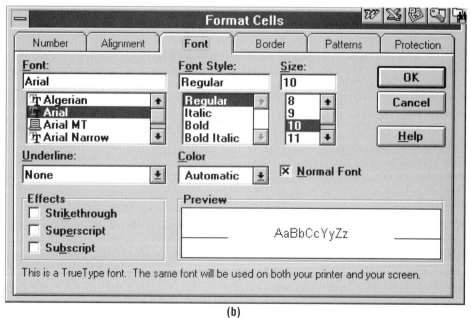

(b)

MOUSE APPROACH

2. Click the ⬇ button of the Font drop-down box (Format toolbar) for its list

3. Click the ↓ button of the Font list until Times New Roman is visible, similar to Figure SS2-30a

KEYBOARD APPROACH

2. Press Ctrl + 1 (or *Format, Cells*), F (or *Font* tab) for the Font tab of the Format Cells dialog box as in Figure SS2-30b

3. Press Alt + F (or *Font*) for the Font text box

CHAPTER 2   ENHANCING SPREADSHEETS: RANGE AND DEFAULT CHANGES, FORMATS AND FUNCTIONS   SS109

4. **Click** *Times New Roman* **to select it**

4. **Type** Times New Roman (or press the ↓ key to move the highlight to it) and then press ↵

The title, "WEEKLY PAYROLL," should now appear in the font face Times New Roman as in Figure SS2-31a.

CHANGING FONT SIZE. A font's size is in terms of points. A point is a unit of measure equivalent to 1/72 of an inch. As displayed in the Font Size drop-down box of the Format toolbar, Excel's default point size is 10 points. To change the point size:

FIGURE SS2-31 ■ CHANGING A FONT

(a) The font face has been changed to Times New Roman. (b) Changing a font's size to 16 points enlarges its typeface. (c) The Bold feature darkens a font's type face for emphasis.

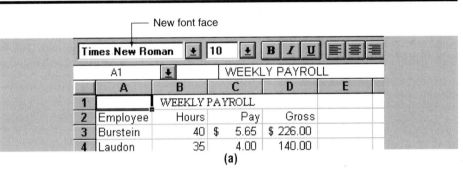

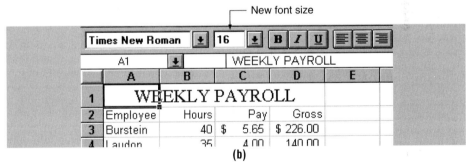

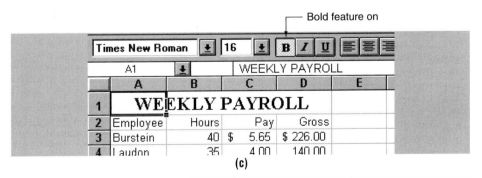

MOUSE APPROACH	KEYBOARD APPROACH
1. Click the ⬇ button of the Font Size drop-down box (Format toolbar)	1. Press Ctrl + 1 (or *Format, Cells*), F (or *Font* tab)
2. Click *16* in the Font Size list	2. Press Alt + S for the Size text box and type 16 (or press the ↓ key to move the highlight to it) and then press ↵

The title, "WEEKLY PAYROLL," should now resemble Figure SS2-31b.

CHANGING FONT STYLE. Font styles available with many fonts include: Regular (the default), *Italic,* **Bold,** and ***Bold Italic.*** You can change the font style using the Font tab (Format Cells dialog box), however, using the toolbar or shortcut keys is more efficient. Try this:

MOUSE APPROACH	KEYBOARD APPROACH
1. Click the *Bold* button (Format toolbar) to boldface the title	1. Press Ctrl + B to boldface the title
2. Click the *Italic* button (Format toolbar) to italicize the title	2. Press Ctrl + I to italicize the title

The title, "WEEKLY PAYROLL," should now appear in Bold Italic. Now, to remove the Italic style:

MOUSE APPROACH	KEYBOARD APPROACH
3. Click the *Italic* button again	3. Press Ctrl + I again

The title, "WEEKLY PAYROLL," should now resemble Figure SS2-31c. Font-style commands are toggle (on/off) commands and, as mentioned earlier, can also be invoked before entering data.

FIGURE SS2-32 ■ CHANGING BACKGROUND AND CHARACTER COLORS

(a) The background color of Cells A2 through D2 are changed to black. (b) The character color of the data in Cells A2 through D2 are changed to white.

4. Resave this workbook as SS2-1E

CHANGING COLOR

Both the background and font colors can be changed. Although the following exercise changes Cells A2 through D2's cell-background color to black and the characters to white, as in Figure SS2-32b, you can use any color available on Excel's color palette.

CHANGING BACKGROUND COLOR. The background color is the color of the interior space of a cell. To change the background color:

1. Select the range A2:D2

MOUSE APPROACH	KEYBOARD APPROACH
2. Click the ▼ button of the Color button (Format toolbar) for the cell color palette	2. Press Ctrl + 1 (or *Format, Cells*), P (or *Pattern* tab) for the Pattern tab of the Format Cells dialog box
3. Click the *Black* palette box	3. Press Alt + C for the Color text box and palette and then use the arrow keys to select the *Black* palette box and press ↵ (or *OK*)

4. Move to Cell A2

The background color of Cells A2:D2 are now black as in Figure SS2-32a. Since the character color is also black, they blend into the background and are not currently distinguishable. This will be corrected in the following section when you change the color of the characters to white.

CHANGING CHARACTER COLOR. The default color of text is black; however, this can easily be changed as follows:

1. Select the range A2:D2

MOUSE APPROACH	KEYBOARD APPROACH
2. Click the ▼ button of the Font Color button (Format toolbar) for the Font color palette	2. Press Ctrl + 1 , F (or *Format, Cells, Font* tab)
3. Click the *White* palette box	3. Press Alt + C the Font color palette and then use the arrow keys to select the *White* palette box and then press ↵ twice (or *OK*)

4. Move to Cell A1

The text in Cells A2 through D2 should appear as Figure SS2-32b.

5. Resave the workbook as SS2-1E

ADDING LINES

Excel's Border commands allow you to draw lines around each cell, or outlines around ranges of cells for emphasis. Only lines, double-lines, color changes and outlines are discussed here.

SS112 SPREADSHEETS WITH MICROSOFT EXCEL 5.0

FIGURE SS2-33 ■ ADDING LINES

(a) Border lines (single and double) have been added to the bottom of Cells A7 through D7, and A8 through D8. (b) Vertical lines have been added to the worksheet. (c) A double-line outline has been drawn around the outer borders of the worksheet.

	A	B	C	D	E
1	WEEKLY PAYROLL				
2	Employee	Hours	Pay	Gross	
3	Burstein	40	$ 5.65	$ 226.00	
4	Laudon	35	4.00	140.00	
5	Martin	38	5.75	218.50	
6	Parker	25	6.75	168.75	
7	Williams	32	3.50	112.00	
8	TOTAL			$ 865.25	
9					
10					

(a)

	A	B	C	D	E
1	WEEKLY PAYROLL				
2	Employee	Hours	Pay	Gross	
3	Burstein	40	$ 5.65	$ 226.00	
4	Laudon	35	4.00	140.00	
5	Martin	38	5.75	218.50	
6	Parker	25	6.75	168.75	
7	Williams	32	3.50	112.00	
8	TOTAL			$ 865.25	
9					
10					

(b)

	A	B	C	D	E
1	WEEKLY PAYROLL				
2	Employee	Hours	Pay	Gross	
3	Burstein	40	$ 5.65	$ 226.00	
4	Laudon	35	4.00	140.00	
5	Martin	38	5.75	218.50	
6	Parker	25	6.75	168.75	
7	Williams	32	3.50	112.00	
8	TOTAL			$ 865.25	
9					
10					

(c)

CREATING LINES. To create lines (including double-lines) as in Figure SS2-33a:

1. **Open the SS2-1E workbook if needed**

2. **Select the range A7:D7**

CHAPTER 2 ENHANCING SPREADSHEETS: RANGE AND DEFAULT CHANGES, FORMATS AND FUNCTIONS SS113

MOUSE APPROACH

3. Click the ⬇ button of the Borders button (Format toolbar) for a palette of borders

4. Click the *Single line* border box (see left margin)

5. Move to Cell A8 and then select the range A8:D8

6. Click the ⬇ button of the Borders toolbar button for a palette of borders again

7. Click the *Double-line* border box (see left margin)

8. Move to Cell A1

KEYBOARD APPROACH

3. Press `Ctrl` + `1` (or *F*ormat, C*e*lls), `B` for Border tab

4. Press `Alt` + `B` for Bottom and then `↵`

5. Move to Cell A8 and then select the range A8:D8

6. Press `Ctrl` + `1` , `B` again

7. Press `Alt` + `B` for Bottom, `Alt` + `E` for Style, use the arrow keys to select a double-line, and then press `↵`

> Tip: In place of Steps 4 through 7 of the Mouse Approach, you can click the top single line, bottom double-line border box of the Border palette.

Your worksheet should appear as Figure SS2-33a, Now, to add vertical lines:

9. Select the range A3:C7

MOUSE APPROACH

10. Click the ⬇ button of the Borders toolbar button for a palette of borders

11. Click *Right Vertical* Border box

12. Move to Cell B2

13. Save the workbook as SS2-1F

KEYBOARD APPROACH

10. Press `Ctrl` + `1` , `B` for Border tab and then press `Alt` + `R` for Right border

11. If needed, press `Alt` + `E` for the Style group and then use the arrow keys to select the Single line box and press `↵`

CHANGING LINE COLOR. Now, to add white vertical lines to Cells B2 and C2:

1. Select the range A2:C2

2. Open the Format Cells dialog box and select the Border tab

MOUSE APPROACH

3. Click *Right* in the Border group

4. Click the ⬇ button of the Color drop-down box for the color palette

5. Click the *White* box in the color palette

6. Click OK

KEYBOARD APPROACH

3. Press `Alt` + `R` for right border

4. Press `Alt` + `C` for the color palette

5. Use the arrow keys to select the *White* box in the color palette

6. Press `↵` twice

7. Move to Cell A1
8. Resave the workbook as SS2-1F

Your worksheet should now appear as Figure SS2-33b.

CREATING AN OUTLINE. The outline feature places a line or lines around a selected range. To create a double-line border around the worksheet:

1. Select the range A1:D8
2. Open the Format Cells dialog box and select the Border tab

MOUSE APPROACH	KEYBOARD APPROACH
3. Click *Outline* in the Border group 	3. Press Alt + O to select outline border
4. Click the *Double-line box* in the Style group	4. Press Alt + E and then use the arrow keys to select the double-line box
5. Click *OK*	5. Press ↵

6. Move to Cell A1

Your worksheet should appear as Figure SS2-33c.

7. Save this workbook as SS2-1G and then close it

PROVIDING ADDITIONAL EMPHASIS

If you have a mouse, you can use the Drawing toolbar to add a variety of additional features such as drop shadows, captions, arrows and other objects.

To add a drop shadow, as in Figure SS2-28, to your SS2-1G workbook:

1. Open the SS2-1G workbook
2. Select the range A1:D8

3. Click the *Drawing* button (Standard toolbar) for the Drawing toolbar

4. Click the *Drop Shadow* button on the Drawing toolbar

At this point, you can use the Drawing toolbar to create other objects in your worksheet. Feel free to experiment with this toolbar on your own. For now, to close the toolbar:

5. Click the *Drawing* button (Standard toolbar) to remove the Drawing toolbar

Note that drop-shadow borders have handles (small square boxes). This means that the drop-shadow border is selected. In Excel, a drop-shadow border is considered an object (drawing). Objects in the Windows environment, like data, must be selected before they can be edited. See the appendix for further information on creating and editing objects in Excel. For now,

6. Click Cell A1 (or any other cell) to deselect the drop shadow

Your worksheet should appear as in Figure SS2-28.

7. Save the workbook as SS2-1H and then close it

CHAPTER 2   ENHANCING SPREADSHEETS: RANGE AND DEFAULT CHANGES, FORMATS AND FUNCTIONS   **SS115**

CHECKPOINT

✓ What is a font?

✓ Open the SS2-1D workbook and change the font face and size of the data in Rows 4 and 5.

✓ Change the background and character colors in the range A7:A11.

✓ Delete any blank rows of the worksheet and place border lines around the data.

✓ Add a Drop-shadow to the worksheet. Save the workbook as ENHANCE and then close it.

CELL REFERENCES

If you *type* every formula in your spreadsheet (a tedious task), you need never worry about different types of cell references. However, it is more likely that you will use the *Copy* and *Paste* commands extensively to *copy* formulas into cells rather than type all of them.

To prepare for these exercises (and practice some of the skills you have learned in this chapter), create the worksheet shown in Figure SS2-28, as follows:

1. **Close any opened workbook and then open a new one**

2. **Make the following default changes:**
    - **Number format: Comma, two decimals (*Format, Style, Modify, Number* tab, *#,##0.00*, OK, OK)**
    - **Column width: 12 (*Format, Column, Standard Width*)**

3. **Use the *Column Width* dialog box (*Format, Column, Width*) to set Column A's width to 25**

4. **Type the cell entries shown in Figure SS2-34**

5. **Right-align the contents of Cells B2..D3**

FIGURE SS2-34 ■ THE INITIAL SS2-3A WORKSHEET BEFORE FORMULAS ARE ADDED

	A	B	C	D	E
1	Bookstore Discounts				
2		Book	0.10	Sale	
3	Title	Price	Discount	Price	
4					
5	The Rough-Faced Girl	16.95			
6	Will's Mammoth	14.95			
7	Foolish Rabbit's Mistake	12.00			
8	Ghost Stories of Japan	8.50			
9	The Hungry Tigress	16.00			
10					
11					

SS116 | SPREADSHEETS WITH MICROSOFT EXCEL 5.0

FIGURE SS2-35 ■ **ABSOLUTE AND RELATIVE REFERENCES**

(a) An absolute reference has been typed. (b) The formula is placed in Cell C5.

C5		fx	=B5*$C$2		
	A	**B**	**C**	**D**	**E**
1	Bookstore Discounts				
2		Book	0.10	Sale	
3	Title	Price	Discount	Price	
4					
5	The Rough-Faced Girl	16.95	=B5*$C$2		
6	Will's Mammoth	14.95			
7	Foolish Rabbit's Mistake	12.00			
8	Ghost Stories of Japan	8.50			
9	The Hungry Tigress	16.00			
10					
11					

(a)

	A	**B**	**C**	**D**	**E**
1	Bookstore Discounts				
2		Book	0.10	Sale	
3	Title	Price	Discount	Price	
4					
5	The Rough-Faced Girl	16.95	1.70		
6	Will's Mammoth	14.95			
7	Foolish Rabbit's Mistake	12.00			
8	Ghost Stories of Japan	8.50			
9	The Hungry Tigress	16.00			
10					
11					

(b)

Your screen should resemble Figure SS2-34. If it does not, repeat Steps 1 through 5.

6. **Save this workbook as *SS2-3A***

RELATIVE AND ABSOLUTE REFERENCES

The standard copy procedure, which you have seen, uses cell references that are relative. A **relative reference** is a cell address that, when copied, is automatically adjusted to reflect its new position in the worksheet. However, you may not want the copied cell address to change at all.

Examine the discount worksheet in Figure SS2-1. If you enter the formula =B5*C2 in Cell C5, the correct discount will be calculated for the first book. However, if this formula was copied down the column, the relative references in it would be changed automatically to =B6*C3, =B7*C4, and so on. This would be incorrect, for although the book price reference in Column B should change relative to each row, the discount percentage reference (C2) *must remain constant*. This problem calls for an **absolute reference**—a cell address reference that always refers to the same cell regardless of where it is copied. Absolute references are easily created:

1. **Open the *SS2-3A* workbook if needed**

2. **Move to Cell C5**

CHAPTER 2   ENHANCING SPREADSHEETS: RANGE AND DEFAULT CHANGES, FORMATS AND FUNCTIONS   SS117

FIGURE SS2-35 ■ *(continued)*

(c) The relative reference in Cell C5 has been changed in each row, whereas the absolute reference remains constant. (d) The completed worksheet has both relative and absolute references.

	A	B	C	D	E
1	Bookstore Discounts				
2		Book	0.10	Sale	
3	Title	Price	Discount	Price	
4					
5	The Rough-Faced Girl	16.95	1.70		
6	Will's Mammoth	14.95	1.50		
7	Foolish Rabbit's Mistake	12.00	1.20		
8	Ghost Stories of Japan	8.50	0.85		
9	The Hungry Tigress	16.00	1.60		
10					
11					

(c)

	A	B	C	D	E
1	Bookstore Discounts				
2		Book	0.10	Sale	
3	Title	Price	Discount	Price	
4					
5	The Rough-Faced Girl	16.95	1.70	15.26	
6	Will's Mammoth	14.95	1.50	13.46	
7	Foolish Rabbit's Mistake	12.00	1.20	10.80	
8	Ghost Stories of Japan	8.50	0.85	7.65	
9	The Hungry Tigress	16.00	1.60	14.40	
10					
11					
12					

(d)

---

3.   Type `=B5` (do not press the Enter key yet)

You need do nothing else to this reference, because you want it to remain relative.

4.   Type `*C2` (do not press the Enter key yet)

To make C2 an absolute reference,

5.   Press **F4** (Absolute)

Notice that dollar symbols have been placed before the column letter and row number in the cell address ($C$2), as in Figure SS2-35a. The dollar symbols indicate that the row and column references are "locked" in the identified worksheet—they are absolute references that will not be changed if this formula is copied. (The F4 function key places these symbols for you, but you may type them yourself instead, as long as you place them correctly.)

6.   Press ↵ to complete the entry

The formula in Cell C5 (and its result of 1.70) should resemble the contents shown in Figure SS2-35b. If it does not, retype it now. When the formula is correctly entered, it can be copied into the remaining cells.

7.   **Copy Cell C5 into the range C6:C9**

Examine the formulas in Cells C5:C9, as shown in Figure SS2-35c. Notice that the relative reference (B5) has been changed in each row, whereas the absolute reference ($C$2) remains unchanged in each formula.

Complete the spreadsheet now by entering a formula with relative references (ones that will change when copied) to calculate the sale price:

8. In Cell D5, enter $=B5-C5$ and then press ↵

9. Copy this formula into cells D6:D9

10. Move to Cell A1

Your worksheet should resemble Figure SS2-35d.

11. Save this workbook as SS2-3B

MIXED REFERENCES

Other circumstances may require the use of a **mixed reference**—a cell-address reference that is part absolute and part relative. Mixed references use one dollar sign to lock in either a row or column coordinate, but leave the other coordinate relative. For example,

1. Close any open workbook and then open a new workbook

2. In Cell B1, type $=$A1$ and press ↵

3. Now copy Cell B1 to the range C1:C10

4. Move to Cell C1

Examine the cell contents of any cell in Column C. Notice that the Column A reference remains, but the row changes relative to its new location. In the mixed reference =$A1, the dollar sign before the A has made the column absolute—it remains constant when copied—whereas Row 1 is free to change. Similarly, in a mixed reference such as =A$1, Column A is relative, whereas Row 1 is absolute.

5. Close the workbook without saving

> Tip: Pressing the F4 key while the cell pointer is on a cell address changes the reference from relative to absolute and then to mixed references. The cycle is =A1 → =$A$1 → =A$4 → =$A4 → =A1.

FIXING CIRCULAR REFERENCES

A **circular reference** is an error condition that occurs in a spreadsheet when a cell formula refers to itself either directly or indirectly. This is usually caused by a mistyped or misplaced formula. Figure SS2-36 displays two examples of circular references. In Figure SS2-36a, Cell B2's formula includes a direct reference to itself—clearly a problem. Figure SS2-36b, on the other hand, displays an *indirect* circular reference—Cell D2's formula refers to a cell, which refers to another cell, which in turn refers back to Cell D2. Create the circular reference in Figure SS2-36a to see the effect:

1. Close any open workbook and open a new one

2. In Cell B2, type $=B1+B2$ and press ↵

FIGURE SS2-36 ■ CIRCULAR REFERENCES

(a) A *direct* circular reference is placed in the same cell. (b) An *indirect* circular reference can involve many cells.

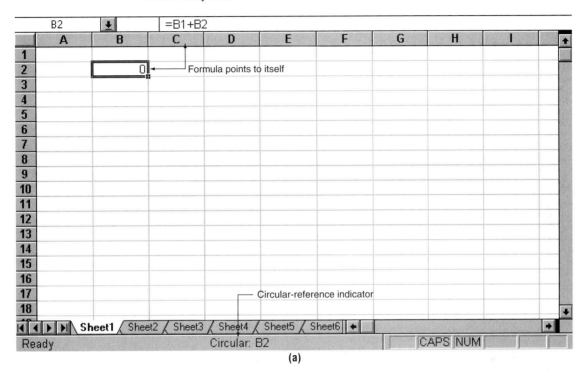

(a)

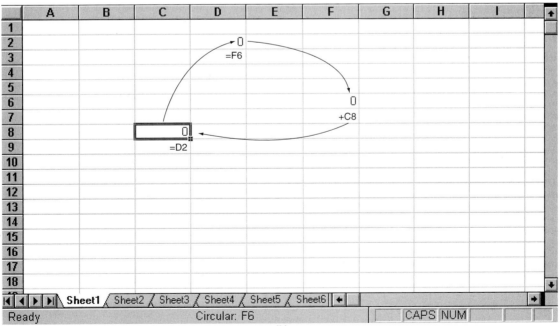

(b)

FIGURE SS2-37 ■ CIRCULAR REFERENCE MESSAGES

(a) If you enter a circular reference, this dialog box appears to warn you. (b) If a circular reference has been entered into a worksheet, the status bar displays its cell position.

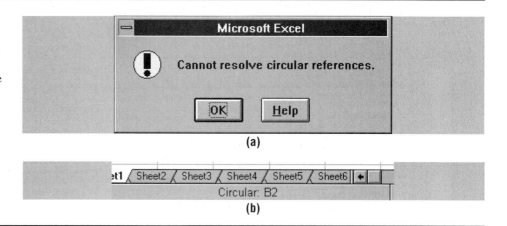

When a circular reference occurs, a dialog box indicating "Cannot resolve circular references," as in Figure SS2-37a, will appear.

MOUSE APPROACH	KEYBOARD APPROACH
3. Click *OK*	3. Press ↵

"Circular: B2" now appears in the status bar, as in Figure SS2-37b. This circular reference indicator will remain the same until changed.

4. In Cell B2, press Delete

5. Close the workbook without saving

CHECKPOINT

✓ Describe the difference between a relative and absolute reference. Which key invokes the absolute reference?
✓ Define the components and effect of a mixed reference.
✓ What is a circular reference and where does Excel identify that one exists in a worksheet?
✓ Open SS2-3A. Delete Column D. Create a border line beneath the column headings. Change the discount rate to 15 percent.
✓ Create a mixed reference in Cell D5 to calculate the final book price by subtracting the discounted price from the book price. Save the workbook as SS2-4A.

FUNCTIONS

Excel offers more than 100 built-in formulas, called *functions,* that perform a variety of useful calculations. You can use functions for arithmetic, statistical, financial, string, or date and time calculations. Functions are also available for creating conditional for-

FIGURE SS2-38 ■ ANATOMY OF A FUNCTION

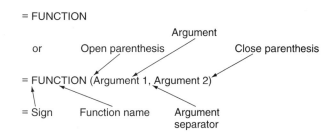

mulas or performing table lookups (see the next chapter). A complete list of Excel's functions is included in the appendix.

FUNCTION STRUCTURE

Although Excel functions perform different tasks, each shares a common structure, as shown in Figure SS2-38. All functions must begin with an "=" symbol and a function name that identifies the desired calculation. In addition, many functions include *arguments* (enclosed in parentheses) that indicate the data or range of cells that should be used in the calculation.

A FUNCTION SAMPLER

Figure SS2-39 lists a few illustrative examples of functions. Each has been applied to the data in Figure SS2-40 to calculate an answer (in Column C of the worksheet). If you want to see the effect of each yourself,

1. Close any open workbook and then open a new one
2. Enter the data in Cells A1 through A5 of Figure SS2-40
3. Enter the data in Cells A7 and A12 of Figure SS2-40
4. Type each function shown in Figure SS2-40 in the corresponding cell in Column C

(That is, start in C1 and type =SUM(A1:A7) Then type each succeeding function in the cell below the previous one.) Examine the result of each function, based on the spreadsheet's data, before entering the next function.

The results in Column C should match the spreadsheet (except for Cell C11, which generates a random number, and C19, which depends on the current date). Check your entries and retype them if your results differ.

5. Save this workbook as *SS2-4* and then close it

USING THE FUNCTION WIZARD

Excel's **Function Wizard** is a feature that can help you quickly identify a function's operation and its required arguments. It also simplifies using functions by providing

SS122 SPREADSHEETS WITH MICROSOFT EXCEL 5.0

FIGURE SS2-39 ■ SOME SAMPLE FUNCTIONS

This is an illustrative sample of a few of the many FUNCTIONs. s = a string or a cell address that contains a string. v = a value or a cell address that contains a value. n = a number.

Function	Explanation
SUM(range)	Calculates the sum of the range
AVERAGE(range)	Calculates the average of nonempty cells
MAX(range)	Lists the highest value in the range
MIN(range)	Lists the lowest value in the range
COUNT(range)	List the number of nonempty cells
STDEVP(range)	Calculates the standard deviation
ROUND(v,n)	Rounds v to n decimal places
SQRT(v)	Calculates the square root of v
ABS(v)	Calculates the absolute value of v
INT(v)	Calculates the integer value of v
RAND( )	Calculates a random number from 0 to 1
LEFT(s,n)	Returns the first n characters of s
RIGHT(s,n)	Returns the last n characters of s
LEN(s)	Counts the characters in s
LOWER(s)	Converts s to lowercase
PROPER(s)	Changes the first letter in s to uppercase and the rest to lowercase
REPT(s,n)	Duplicates s n times
PMT(p,i,n)	Calculates a periodic payment amount needed to pay off a loan of *rate* interest for the period, *nper* payments, *pu* principal or present value
NOW	Calculates a value that corresponds to the current date and time
DATE(y,m,d)	Calculates a date number for a set of year, month, and day values

---

a two-step function-entry guide. This process, as illustrated next, involves first selecting a desired function from a list and then filling in its arguments.

1.   **Open workbook SS2-4 if needed**

2.   **Move to Cell C20**

CHAPTER 2   ENHANCING SPREADSHEETS: RANGE AND DEFAULT CHANGES, FORMATS AND FUNCTIONS   SS123

FIGURE SS2-40 ■ **A WORKSHEET SAMPLER OF FUNCTIONS**

Note: Your results in Column C should match, except for Cell C11, which generates a random number and C19, which depends on the current date.

	A	B	C	D	E	F	G
1	11		78.6		◄		=SUM(A1:A7)
2	1		13.1		◄		=AVERAGE(A1:A7)
3	49		49		◄		=MAX(A1:A7)
4	0		-3		◄		=MIN(A1:A7)
5	-3		6		◄		=COUNT(A1:A7)
6			17.91973		◄		=STDEVP(A1:A7)
7	20.6		21		◄		=ROUND(A7,0)
8			7		◄		=SQRT(A3)
9			3		◄		=ABS(A5)
10			20		◄		=INT(A7)
11			0.996198		◄		=RAND()
12	SAMPLE		SAM		◄		=LEFT(A12,3)
13			LE		◄		=RIGHT(A12,2)
14			6		◄		=LEN(A12)
15			sample		◄		=LOWER(A12)
16			Sample		◄		=PROPER(A12)
17			SAMPLESAMPLE		◄		=REPT(A12,2)
18			($49.02)		◄		=PMT(A2,A1,A3)
19			16740		◄		=INT((NOW())-DATE(A3,A2,A1))
20							

MOUSE APPROACH

3. Click *Insert*, *Function* for the Function Wizard

KEYBOARD APPROACH

3. Press Shift + F3 for the Function Wizard

Note that the Function Wizard's title bar displays "Function Wizard"—Step 1 of 2.

MOUSE APPROACH

4. Click *All* in the Function Category list box to select it

5. Use the vertical scroll bar of the Function Name list box to scroll to PMT and then click it.

KEYBOARD APPROACH

4. Press Alt + C and then use the arrow keys to select All in the Function Category list box

5. Press Alt + N , P , and then ↓ five times to select PMT in the Function Name list box

Your Function Wizard's dialog box should resemble Figure SS2-41a. (Note that the position of PMT in your Function Name list box may differ.) Just below the Function Category the selected function is displayed with its required arguments and a brief description of its operation.

SS124 SPREADSHEETS WITH MICROSOFT EXCEL 5.0

FIGURE SS2-41 ■ THE FUNCTION WIZARD

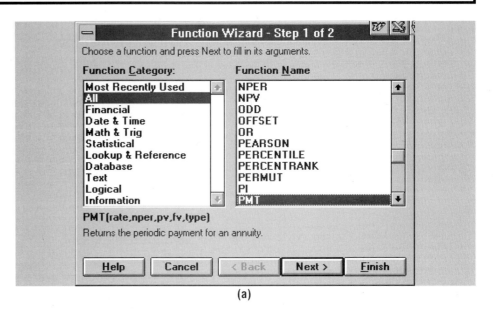

(a)

(b)

MOUSE APPROACH	KEYBOARD APPROACH
6. Click the *Next* button for the Function Wizard—Step 2 of 2 dialog box	6. Press ↵ for the Function Wizard—Step 2 of 2 dialog box

7. Type A2 in the rate text box and then press Tab

8. Type A1 in the nper (number of periods) text box and then press Tab

9. Type A3 in the pv (present value)

Your Function Wizard—Step 2 of 2—dialog box should resemble Figure SS2-41b.

CHAPTER 2   ENHANCING SPREADSHEETS: RANGE AND DEFAULT CHANGES, FORMATS AND FUNCTIONS   SS125

To the right of each cell reference that you entered is the current data it contains. Note also that the Value box (upper-right corner) displays the result of the function ($49.02).

MOUSE APPROACH	KEYBOARD APPROACH
10. Click the _Finish_ button	**10. Press** ↵

The result of the PMT function, ($49.02) in Cell C20, should be the same as in Cell C18.

> **Tip:** The Function Wizard can also be used to place a function within a formula using cell references and mathematical operators and within another function. For example, the formula in Cell C19 "=INT((NOW())-DATE(A3,A2,A1))"

11. Close the workbook without saving

CHECKPOINT

✓ What is a function and the different ways that it can be entered?
✓ Can functions be inserted within a function? Give an example.
✓ Open SS2-4a. Type in function formulas to calculate the total and average book prices in Rows 11 and 12.
✓ Use the Function Wizard to insert function formulas to calculate the maximum and minimum book prices in Rows 13 and 14.
✓ Use a data function to place the system date in the cell next to your name. Resave the workbook as SS2-4a.

MANAGING LARGE SPREADSHEETS

As spreadsheets grow large, they become more difficult to manage on the screen. Row or column data may disappear off the screen as the cell pointer is moved, making it harder to enter data in the proper cells. Results generated by "What if?" scenarios may be located far from data-entry cells, and thus not easily read as changes are made. Excel offers two command windows—*Titles* and *Split*—that alleviate the problems associated with large spreadsheets. Note that these features affect only the screen; they do not alter how worksheets print.

FREEZING

The **Freeze Panes** command (window menu) freezes columns, rows, or both along the top and left of the worksheet. Once frozen, these cells remain in constant view no matter where the cell pointer moves in the worksheet.

FREEZING PANES.   The following exercise demonstrates the procedure for freezing panes on the screen:

1.   Open the SS2-1H workbook

Position the cell pointer one row *below* the rows you want to freeze and one column to the *right* of the columns to freeze. In this example, you will freeze Rows 1 through 2 and Column A.

SS126 | **SPREADSHEETS WITH MICROSOFT EXCEL 5.0**

FIGURE SS2-42 ■ FREEZING PANES

(a) The cell pointer is positioned below the row and to the right of the column to be frozen. (b) Frozen columns remain on the screen as it scrolls right. (c) Frozen rows remain on the screen as it scrolls down.

	A	B	C	D	E	F	G	H	I	
1	WEEKLY PAYROLL									
2	Employee	Hours	Pay	Gross						
3	Burstein	40	$ 5.65	$ 226.00						
4	Laudon	35	4.00	140.00						
5	Martin	38	5.75	218.50						
6	Parker	25	6.75	168.75						
7	Williams	32	3.50	112.00						
8	TOTAL			$ 865.25						
9										
10										
11										

(a)

	A	C	D	E	F	G	H	I	J	
1	WEPAYROLL									
2	Employee	Pay	Gross							
3	Burstein	$ 5.65	$ 226.00							
4	Laudon	4.00	140.00							
5	Martin	5.75	218.50							
6	Parker	6.75	168.75							
7	Williams	3.50	112.00							
8	TOTAL		$ 865.25							
9										
10										
11										

(b)

---

2. **Move to Cell B3, as shown in Figure SS2-42a**

The columns to the left of this cell, and the rows above it, can now be frozen.

MOUSE APPROACH	**KEYBOARD APPROACH**
3. Click _Window_, _Freeze Pane_ to freeze both rows and columns	3. Press **Alt** + **W** , **F** to freeze both rows and columns

4. **Move the cell pointer to Cell J3**

Note how Column A remains on the screen, as in Figure SS2-42b. To return to the first cell past the frozen panes (Cell B3),

5. **Move to Cell B3**

6. **Move to Cell B20**

Note how Rows 1 and 2 remain on the screen, as in Figure SS2-42c.

CHAPTER 2   ENHANCING SPREADSHEETS: RANGE AND DEFAULT CHANGES, FORMATS AND FUNCTIONS   **SS127**

FIGURE SS2-42 ■ *(continued)*

	A	B	C	D	E	F	G	H	I
1	**WEEKLY PAYROLL**								
2	Employee	Hours	Pay	Gross					
6	Parker	25	6.75	168.75					
7	Williams	32	3.50	112.00					
8	TOTAL			$ 865.25					
9									
10									
11									
12									
13									
14									
15									
16									
17									
18									
19									
20									

(c)

You can freeze panes anywhere. You should consider doing so especially on large spreadsheets where the benefit of titles becomes significant.

> **Tip:** To freeze just the rows, click the row number of the row below the row you want to freeze and then click *Window, Freeze Pane.* To freeze only the columns, click the column letter of the column to the right of the columns you want frozen, and then click *Window, Freeze Pane.*

UNFREEZING PANES.   You need not be in any particular cell to unfreeze titles. Simply,

MOUSE APPROACH

1.   Click *Window*

2.   Click *Unfreeze Panes*

KEYBOARD APPROACH

1.   Press Alt + W

2.   Press F

SPLITTING

The **Split** command splits the worksheet window into two or three separate *panes,* either horizontally, vertically, or both. This allows you to see two or four different parts of the spreadsheet at the same time. These panes are two (or four) copies of the same spreadsheet.

SPLITTING PANES.   The following exercise creates a vertical window (but could just as easily create a horizontal one).

SS128 **SPREADSHEETS WITH MICROSOFT EXCEL 5.0**

1. **Open the *SS2-1H* worksheet (if needed)**

When creating a pane, you must first position the cell pointer in the row that will be the top edge of the new pane (if horizontal), or the column that will be its left edge (if vertical). You will use Column D:

2. **Move to Cell D1, as shown in Figure SS2-43a**

MOUSE APPROACH

3. **Click *Window* for the Window menu**

4. **Click *Split***

KEYBOARD APPROACH

3. **Press Alt + W for the Window menu**

4. **Press S for the Split**

Note how two panes appear side by side as in Figure SS2-43b.

FIGURE SS2-43 ■ SPLITTING

(a) The cell pointer is placed where the window will be split. (b) The cell pointer is in the right pane but can be switched to the left by clicking any cell in the left pane or by pressing the F6 key.

	A	B	C	D	E	F	G	H	I	
1	**WEEKLY PAYROLL**									
2	Employee	Hours	Pay	Gross						
3	Burstein	40	$ 5.65	$ 226.00						
4	Laudon	35	4.00	140.00						
5	Martin	38	5.75	218.50						
6	Parker	25	6.75	168.75						
7	Williams	32	3.50	112.00						
8	TOTAL			$ 865.25						
9										
10										

(a)

	A	B	C	D	E	F	G	H	I	
1	**WEEKLY PAYROLL**									
2	Employee	Hours	Pay	Gross						
3	Burstein	40	$ 5.65	$ 226.00						
4	Laudon	35	4.00	140.00						
5	Martin	38	5.75	218.50						
6	Parker	25	6.75	168.75						
7	Williams	32	3.50	112.00						
8	TOTAL			$ 865.25						
9										
10				← Split bar						

(b)

CHAPTER 2   ENHANCING SPREADSHEETS: RANGE AND DEFAULT CHANGES, FORMATS AND FUNCTIONS   SS129

SWITCHING PANES.   You can now move the cell pointer in the right pane as needed. If you wish to adjust the left pane, you must switch the cell pointer to it.

MOUSE APPROACH	KEYBOARD APPROACH
1. Click *Cell C1* (or any cell) in the left pane	1. Press F6 to switch to the left pane

You can now move in the pane.

MOUSE APPROACH	KEYBOARD APPROACH
1. Click *Cell D1* (or any cell) in the right pane	1. Press F6 to switch back

REMOVING THE SPLIT.   When you no longer need two (or more) panes on the screen, you can clear them as follows:

MOUSE APPROACH	KEYBOARD APPROACH
1. Click *Window,* for the Window menu	1. Press Alt + W for the Window menu
2. Click *Remove Split*	2. Press S to remove split

You may practice the split procedure by creating a horizontal pane by moving the cell pointer to Column A and the respective row and then invoking the Split command (Window menu). You can also create a vertical and horizontal split by placing the cell pointer in any desired cell except for Row 1 or Column A and then invoking the Split command.

3.   **Close the workbook without saving**

CHECKPOINT

✓   What is the difference between Freezing and Splitting?
✓   Open workbook SS2-3B. Freeze titles in Column A.
✓   Set a vertical pane in Column C. Switch to the spreadsheet on the right.
✓   Split the worksheet at column C. Move to the other side of the split bar and then unsplit the worksheet. Unfreeze the column and then close any open worksheet.

PRINTING TECHNIQUES

Large spreadsheets may also require the use of additional print features to enhance the appearance of the spreadsheet on paper. Such features include creating page breaks and using print options.

PAGE BREAKS

Excel automatically creates a new page when printed data fill a page (as determined by top and bottom margins). However, you can control page breaks yourself by adding

SS130 | **SPREADSHEETS WITH MICROSOFT EXCEL 5.0**

FIGURE SS2-44 ■ PAGE BREAKS

Page breaks can be inserted as needed.

	A	B	C	D	E	F	G	H	I
1	WEEKLY PAYROLL								
2	Employee	Hours	Pay	Gross					
3	Burstein	40	$ 5.65	$ 226.00					
4	Laudon	35	4.00	140.00					
5	Martin	38	5.75	218.50					
6	Parker	25	6.75	168.75					
7	Williams	32	3.50	112.00			Page-break indicator		
8	TOTAL			$ 865.25					
9									
10									

a row in your spreadsheet with special print-control characters. The following exercise, which creates a page break after Row 8, shows you how to do this.

1. Open the *SS2-1G* workbook

The cell pointer should be first placed in the *leftmost* column of the range you are printing, in the row where you want the new page to start.

2. Move to Cell A6

MOUSE APPROACH	**KEYBOARD APPROACH**
3. Click *Insert, Page Break*	3. Press **Alt** + **I** , **B**

As shown in Figure SS2-44, Excel inserts a row of dimmed dashed lines representing a forced page break. When this worksheet is printed, a new page will begin at Row 9.

To remove a page break:

4. Move to Cell A6 (if needed)

MOUSE APPROACH	**KEYBOARD APPROACH**
5. Click *Insert, Remove Page Break*	5. Press **Alt** + **I** , **B**

PAGE SETUP OPTIONS

A number of *Page Setup* options are available through the *Page Setup* dialog box. This dialog box can be accessed through the *File* menu, the *Print* dialog box, or the *Print Preview* dialog box. As displayed in Figure SS2-45, the Page Setup dialog box includes the following options:

■ *Page tab:* Changes orientation scales data so you can fit more on each page

CHAPTER 2 ENHANCING SPREADSHEETS: RANGE AND DEFAULT CHANGES, FORMATS AND FUNCTIONS SS131

FIGURE SS2-45 ■ THE PAGE SETUP DIALOG BOX

Page Setup

| Page | Margins | Header/Footer | Sheet |

Orientation
- ● Portrait
- ○ Landscape

Scaling
- ● Adjust to: 100 ⬍ % normal size
- ○ Fit to: 1 ⬍ page(s) wide by 1 ⬍ tall

Paper Size: Letter 8 ½ x 11 in ⬇

Print Quality: 300 dpi ⬇

First Page Number: Auto

OK
Cancel
Print...
Print Preview
Options...
Help

- ■ *Margin tab:* Adjusts margins
- ■ *Header/Footer tab:* Places a header at the top or a footer at the bottom of each page
- ■ *Sheet tab:* Prints column and row titles on each page and offers other printing options

SCALING PAGE DATA. When you are working with a large worksheet, the Scaling group options of the Page tab (*Page Setup* dialog box) allow you to compress the data size. Data, columns, or rows can be compressed to a single page or custom compressed. Try this:

MOUSE APPROACH	KEYBOARD APPROACH
1. Click *File, Page Setup* for its dialog box	1. Press **Alt** + **F** , **U** for the *Page Setup* dialog box

The *Page Setup* dialog box, as shown in Figure SS2-45, should appear on your screen.

You can select either the *Adjust to* (the default) or *Fit to* option button in the scaling group to control the compression of your worksheet data. The *Adjust to* option is preset to 100% and allows you to control the size of the printed data. To change it, you can either click the up or down triangle buttons to the right of the *Adjust to* text box or type in a desired size. Try this:

SS132   SPREADSHEETS WITH MICROSOFT EXCEL 5.0

MOUSE APPROACH	KEYBOARD APPROACH
2. Click the ▼ button of the Adjust to text box until the size is reduced to 75%	2. Press `Alt` + `A` and then type `75`
3. Click *Print Preview*	3. Press `Alt` + `W` for Print Preview
4. Click *Zoom*	4. Press `↵` for Zoom

Your worksheet now appears scaled to 75% of its original size. You can print the worksheet instead of print previewing it by replacing Steps 3 and 4 with clicking the *Print* button (or pressing `Alt` + `P`). Now, reset the scaling to 100%.

MOUSE APPROACH	KEYBOARD APPROACH
5. Click *Setup* for its dialog box	5. Press `Alt` + `S` for the Setup dialog box
6. Click the ▲ button of the Adjust to text box to increase to 100%	6. Press `Alt` + `A` and then type `100`

The Fit to option is helpful when you want to compress a large worksheet's width and/or length to that of a page or a desired number of pages. Like the Adjust to option, the Fit to option can be changed either by clicking the up or down triangle buttons to the right of its text boxes or by typing in a desired size. For now,

MOUSE APPROACH	KEYBOARD APPROACH
7. Click *OK* to return to the Print Preview window	7. Press `↵` to return to the Print Preview window
8. Click *Close* to return to your worksheet	8. Press `Esc` to return to your worksheet

REPEATING COLUMN OR ROW TITLES. *Print titles* are the printed versions of frozen panes; that is, for print titles, you can select columns, rows, or both to be repeated on every page of a printed spreadsheet. This option is useful for multipage worksheets where top or side labels would normally appear only on the first page. To select print titles,

1. Open the *SS2-1G worksheet* (if needed)

MOUSE APPROACH	KEYBOARD APPROACH
2. Click *File, Page Setup* for its dialog box	2. Press `Alt` + `F`, `U` for the Page Setup dialog box
3. Click the *Sheet* tab	3. Press `S` for Sheet tab

The Print Titles group of the Sheet tab allows you to specify the range of rows to repeat at the top of a page and/or columns to repeat at the left of a page. To specify the top two rows as a print title:

MOUSE APPROACH	KEYBOARD APPROACH
4. Click the *Rows to Repeat at Top* text box	4. Press `Alt` + `R` for the Rows to Repeat at Top text box
5. Type `1:2` to repeat Rows 1 through 2	5. Type `1:2` to repeat Rows 1 through 2
6. Click *Print Preview*	6. Press `Alt` + `W` for the Print Preview window

CHAPTER 2   ENHANCING SPREADSHEETS: RANGE AND DEFAULT CHANGES, FORMATS AND FUNCTIONS   **SS133**

If this worksheet contained multiple pages, Rows 1 and 2 would appear on the top of each printed page. To print column titles on each page of a multiple-page worksheet, you would select the *Columns to Repeat at Left* text box of the Sheet tab and type in the first column letter of the range, a colon, and then the last column letter. For example, if you desired to print the column titles of Columns A through C on each page of a multiple-page worksheet, type A:C in the Columns to Repeat at Left text box.

7. **Exit the Print Preview window**

8. **Close the worksheet without saving**

OTHER PRINT OPTIONS. The Print group box of the *Page Setup* dialog box (Figure SS2-46a) contains five print-display check boxes: Gridlines (the default), Notes (prints any cell notes defined in the worksheet), Draft Quality (prints without grid lines and less graphics), Black and White (prints worksheet in pure black and white), and Row and Column Headings (includes row numbers and column letters). Try this:

1. **Open the *SS2-1F* workbook**

MOUSE APPROACH

2. **Click *File, Page Setup***

3. **Click the *Sheet* tab**

4. **Click *Gridlines* to remove the "X" from the check box**

5. **Click *Row and Column Headings***

6. **Click *Print Preview***

7. **Click *Zoom* (if needed)**

KEYBOARD APPROACH

2. **Press Alt + F , U**

3. **Press S for Sheet tab**

4. **Press Alt + G to remove the "X" from the Gridlines check box**

5. **Press Alt + L to place an "X" in the Row and Column Heading check box**

6. **Press Alt + W for the Print Preview window**

7. **Press ↵ to Zoom (if needed)**

Your worksheet should appear as Figure SS2-46b. Note that only the border lines that you created appear in the worksheet. In addition, the row numbers and column letters also appear.

8. **Exit the Print Preview window and close the worksheet without saving**

9. **Exit Excel and then Windows (if desired)**

A FINAL NOTE ABOUT PRINT OPTIONS. Excel comes with a variety of Print options that can be controlled through the Page Setup dialog box (File menu). Print options are saved with your spreadsheet; they need not be reentered each time you want to print. In addition, as mentioned earlier, some printers may not support all Excel print options. In these cases, the worksheet image that appears in the Print Preview window may differ from your printed page. For example, some printers may not print reverse color (white text on a black background), italics, underlining and graphics as they appear in the Print Preview window. In addition, you may have to restart your printer to cancel previous settings.

FIGURE SS2-46 ■ **OTHER PRINT OPTIONS**

(a) The Print group options of the Sheet tab have check boxes to control certain displays of a worksheet. (b) Deactivating the Gridline check box and selecting the Row and Column Headings check box will result in this worksheet when printed.

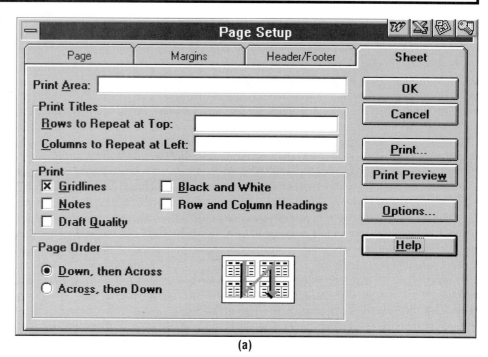

(a)

(b)

CHECKPOINT

✓ Open the SS2-3B workbook. Place a page break between *Will's Mammoth* and *Foolish Rabbit's Mistake*.
✓ Print Preview the worksheet and then remove the page break.
✓ Using the *Page Setup* dialog box, create title rows that include Rows 1 through 3.
✓ Activate the Row and Column headings and deactivate gridlines options.
✓ Print the worksheet and save it as SS2-5.

SUMMARY

Specific mouse actions or keystrokes for the following commands can be reviewed in the chapter or in the appendix.

CHAPTER 2   ENHANCING SPREADSHEETS: RANGE AND DEFAULT CHANGES, FORMATS AND FUNCTIONS   SS135

- Commands that use ranges affect only specified cells, not the entire spreadsheet. Range data alignment changes previously typed data in their cells. Range format changes adjust number displays, but not the number itself. Popular formats include General (the default), which automatically selects the correct format, and Accounting, which contains built-in format codes that will display numbers with dollar signs, comma, 2-decimal, and in brackets (negative numbers).

- The Copy and Paste commands replicate the contents of a cell (or cell range) into other cells. Other commands related to *Copy and Paste* include *Transpose* (which exchanges rows and columns) and *Cut and Paste* (which erases the original cells).

- Range names can be used in place of specific cell addresses in all commands and formulas.

- Default changes affect the entire worksheet by changing configuration or default settings. Default format and column-width changes affect all cells that have not been set with range changes. Default alignment changes set a new default for data entry; they do not affect existing range alignment changes.

- The default column width for the entire worksheet can be changed. Column width can also be changed individually, or by column range (for adjacent columns). In addition, columns can be hidden completely.

- Font (character type style) changes include font face, size, style (bold or italic) and color. All can be changed using either toolbar buttons or the Font tab of the Format Cells dialog box. Cell background color can also be changed by using toolbar buttons or the Pattern tab of the Format Cells dialog box.

- Border lines can be added to cell walls by using the Border button (Format toolbar) or the Border tab of the Format Cells dialog box.

- Drop-shadow backgrounds and other graphic images can be added to a worksheet using the Drawing toolbar and a mouse.

- Cell references can be relative, absolute, or mixed. Relative references (such as =A1) are automatically adjusted to reflect their new location, absolute references (such as =$A$1) remain constant, and mixed references (such as =A$1) have only one coordinate absolute.

- Circular references occur when a formula refers to itself directly or indirectly. They are indicated by the "Circular" (cell reference)" message in the status bar.

- Functions perform useful calculations for arithmetic, statistical, financial, string, logical, and date and time applications. All functions begin with an = symbol and may include arguments to indicate data or ranges.

- Screen techniques to manage large spreadsheets include the use of freezing and splitting panes that allow you to view different parts of the spreadsheet on one screen. Print techniques include scaling (compressing) page data, and displaying column or row titles, column or row indicators, and removing grid lines.

KEY TERMS

Absolute reference (SS116)	Default changes (SS95)	Paste (SS85)
Alignment (SS72)	Destination range (SS83)	Range name (SS90)
Circular reference (SS118)	Font (SS70)	Relative reference (SS116)
Copying (SS82)	Format (SS83)	Source range (SS83)
Cut (SS88)	Freeze Panes (SS125)	Split (SS127)
	Mixed reference (SS118)	Transpose (SS89)
	Panes (SS133)	

SS136 | SPREADSHEETS WITH MICROSOFT EXCEL 5.0

QUIZ

TRUE/FALSE

1. Only the alignment of text in a cell can be changed.
2. The General format automatically selects the correct number format for data entered.
3. The Cut and Paste commands move cell content to a new location.
4. Transposing cells changes them from text to formulas.
5. Any range can be replaced with a range name.
6. Default alignment changes affect all existing data in a spreadsheet.
7. Data entered into a new cell is automatically assigned the default settings.
8. A font is a type style.
9. Borders are lines that can be placed horizontally.
10. Worksheets can be split horizontally or vertically.

MULTIPLE CHOICE

11. _ refers to the way a number is displayed in a cell.
    a. Range
    b. Format
    c. Freeze
    d. Value
12. Which of the following numbers has been formatted as currency with two decimals?
    a. 1234.56
    b. $1234.2
    c. $1,234
    d. $1,234.00
13. Which item must be specified first when copying cells?
    a. Range name
    b. Worksheet name
    c. Range destination
    d. Source range
14. Which command (or commands) transfers cell contents to a new location and then erases the original cell?
    a. *Cut* and *Paste*
    b. *Copy* and *Paste*
    c. *Transpose*
    d. *Format*
15. All of the following are worksheet enhancement changes except,
    a. Transpose adjustments
    b. Font changes
    c. Border line changes
    d. Drop-shadow borders
16. It is most effective to issue default changes
    a. after text is returned.
    b. after all formatting has been completed.
    c. before data are entered into cells.
    d. before printing or saving a worksheet.

17. The default number format is
    a. general.
    b. accounting.
    c. currency.
    d. worksheet.
18. Number signs (####) that fill a cell indicate that
    a. the cell is too narrow to show a number.
    b. the cell is too narrow to show text.
    c. the cell has a border line in it.
    d. the data in the cell must be retyped.
19. Which of these commands cannot be used to change column width?
    a. Dragging the right border next to the column letter
    b. Clicking *Format, Column Width*
    c. Pressing Alt + O , C , W
    d. Clicking *Column Width,* and then *Worksheet*
20. How would you describe the reference (or references) contained in the formula =$A$1*B3?
    a. A mixed reference
    b. An absolute reference followed by a relative reference
    c. A relative reference followed by an absolute reference
    d. A currency format followed by a fixed format

MATCHING

Select the lettered item from the following figure that best matches each phrase:

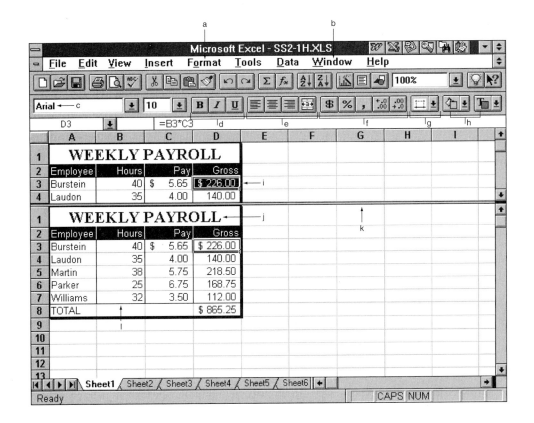

SS138 SPREADSHEETS WITH MICROSOFT EXCEL 5.0

21. Toolbar buttons that change the alignment of data in a cell.
22. The result of a font change.
23. Contains a formula that is formatted—accounting currency, 2 decimals.
24. Created by invoking the split command.
25. Toolbar buttons that can be used to change the background color of a cell or characters.
26. Can be created by using the Border tab of the Format Cells dialog box.
27. Contains commands to change the format of cells, row and column settings, and style settings.
28. Contains commands to split or freeze panes.
29. Can be used to quickly change the format of number displays by mouse.
30. Can be used to quickly invoke certain font-style changes.

ANSWERS

True/False: 1. F; 2. T; 3. T; 4. F; 5. T; 6. F; 7. T; 8. T; 9. T; 10. T
Multiple Choice: 11. b; 12. d; 13. d; 14. a; 15. a; 16. c; 17. a; 18. a; 19. d; 20. b
Matching: 21. e; 22. j; 23. i; 24. k; 25. h; 26. l; 27. a; 28. b; 29. f; 30. d

EXERCISES

I. OPERATIONS

Provide the Excel Mouse Approach and Keyboard Approach actions (as appropriate) required to do each of the following operations.

1. Right-align cells B5:F8.
2. Change the format of cells C1:C6 to "accounting-comma, two decimals."
3. Display accounting-currency, two decimals in cells D5:D20.
4. Copy Cell B6 to Cell B7.
5. Copy Cell C7 to Cells C8:C15.
6. Copy Cells A1:A8 to Cells B1:B8.
7. Create a range name called JANUARY for range F5:F25.
8. Change the column width to 20 by the Drag-and-Drop technique.
9. Change the column width of Columns E and F to 10.
10. Reset the width of Column F to the default setting.
11. Add a border line to Cells A5:H5.
12. Create an absolute reference to Cell T6.
13. Freeze vertical titles in Columns A and B.
14. Create an unsynchronized horizontal pane at Row 5.

II. COMMANDS

Describe fully, using as few words as possible in each case, what command is initiated or what is accomplished in Excel by the actions described below. Assume that each exercise part is independent of any previous parts.

1. Pressing the `Shift` + `F3` keys
2. Clicking the `↓` button of the font drop-down box
3. Dragging the right border next to a column letter
4. Pressing the `F5` key
5. Clicking the toolbar button containing a picture of two documents
6. Pressing the `Ctrl` and `N` keys
7. Pressing `F6` after invoking the split command
8. Pressing the `Ctrl` and `1` keys
9. Clicking the toolbar button that looks like a clipboard with paper
10. Pressing the `'` (apostrophe) keys, `10` and then the Enter key

III. APPLICATIONS

Perform the following operations and briefly describe how you accomplished each operation and what its results were.

APPLICATION 1: CLUB BUDGET

Save the workbook as "CLUB2" after each operation is completed so that you can continue this exercise later. (Remember to set the default drive to A before saving the workbook.)

1. Open the "CLUB1" workbook (created in the previous chapter).
2. Right-align the data in Cells C6 through F6.
3. Format the range C8:F8 and C14:F14 with the accounting-currency, two-decimal format _($*#,##0.00_).
4. Format the range C9:F12 with the accounting-comma, two-decimal format _(*#,##0.00_).
5. Delete the empty Row 7 and then Row 12.
6. Place a single-lined border in the range C11:F11 and then place a double-lined border in the range C12:F12.
7. Change the standard (default) column width to 12 and then the column width of Column F to 15.
8. Insert three columns to the left of Column F (previous chapter skill).
9. Copy the range C7:E12 to the range F7:H12.
10. Type `APR` in Cell F7, `MAY` in Cell G7, and `JUN` in Cell H7.
11. Delete the range I7:I11, place a SUM function to total the range C7:H7 and then copy the formula to the range I8:I11.

12. Format the range I8:I11 in accounting-comma, two decimals _(*#,##0,00_).
13. Change the numbers in Cells F7 to 80, G9 to 75, H11 to 325.
14. Change the font of Cell A4 to Times New Roman, 14 points and then boldface that cell's content and the range C6:I6.
15. Save the workbook as "CLUB2," print the entire worksheet without gridlines, and then exit the program.

APPLICATION 2: ADDITIONAL GPA

Save the workbook in this exercise as "GPA2" after each operation is completed so that you can continue this exercise later.

1. Open the "GPA1" workbook (created in the previous chapter).
2. Center all the data in Cells B6 through C12. Right-align the data in Cells D6 through F6.
3. Format Cells D8 through F14 to "0 decimals (0)."
4. Insert a row below Row 10 (previous chapter skill).
5. Copy Cells A10 through F10 into the new Row 11. Type ART205 in Cell A11, 9301 in Cell B11, A in Cell C11, 2 in Cell D11, and 4 in Cell E11.
6. Move the word "Grades" in Cell A4 to Cell C3.
7. Create the name CREDITS for the range D8 to D13. In Cell D15, enter an =SUM function that totals the range named CREDITS. Copy the formula to Cell E15 so that the SUM function totals Column E.
8. Change the default column width to 8, and the default alignment to right-aligned.
9. Change the column width of Columns A and B to 7.
10. Reset Column B's width to the default setting.
11. Hide Column B, print the spreadsheet, then unhide the column.
12. Type PART OF in Cell G5 and TOTAL in Cell G6. Create a formula in Cell G8 to divide F8 (relative reference) by F15 (absolute reference). Copy this formula into Cells G9 through G13. Format Column G to "percent, 2 decimal (0.00%)."
13. Add border lines where appropriate (in Rows 7 and 14).
14. Place a formula in Cell F4 to calculate the current GPA as (Total Points)/(Total Credits). Format this cell to "2 decimals (0.00)." Place the title "GPA" in Cell E4.
15. Print the spreadsheet and then save it again as GPA2.

APPLICATION 3: CHECKBOOK

Save the workbook as "CHECK2" after each operation is completed so that you can continue this exercise later. (Remember to set the default drive to A before saving the workbook.)

1. Open the CHECK1 workbook (created in the previous chapter).
2. Format the range E8:G12 with the accounting-comma, two-decimal format _(*#,##0.00_).
3. Change the column width of Column C to 20, delete Row 7 and Column D.

4. Add single-lined borders to the right walls of the range A6:D11, and then double-lined borders to the right walls of the range E6:E11.
5. Change the Font and Font size of the text in Cell A4 to Times New Roman 16 points and boldface the text; then center-align it across the range A4:F4.
6. Change the character color to white in the range A6:F6 and then background color of the same range to black.
7. Change the color of the single-lined borders on the right walls of Cells A6:D6 and the double-lined border on the right wall of Cell E6 to white.
8. Place a double-lined outline border around the range A4:F11 and then delete Row 5.
9. Right-align the data in cells A5, B5, D5, E5 and F5.
10. Insert a row between the rows beginning with 12-Jan and 15-Jan. Type 14-Jan in Cell A10, Transfer from savings in Cell C10, and 2000 in Cell E10.
11. Copy the formula in Cell F9 to Cells F10 and F11. (Use the Paste Special command of the Edit menu to paste "only" the formula.)
12. Italicize "Deposit pay check" in Cells C6 and C11.
13. Save the workbook as "CHECK2," print the entire worksheet with the grid option off, and then exit the program.

APPLICATION 4: INVESTMENTS

Save the workbook as "INVEST2" after each operation is completed so that you can continue this exercise later. (Remember to set the default drive to A before saving the workbook.)

1. Open the INVEST1 workbook (created in the previous chapter).
2. Change the font in Cell A4 to Times New Roman, 18 points, boldfaced and then center-align the text in across the range A4:I4.
3. Delete Row 8.
4. Change the default (standard column width) to 12, change the column width of Column A to 20, delete Column B, change the width of Column B and E to nine.
5. Right-align the data in the range C6:H7 and B7:B12.
6. Format the ranges C8:D12, F8:H8, and F14:H14 to accounting-currency, two decimals _($*#,##0.00_).
7. Format the range E8:E12 to accounting-comma, no decimals (*#,##0_) and the range F9:H12 to accounting-comma, two decimals _(*#,##0.00_).
8. Type RETURN ON in Cell I6 and INVEST in Cell I7. Create a formula in Cell I8 to divide H8 (relative reference) by G8 (absolute reference). Copy this formula into Cells I9 through I12.
9. Right-align the range I6 and I7, and then format I8:I12 to percentage, two decimals (0.00%).
10. Place a single-lined border at the bottom of Cells A7 through I7 and A12 through I12 and a double-lined border at the bottom of the Cells F14 through G14.
11. Hide Columns B through E, print the spreadsheet without gridlines and then unhide the columns.
12. Insert a column in D. Type the word DATE in Cells B6 and D6, SOLD in

B7 and PURCH in D7, 7/10/YY in D8, 9/15/YY in D9, 10/25/YY in D10, 12/20/YY in D11, and then 5/3/YY in D12.
13. Right-align the range D8:D12 and then change Column D's width to nine.
14. Save the workbook as "INVEST2." Print the entire worksheet without gridlines, in landscape orientation, scaled to print on one page. Exit the program.

APPLICATION 5: ADDITIONAL INVENTORY

Save the worksheet as "STOCK2" after each operation is completed so that you can continue this exercise later.

1. Open the "STOCK1" workbook (created in the previous chapter).
2. Right-align the data in Cells B6 through D6.
3. Format cells B8 and D8 to "accounting-currency, 2 decimals _($*#,##0.00_)" Format the rest of the cells in Columns B and D to "accounting-comma, 2 decimals _(*#,##0.00_)." Format Cell D14 to "accounting-currency, 2 decimals."
4. Move the word *Inventory* in Cell A4 to Cell C4.
5. Create the name COUNT for the range C8:C12. In Cell C14, enter an =SUM function that totals the range named COUNT.
6. Change the default column width to 12, and the default alignment to right-aligned.
7. Change the column width of Columns A and B to 15.
8. Reset Column B's width to the default setting.
9. Hide Columns B and C, print the spreadsheet, and then unhide the two columns.
10. Type PART OF in Cell E5, and TOTAL in Cell E6. Create a formula in Cell E8 to divide D8 (relative reference) by D14 (absolute reference). Copy this formula into Cells E9 through E12. Format Column E to "percent, 1 decimal."
11. Insert a row below Row 9 (previous chapter skill).
12. Copy cells A9 through E9 into the new Row 10. Type Templates (left-justified) in Cell A10, .7 in Cell B10, and 100 in Cell C10.
13. Add border lines where appropriate.
14. Print the spreadsheet and then save it again as "STOCK2."

APPLICATION 6: ADDITIONAL TICKETS

Save the workbook in this exercise as "TICKET2" after each operation is completed so that you can continue this exercise later.

1. Open the "TICKET1" workbook (created in the previous chapter).
2. Right-align the data in Cells B6 through F6. Insert a row below Row 6.
3. Format Cells B8 and F8 to "accounting-currency, 0 decimals _($*#,##0.00_)." Format the rest of the cells in Columns B and F to "accounting-comma, 0 decimals _(*#,##0.00_)." Format Cell F14 to "accounting-currency, 0 decimals."
4. Insert a row below Row 11 (previous chapter skill).
5. Copy Cells A11 through F11 into the new Row 12. Type Rear Mezz in Cell A12, 20 in Cell B12, 100 in Cell C12, and 0 in Cell D12.
6. Move the word "Tickets" in Cell A4 to Cell C3.

7. Create the name SEATS for the range C8 to C13. In Cell C15, enter a SUM function that totals the range named SEATS. Copy the formula to Cell D15 so that the SUM function totals Column D. Format Columns C, D, and E to "accounting-comma, 0 decimals _(*#,##0_)."
8. Change the default column width to 10, and the default alignment to right-aligned.
9. Change the column width of Columns A and B to 12.
10. Reset Column B's width to the default setting.
11. Hide Columns B and C, print the spreadsheet, and then unhide the two columns.
12. Type PART OF in Cell G5, and TOTAL in Cell G6. Create a formula in Cell G8 to divide F8 (relative reference) by F15 (absolute reference). Copy this formula into Cells G9 through G13. Format Column G to "percent, 2 decimals (0.00%)."
13. Add border lines where appropriate (in Rows 7 and 14).
14. Print the spreadsheet and then save it again as "TICKET2."

MASTERY CASES

The following Mastery Cases allow you to demonstrate how much you have learned about this software. Each case describes a fictitious problem or need that can be solved using the skills you have learned in this chapter. While minimum acceptable outcomes are specified, you are expected and encouraged to design your response (files, data, lists) in ways that display your personal mastery of the software. Feel free to show off your skills. Use "real" data from your own experience in your solution, although you may also fabricate data if needed.

These Mastery Cases allow you to display your ability to:

- Use ranges in commands
- Reset worksheet defaults
- Adjust column width
- Enhance a worksheet with fonts, colors and lines
- Use absolute cell references
- Use Print Options

CASE 1. MODIFYING YOUR EXAM GRADES: Open the exam grades workbook that you created for Mastery Case 1 of Chapter 1. Right-align appropriate titles. Change the font and font size of the title characters. Select an appropriate format for the grades. Adjust column widths to the minimal width necessary for each column. Add border lines to further enhance the spreadsheet. Save and print the worksheet *without* gridlines.

CASE 2. MODIFYING YOUR HOLIDAY SHOPPING BUDGET: Open the holiday-shopping workbook that you created for Mastery Case 2 of Chapter 1. Change the font and font size of the titles. Format the first row of numbers and the totals as accounting-currency, two decimals. Format all other numbers as accounting-comma, two decimals. Add a PERCENT DIFFERENCE column and place formulas to yield

the difference in a percentage for each gift and then format appropriately. Add border lines to further enhance the worksheet. Save and print *without* gridlines.

 CASE 3. MODIFY YOUR SALES REPORT: Open the sales report workbook that you created for Mastery Case 3 of Chapter 1. Add two columns to calculate TAX and ADJUSTED TOTAL. Place your state sales tax rate in a cell above the TAX title; use the actual rate or invent your own. Insert cell formulas in the tax column that will multiply the TOTAL by that tax rate (use an absolute reference). Create appropriate formulas to calculate the ADJUSTED TOTAL to reflect the sales tax. Adjust format, column width, and fonts to best present your data. Save and print your report.

SPREADSHEETS WITH MICROSOFT EXCEL 5.0

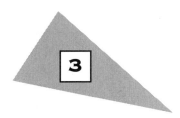

ADVANCED SPREADSHEETS:
CHARTS, DATA MANAGEMENT, MACROS, MULTIPLE WORKBOOKS, MULTIPLE SHEETS, AND SHARING DATA

OUTLINE

OVERVIEW

PREPARING FOR THIS CHAPTER

MODULE 1: CHARTS
Creating a Chart
Manipulating a Chart
Editing Chart Parts
Chart Types
"Exploding" Data
Printing a Chart

MODULE 2: CONDITIONAL FUNCTIONS
The IF Function
Table Lookups—
VLOOKUP and HLOOKUP

MODULE 3: DATA MANAGEMENT
Module 3a: Generating a Sequence of Numbers

Module 3b: Sorting Data
Module 3c: Creating a Data Distribution
Module 3d: Information Retrieval—Data Queries
Module 3e: Using Data Functions

MODULE 4: MACROS
Creating a Macro
Running a Macro
Assigning a Macro
Adding Another Macro
Editing a Macro

MODULE 5: USING MULTIPLE WORKBOOKS
Switching between Windows
Arranging Windows
Resizing Windows

Manipulating Data between Workbooks

MODULE 6: USING MULTIPLE SHEETS
Using Sheet Tabs
Manipulating Data between Sheets

MODULE 7: PROTECTING THE SPREADSHEET
Setting the Unprotected Range
Activating the Protection Feature

MODULE 8: SHARING DATA AMONG APPLICATIONS
Exporting and Importing
Exporting Data from Excel
Importing Data into Excel
Linking Data from Other Office Applications

OBJECTIVES

After completing this chapter you will be able to do any of the following (based on your selection of modules)

1. Create column (bar) charts, line charts, and pie charts from columnar data.

2. Distinguish among the purposes and procedures for using conditional functions such as IF, VLOOKUP, and HLOOKUP.

3. Use database techniques to create number sequences and data distributions, as well as to sort, query, and copy data within the spreadsheet to a query table.

4. Understand, create, and invoke macros.

5. Use data from other spreadsheets by linking, copying, and combining cells from other spreadsheet files or sheets.

6. Explain and demonstrate data-protection techniques.

7. Explain and demonstrate import and export techniques in Excel.

SS145

OVERVIEW

Chapter 3 presents an advanced set of spreadsheet techniques, including charts, conditional functions, databases, spreadsheet links, macros, and spreadsheet security. Each procedure is presented as a separate module that can be studied independently of the others. Study the modules that are most useful to you.

Using files available on disk and others created by the reader, the chapter presents a series of eight learning modules. Module 1 examines creating charts from spreadsheet data. Conditional functions are presented next in Module 2—including an IF function and table lookup functions. Module 3 introduces the reader to database techniques—including fill sequences, sorts, data distributions, queries, and query tables. Each submodule of this section can be studied separately as desired. This is followed by Module 4, which presents methods for automating procedures with macros. Modules 5 and 6 examine techniques for linking workbooks and sheets. Module 7 looks at protection techniques for improving data security. The chapter concludes with sharing data among programs (Module 8).

PREPARING FOR THIS CHAPTER

This text comes with a data diskette that contains files for use with this chapter. These files reduce the amount of initial data entry you must do in each module. If you do not have this disk (or you want to practice entering data), you can create the files as you need them.

The files from the Dryden data diskette must first be copied onto your data disk so they will be available for use. Check with your instructor or lab technician to see if the files are available, or do the following steps to use Windows *File Manager* application. (It is assumed that you are already in Windows.)

1. **Place the Dryden data diskette in drive A**
2. **Locate the Main program group in Program Manager's workspace**

If Main is already a window, go to Step 4. Otherwise do Step 3 to enlarge it to a window:

MOUSE APPROACH

3. **Double-click the *Main* group icon to resize it to a window**
4. **Double-click the *File Manager* icon**
5. **Click *File*, *Copy* for its dialog box**

KEYBOARD APPROACH

3. **Press** `Ctrl` + `F6` **to move the highlight to the *Main* group icon and then press** `↵` **to resize it to a window**
4. **Press the arrow key (or keys) to move the highlight to File Manager and then press** `↵` **to start it**
5. **Press** `F8` **for the *Copy* dialog box**

6. **Press** `Alt` + `F` **to highlight the contents of the From text box**
7. **Type** `A:\EXCEL\*.*` **into the From text box**
8. **Press** `Tab` **to move the insertion point to the To text box**
9. **Type** `C:\FILES\` **into the To text box**

CHAPTER 3 ADVANCED SPREADSHEETS **SS147**

FIGURE SS3-1 ■ COPYING FILES WITH *FILE MANAGER'S COPY* DIALOG BOX

(a) Files from the Excel Directory of the Dryden data diskette in drive A are copied to the FILES directory on the hard disk in drive C using the Copy dialog box. (b) A file from the WORD directory (Dryden Data disk) is copied to the FILES directory. (c) Files from the FILES directory are copied to your data diskette using the Copy dialog box.

Copy

Current Directory: C:\
From: A:\EXCEL*.*
To: ● C:\FILES\
○ Copy to Clipboard

OK
Cancel
Help

(a)

Copy

Current Directory: C:\
From: A:\WORD\EXWP3-6.DOC
To: ● C:\FILES\
○ Copy to Clipboard

OK
Cancel
Help

(b)

Copy

Current Directory: C:\
From: C:\FILES*.*
To: ● A:
○ Copy to Clipboard

OK
Cancel
Help

(c)

Your From and To text boxes should appear as shown in Figure SS3-1a. If they do not, press `Esc` and repeat Steps 5 through 9.

MOUSE APPROACH	KEYBOARD APPROACH
10. Click the *OK* button	10. Press `↵`
11. Click the *Yes* button to create the FILES directory and then copy the files	11. Press `↵` again to create the FILES directory and then copy the files
12. Click *File, Copy*	12. Press `F6` for the Copy dialog box
13. Press `Alt` + `F` to highlight the contents of the *From* text box	
14. Type `A:\WORD\EXWP3-6.DOC` into the *From* text box	
15. Press `Tab` to move the insertion point to the *To* text ox	
16. Type `C:\FILES\` into the To text box	

The From and To text boxes should appear as shown in Figure SS3-1b. If they do not, press `Esc` and repeat Steps 13 through 16.

SS148 | **SPREADSHEETS WITH MICROSOFT EXCEL 5.0**

MOUSE APPROACH	KEYBOARD APPROACH
17. Click *OK*	17. Press ↵
18. Click *File, Copy*	18. Press F8 for the Copy dialog box
19. Place your data diskette into drive A	
20. Press Alt + F to highlight the contents of the *From* text box	
21. Type C:\FILES*.* into the *From* text box	
22. Press Tab to move the insertion point to the *To* text box	
23. Type A:	

The From and To text boxes should appear as shown in Figure SS3-1c. If they do not, press Esc and repeat Steps 17 through 22.

MOUSE APPROACH	KEYBOARD APPROACH
24. Click the *OK* button to copy	24. Press ↵ to copy
25. Click *File, Delete* for its dialog box	25. Press Delete for the Delete dialog box
26. Type C:\FILES and then click the *OK* button	26. Type C:\FILES and then press ↵
27. Click the *Yes to All* button (as many times as necessary) to delete the FILES directory	27. Press A for *Yes to All* (as many times as necessary) to delete the FILES directory
28. Double-click the File Manager's *control-menu* box to exit and return to Program Manager	28. Press Alt + F4 to exit File Manager and return to Program Manager

---

MODULE 1: CHARTS

Most people understand information faster when it is presented as a **chart**—a pictorial representation of data. The chart features in Excel allow you to quickly develop charts from worksheet data, such as the one shown in Figure SS3-2b. The following exercises demonstrate how to construct, save, and print charts. To prepare for these exercises, open or create the spreadsheet shown in Figure SS3-2a as follows:

1.   **Start Excel, switch to Drive A, and then open the *GADGETS* workbook from your data disk**

2.   **If you do not have this workbook (or if you prefer to create one yourself), type it now, matching the data shown in Figure SS3-2a, and save it as *GADGETS***

The following exercise creates column (bar) chart shown in Figure SS3-2b. A **column (bar) chart** displays numeric data as a set of evenly spaced bars whose relative heights indicate values in the range being charted.

To create a simple column chart, follow five basic steps: (1) select the range of data to be charted, (2) invoke the *Chart* command (*Insert* menu), (3) point to the first cell in the left corner of the chart's desired location (destination), (4) click, and (5) follow Excel's ChartWizard's five steps.

CHAPTER 3 ADVANCED SPREADSHEETS SS149

FIGURE SS3-2 ■ TRANSFORMING WORKSHEET DATA INTO A CHART DISPLAY

(a) GADGETS worksheet.
(b) Completed column (bar) chart of GADGETS data.

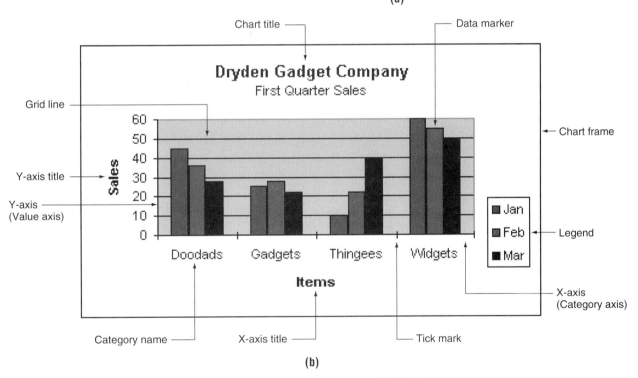

CREATING A CHART

The following chart-creating technique uses Excel's ChartWizard. This feature uses five ChartWizard dialog boxes to walk you through the chart-creating process. This technique requires a mouse, although some keyboard commands have been supplied.

To create a column chart (Excel's default chart),

1. **Move to Cell A3**

SS150 SPREADSHEETS WITH MICROSOFT EXCEL 5.0

FIGURE SS3-3 ■ **PREPARING TO CREATE A CHART**

(a) Selecting chart data.
(b) The chart submenu.

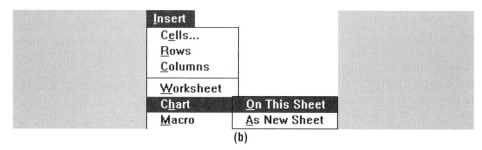

(a)

(b)

---

2. Select the range A3:D7 as in Figure SS3-3a

Be sure not to include the total Column E in the data range.

MOUSE APPROACH	KEYBOARD APPROACH
3. Click *Insert, Chart* for the Chart submenu	3. Press Alt + I , H for the Chart submenu

A Chart submenu should appear as in Figure SS3-3b. At this point, you can either insert the chart on the current sheet or on a new sheet. Placing a chart on a new sheet inserts it on a sheet separate from the current worksheet. See the appendix for this operation. For now, to insert a chart within the current sheet,

MOUSE APPROACH	KEYBOARD APPROACH
4. Click *On This Sheet*	4. Press O to select *On This Sheet*

Your mouse pointer will now change to a charting pointer (see left margin). The next step is done exclusively by mouse.

5. Point to the upper-left corner of *Cell A9* and click

The ChartWizard-Step 1 of 5 dialog box should appear as in Figure SS3-4a. At this point, compare your selected range of data to be charted to the Range text box. It should read "=$A$3:$D$7." If not, click cancel and repeat Steps 1 through 5.

MOUSE APPROACH	KEYBOARD APPROACH
6. Click the *Next >* button for the Step 2 of 5 dialog box	6. Press ↵ for the Step 2 of 5 dialog box

CHAPTER 3   ADVANCED SPREADSHEETS   SS151

The ChartWizard-Step 2 of 5 dialog box will now appear as in Figure SS3-4b. You can now select a chart type by clicking its button (or by pressing the Alt and underlined letter of the chart type). To accept the default (Column chart),

MOUSE APPROACH	KEYBOARD APPROACH
7. Click the *Next >* button for the Step 3 of 5 dialog box	7. Press ↵ for the Step 3 of 5 dialog box

This dialog box, as in Figure SS3-4c, allows you to select a format (for the chart type previously selected) by clicking the desired format button (or by pressing the desired format number). Again, to accept the default setting,

MOUSE APPROACH	KEYBOARD APPROACH
8. Click the *Next >* button for the Step 4 of 5 dialog box	8. Press ↵ for the Step 4 of 5 dialog box

Note the Sample Chart display in this dialog box as in Figure SS3-4d. This is a picture of how the chart will look in the worksheet. This dialog box can also be used to

FIGURE SS3-4 ■ CREATING A CHART USING THE CHARTWIZARD

(a) The ChartWizard chart-data range dialog box.
(b) The ChartWizard chart-type dialog box.

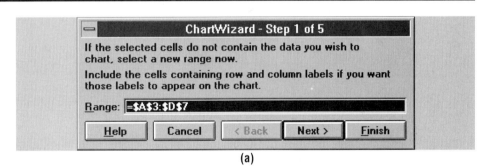

(a)

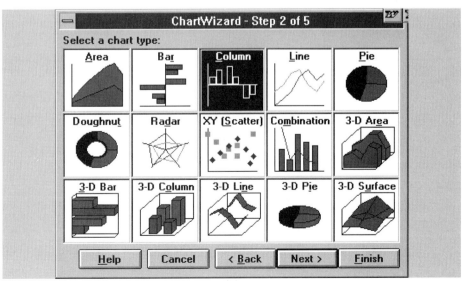

(b)

(continued)

FIGURE SS3-4 ■ *(continued)*

(c) The ChartWizard chart-format dialog box. (d) The ChartWizard Data series dialog box.

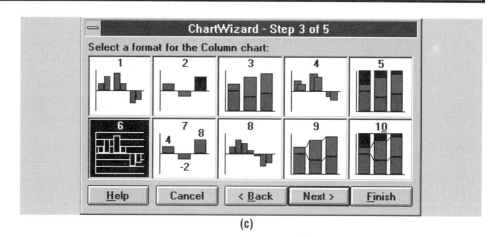

(c)

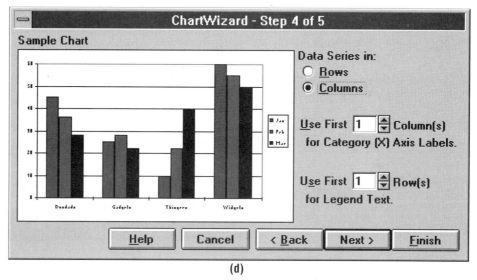

(d)

switch the orientation of the data series between rows and columns. The Columns option button should be selected as in the figure. If not, do Step 9, otherwise go to Step 10.

MOUSE APPROACH	KEYBOARD APPROACH
9. If needed, click the *Columns* option button	9. If needed, press Alt + C to select the Columns option button
10. Click the *Next >* button for the Step 5 of 5 dialog box	10. Press ↵ for the Step 5 of 5 dialog box

This dialog box is used to add a legend and titles. The legend is automatically created, as in this case, when the data is included in the data range in Step 2 above. To add chart and axis titles,

FIGURE SS3-4 ■ *(continued)*

(e) The ChartWizard's titles dialog box.

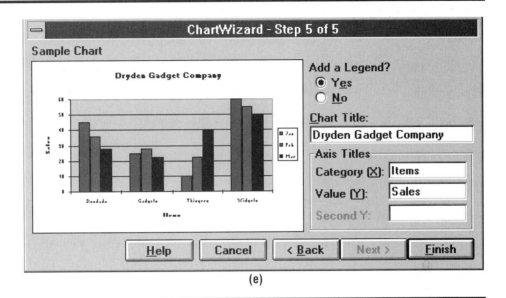

(e)

MOUSE APPROACH

11. Click the *Chart Title* text box

KEYBOARD APPROACH

11. Press `Alt` + `C` for the Chart Title text box

12. Type *Dryden Gadget Company* in the Chart Title text box

13. Press `Tab` to move to the Category (X) text box

14. Type *Items* in the Category (X) text box and press `Tab`

15. Type *Sales* in the Category (Y) text box

Your ChartWizard-Step 5 of 5 dialog box should appear as in Figure SS3-4e. If not, repeat Steps 11 through 15. Now, to complete the chart,

MOUSE APPROACH

16. Click the *Finish* button

KEYBOARD APPROACH

16. Press `↵`

Your worksheet should resemble Figure SS3-5a. Note that the column titles are currently not readable. This will be adjusted soon when the chart is resized.

The small square boxes on the frame of the Chart are called **selection handles,** and they indicate that its outer frame is selected. Later, these handles will be used to resize the chart by mouse. A Chart toolbar also appears on your screen and can also be used to edit the chart.

17. Move to Cell A1 by clicking it (this will also remove the handles from the chart)

18. Save this workbook as *GADGET1*

FIGURE SS3-5 ■ RESIZING A CHART

(a) Clicking the chart selects it and turns on the Chart toolbar. (b) Clicking the vertical scroll bar will position the viewing area of the worksheet.

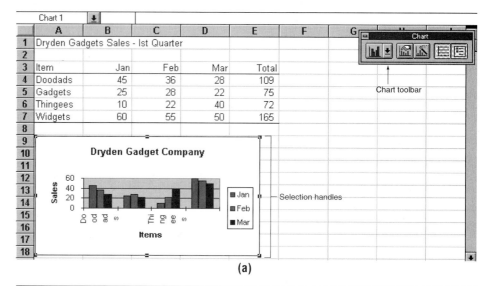

(a)

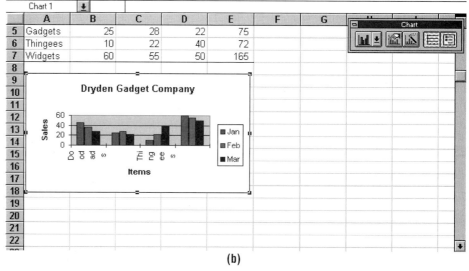

(b)

MANIPULATING A CHART

A chart is considered an object (picture) in the Windows environment. As such, it can be resized, moved and copied. Resizing a chart involves enlarging or reducing its size. Moving a chart relocates it from its current position *(source)* to a new location *(destination)*. Copying involves duplicating the chart in a new location.

Before a chart can be resized, moved or copied, its frame must be selected. To select the chart's frame, click anywhere on the chart. At this point, a chart can be resized by dragging one of its selection handles. Move by dragging the entire chart to a new location, or copy, by holding the Ctrl key while dragging to a new location.

CHAPTER 3   ADVANCED SPREADSHEETS   SS155

> Tip: The cut or copy and Paste or Paste Special commands can also be used to move or copy a selected chart.

RESIZING THE CHART FRAME.   To resize a chart,

1. Open the *GADGET1* workbook, if needed

2. Click anywhere on the chart to select it (selection handles and the Chart toolbar should appear as in Figure SS3-5a)

3. Click the ↓ button of the vertical scroll bar four times to position the viewing area of the worksheet as in Figure SS3-5b

4. Slowly point to the bottom-right selection handle of the chart until the pointer changes to a double arrow (see left margin)

5. Drag the selection handle (and the outline of the chart border) to the bottom-right corner of Cell F21

6. Release the mouse

Your chart should now resemble Figure SS3-5c. Note that the column titles are now readable.

7. Resave the workbook as *GADGET1*

MOVING A CHART.   To move a chart,

1. If needed, click the chart to place selection handles on the frame

2. Point anywhere within the chart

FIGURE SS3-5 ■ *(continued)*

(c) Dragging a selection handle will resize the chart.

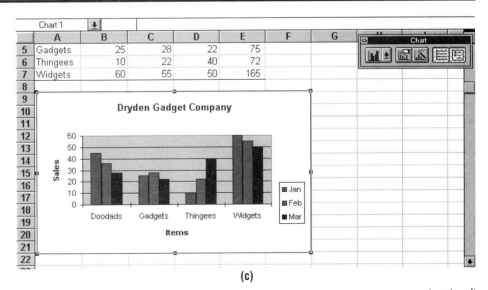

(c)

(continued)

FIGURE SS3-5 ■ *(continued)*

(d) Dragging the chart frame will move the chart.

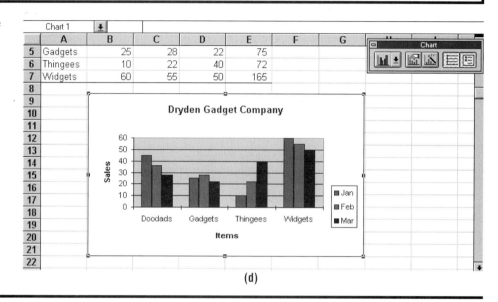

(d)

3. Drag the chart to move it one column to the right as in Figure SS3-5d
4. Resave the workbook as *GADGET1*

Tip: You can also use the Cut and Paste commands (Edit menu) to move a chart after its frame is selected.

COPYING A CHART. To copy a chart,

1. If needed, click the chart to select its frame
2. Point anywhere within the chart
3. Press and hold **Ctrl** while dragging to the right of the current chart (or any desired empty area in the worksheet)

Note: A plus (+) sign appears to the right of the mouse pointer when you are dragging. This indicates that you are copying.

4. Release your mouse

You should now have two of the same charts next to each other.

5. Close the workbook without saving

Tip: You can also use the Copy and Paste commands (Edit menu) to copy a chart after its frame is selected.

EDITING CHART PARTS

Clicking a chart once, as seen earlier, selects its frame. This allows you to resize, move or copy it by mouse. Once a chart's frame is selected, double-clicking a chart will turn on the chart edit mode, which allows you to edit its contents.

ADDING A SUBTITLE. Try this to add a subtitle to the chart:

1. **Open the GADGET1 workbook and then click the chart once**

Your Status bar should display the message "Double-click chart to edit."

2. **Double-click the chart**

The frame of the chart should appear as in Figure SS3-6a. At this point, you can edit any part of the chart by first clicking it. The Insert and Format menus also change to reflect Chart editing commands.

3. **Click the title "Dryden Gadget Company"**

4. **Point to the end of the title after "y" and click to place the insertion point there**

FIGURE SS3-6 ■ **EDITING A CHART**

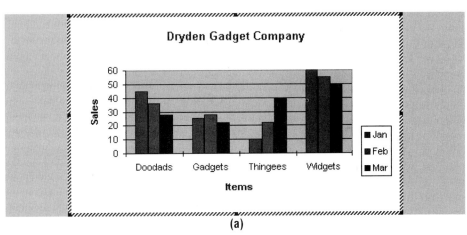

(a) Double-clicking a selected chart puts it in edit mode. Note the frame of the chart. (b) Clicking on the title places an insertion point there for editing text.

(a)

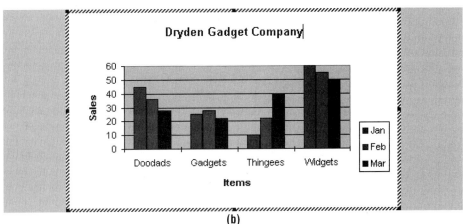

(b)

An insertion point should appear at the end of the title as in Figure SS3-6b. The message "Title" also appears in the Name box of the Formula bar.

5. Press ↵ to move the insertion point to the next line

6. Click the ▼ button of the *font size* drop-down box (Formatting toolbar) and then click 8

7. Click the *Bold* (B) toolbar button (to turn it off)

8. Type First Quarter Sales

You can edit other parts of the chart or turn off the edit mode. To turn off the chart edit mode,

9. Double-click Cell F7 (or any cell outside the chart)

Your chart should resemble Figure SS3-2b. Examine your screen and the figure to learn each part's name.

10. Resave the workbook as *GADGET1*

> Tip: Double-clicking some chart parts when in the chart edit mode will open a dialog box. These boxes can be used to edit the chart part's attributes.

GRIDLINES. Gridlines can improve the readability of charts. Excel automatically places horizontal (Y-axis) gridlines in major intervals on a column chart, as in Figure SS3-2b. You can modify the chart to have the gridlines appear at minor intervals to provide greater reference readability or you can remove the gridlines. You can also add vertical (X-axis) gridlines with major or minor intervals. These changes can be made through the Gridlines dialog box, which is accessed through the Insert menu. Try this to remove the gridlines,

1. Click the Chart to select it

2. Double-click the Chart for the Chart edit mode

3. Click *Insert, Gridlines, Major Gridlines, OK*

The gridlines should now disappear from your chart. Now, use the Gridlines dialog box to reinsert the gridlines.

4. Click *Insert, Gridlines, Major Gridlines, OK*

5. Double-click the outside of the chart to deselect it

6. Close the workbook without saving

CHART TYPES

Excel offers 15 types of charts that may be selected as you create a chart (see the Creating a Chart section) or after you're done. Each chart type also has many variations, called *subtypes,* that can also be used. Do the following to prepare for the exercises in this section.

1. Open the *GADGET1* workbook

2. Click the ↓ button of the vertical scroll bar to reposition the viewing area of the chart and workbook as in Figure SS3-7a

CHAPTER 3   ADVANCED SPREADSHEETS   SS159

FIGURE SS3-7 ■ PREPARING TO CHANGE CHART TYPES

(a) Repositioning the viewing area at the workbook. (b) Selecting and resizing the chart.

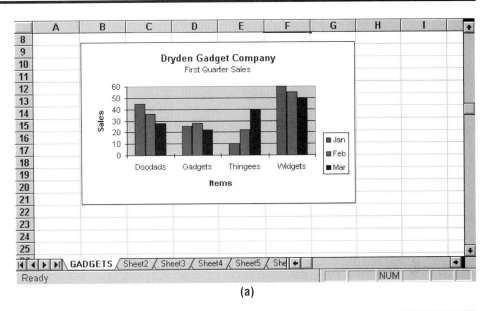

(a)

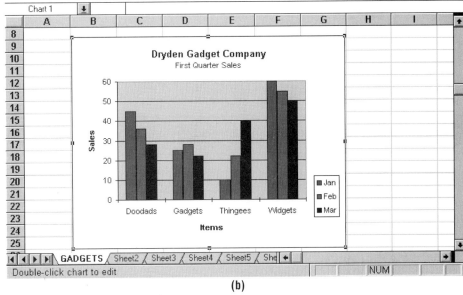

(b)

---

3. **Click the chart**

4. **Slowly point to the bottom-center selection handle of the chart until the pointer changes to a double arrow (see left margin)**

5. **Drag the selection handle (and the outline of the chart border) four cells down and then release**

Your chart should fill the workbook as in Figure SS3-7b.

CHANGING THE CHART TYPE. To change the chart type of an existing chart you must first select a chart, turn on the edit mode, and then select *Format, Chart Type* for its dialog box.

To change to a Line chart,

1. **Double-click it to select it and turn on the chart edit mode**

MOUSE APPROACH	**KEYBOARD APPROACH**
2. Click *Format, Chart Type* for its dialog box	2. Press Alt + O , T for the Chart Type dialog box
3. Click the *Line Chart* button	3. Press Tab three times and then → once to select the Line Chart
4. Click *OK*	4. Press ↵

Your line chart should appear as Figure SS3-8a. A **Line Chart** displays numeric data as a set of points along a line. It is useful for showing trends over time. Now, using the same technique as above, change the chart to a pie chart. At this point, you can also double-click any cell outside the chart to unselect it. For now, keep the chart in edit mode and try the following other chart type changes.

5. **Use the Chart Type dialog box to select a pie chart** (*Format, Chart Type*)

A pie chart similar to Figure SS3-8b should now appear. A **Pie Chart** displays data as parts of a whole circle, where each data "slice" corresponds to a percentage of the total.

Excel also offers 3-D charts. These charts are also accessible through the Chart Type dialog box. Try this,

6. **If needed, select the chart and invoke the chart edit mode**

FIGURE SS3-8 ■ **CHANGING CHART TYPE**

(a) Line chart.

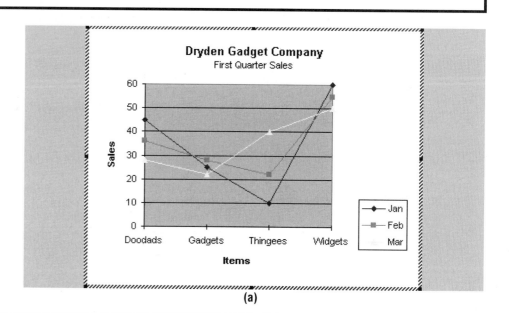

(a)

CHAPTER 3   ADVANCED SPREADSHEETS   SS161

MOUSE APPROACH	KEYBOARD APPROACH
7. Click *Format*, Chart *T*ype for its dialog box	7. Press Alt + O , T for the Chart Type dialog box
8. Click the *3*-D option button	8. Press Alt + 3 for the 3-D option button
9. Click the *3-D Bar* chart button	9. Press Tab and then use the arrow keys to select the 3-D Bar chart button
10. Click *OK*	10. Press ↵

Now, re-align the X-axis title—Sales—to horizontal.

11. Click the X-axis title—Sales—to select it

MOUSE APPROACH	KEYBOARD APPROACH
12. Click *F*ormat, S*e*lected Axis Title for its dialog box	12. Press Ctrl + 1 for the Format Axis Title dialog box
13. If needed, click the *Alignment* tab	13. If needed, press A for the Alignment tab
14. Click the horizontal "Text" orientation button	14. Press Alt + O for the orientation group and then use the arrow keys to select the horizontal "Text" orientation button
15. Click *OK*	15. Press ↵

16. Click the *Legend* to select it (Mar, Feb, Jan)

FIGURE SS3-8 ■ *(continued)*

(b) Pie chart.

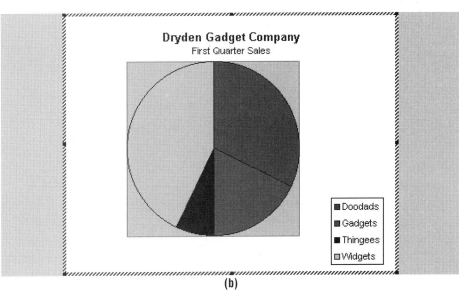

(b)

(continued)

(c) 3D-bar chart.

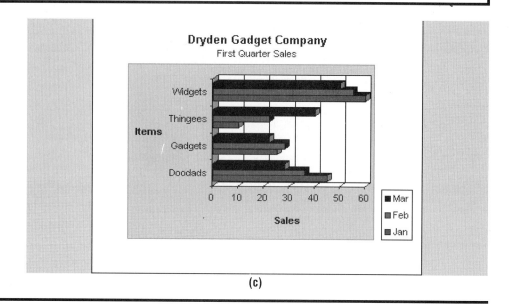

(c)

17. Drag the Legend up to align with the bottom of the chart's plot area, as in Figure SS3-8c

18. Double-click Cell A9 or any cell outside the chart to deselect it and turn off the chart edit mode

Your chart should resemble Figure SS3-8c. A *3-D Bar Chart* is a bar chart with horizontal orientation.

19. Save this workbook as *GADGET2* and close it

CHANGING THE CHART SUBTYPE. Each Chart type has a variety of subtype displays. Subtype displays are selected through the *Option* feature of the Chart Type dialog box. Try this,

1. Close any open workbook
2. Open the *GADGET1* workbook
3. Click and then double-click the Chart to switch to Chart edit mode

MOUSE APPROACH	KEYBOARD APPROACH
4. Click *Format, Chart Type* for its dialog box	4. Press Alt + O , T for the Chart Type dialog box
5. Click the *Options* button for the Format Column Group dialog box	5. Press Alt + O for the Format Column Group dialog box
6. If needed, click the *Subtype* tab	6. Press A for the Subtype

CHAPTER 3 ADVANCED SPREADSHEETS SS163

> **FIGURE SS3-8** ■ *(continued)*

(d) Stacked column (subtype) chart.

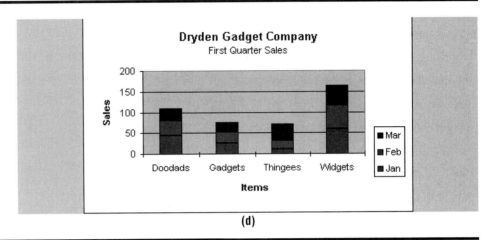

(d)

7. Click the *Stacked Column* chart button (center button)

8. Click *OK*

7. Press Alt + S for Subtype and then → to select the *Stacked Column* chart button (center button)

8. Press ↵

9. Double-click any cell outside the chart to turn off the chart edit mode.

Your chart should resemble Figure SS3-8d. A *Stacked Column* chart places each set of data in bars on top of the previous set in one column to display the total.

10. Close the workbook without saving

"EXPLODING" DATA

As shown in Figure SS3-8a, a pie chart displays data as parts of a circle. In an *exploded* pie chart, one or more data slices are separated from the whole for emphasis (shown in Figure SS3-9b). You will now learn how to "explode" a pie chart and then resize it for better viewing.

EXPLODING A PIE CHART. The quickest way to create an exploded pie chart is to drag the desired slices away from the pie. Try this:

1. Open the *GADGET1* workbook

2. Select the chart frame and then activate the chart edit mode

3. Use the Chart Type dialog box to select a pie chart *(Format, Chart Type, Pie, OK)*

Your pie chart should again resemble Figure SS3-8b. Now, add titles and percentage labels for each of the pie's slices using the Autoformat dialog box.

MOUSE APPROACH

4. Click *Format, Autoformat* for its dialog box

KEYBOARD APPROACH

4. Press Alt + O , A for the Autoformat dialog box

5. Click number 7 format button (see left margin)
6. Click *OK*

5. Press Alt + F for the Format group and then use the arrow keys to select the number 7 pie format
6. Press ↵

Your chart should now display percentage and label information as in Figure SS3-9a. Now to explode its slices,

7. Point to the *Widgets* slice (light gray) of the pie chart
8. Drag it away from the pie chart until it resembles Figure SS3-9b
9. Double-click any cell outside the chart to deselect and turn off the chart edit mode

Your pie chart should now resemble Figure SS3-9b. Note that the slices are reduced in size. This will be adjusted next.

FIGURE SS3-9 ■ EXPLODING A PIE CHART

(a) We will add format information to a chart.
(b) Dragging a pie's slice explodes the pie chart.

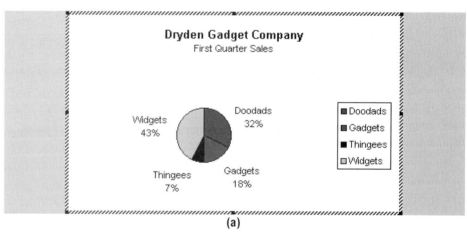

(a)

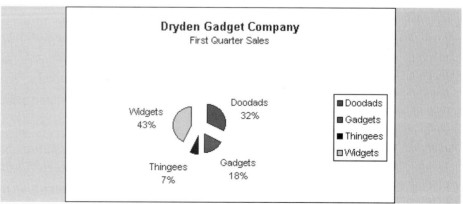

(b)

RESIZING CHART COMPONENTS. Like resizing a chart's frame, resizing its components involves first selecting the item and then dragging one of the selection handles. The next exercise enlarges the *plot area* (the area containing the graph) for better viewing, as in Figure SS3-9d.

1. **Click and then double-click the chart to turn on the chart edit mode**
2. **Point to the center of the plot area and click to select it**

A square selection box with selection handles at each corner should appear as in Figure SS3-9c.

3. **Slowly point to the top-left selection handle until the pointer turns into a double arrow**
4. **Drag the *selection handle* away from the center to enlarge the plot area as in Figure SS3-9d**
5. **Double-click any cell outside the chart to turn off the chart edit mode**

FIGURE SS3-9 ■ *(continued)*

(c) The plot frame of a chart is selected. (d) Dragging a plot-frame selection handle resizes the chart.

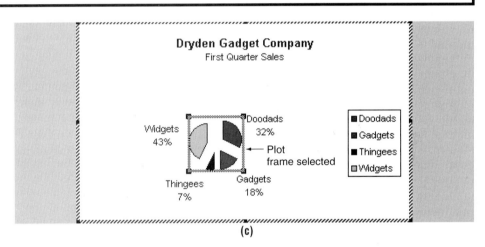

(c)

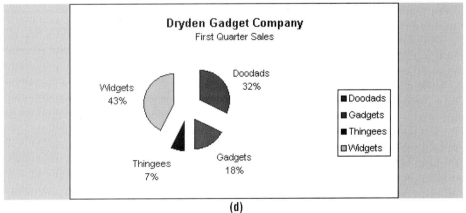

(d)

Your Chart should resemble Figure SS3-9d.

6. Save the workbook as *GADGET3*

PRINTING A CHART

A chart may be printed with its related worksheet data or alone.

PRINTING A WORKSHEET WITH A CHART. To print a chart in its related worksheet,

1. Open the *GADGET1* workbook and turn on your printer

MOUSE APPROACH	KEYBOARD APPROACH
2. Click *File*, *Print*, OK	2. Press Ctrl + P , ↵

PRINTING A SPECIFIC CHART. To print a specific chart in a worksheet,

1. Click and then double-click the chart to select it and turn on the edit mode

MOUSE APPROACH	KEYBOARD APPROACH
2. Click *File*, *Print*, OK	2. Press Ctrl + P , ↵

3. Close the workbook without saving and exit Excel

CHECKPOINT

✓ On a new workbook, list five names in Column A and five math test scores in Column B. Create a column chart displaying these data.
✓ On the worksheet, add reading scores in Column C. Add these new data to the chart and show the data in line-chart form. Adjust or add titles accordingly.
✓ Adjust the data to display only the reading scores in a pie chart with the first score exploded.
✓ Change the format of the exploded pie chart to include percentages and other label information.
✓ Resize the exploded pie chart and print it.

MODULE 2: CONDITIONAL FUNCTIONS

Conditional functions include logical and other special functions—such as IF and lookup tables. These functions add limited decision-making capabilities to your worksheet by automatically selecting alternate results based on a condition that you have specified.

THE IF FUNCTION

The **IF function** is a logical spreadsheet function of the form IF(test,t,f). It takes one of two actions (*t* or *f*) depending on the truth of the stated condition (test). If *test* is *true*, IF performs action *t;* if the *test* is false, it performs *f.* For example, the function

IF(A1 = A2,1,0) placed in Cell A3 will return a 1 in A3 if A1 equals A2, or a 0 if it does not.

A condition is typically expressed as a *logical formula* (a formula that uses one of the logical operators shown in Figure SS3-10a) or a range that contains a logical formula. However, the condition can be *any* formula, cell reference, string, or number. Any condition that equals zero is considered to be *false*. (Blank cells and labels are automatically false.) Anything else is true. The actions to be taken (*t* or *f*) can be constant values or formulas.

Examine the IF examples in Figure SS3-10b. See if you can determine why each IF statement acted the way it did. Note that IF functions can also be nested one inside the other to create tests for multiple conditions (see Examples 9 and 10 in Figure SS3-10b). You may want to type each condition in a cell in Column C and compare your results with those in the figure.

USING IF FUNCTIONS. An IF function is useful when there are two possible courses of action. Figure SS3-11 displays a few practical applications of this concept.

1. **Close any open workbook**

2. **Open the *PAYROLL* workbook from your data disk**

3. **Examine each formula as it is discussed in the text**

(If you do not have this workbook, examine the functions shown at the bottom of Figure SS3-11.)

Column B uses an IF function to mark employees whose sales do not exceed quota. For example, Cell B5 remains blank because *sales* (C5) exceeds *quota* (D5). However, Cell B6 shows a minus sign because C6 does not exceed D6.

Gross pay is divided into two columns: Column G shows the *regular* portion of gross up to the first 40 hours; Column H shows the additional *overtime* pay (or 0 if hours do not exceed 40).

USING CONDITIONS WITHOUT IFS. Note that Column I provides alternatives without actually using an IF function. It calculates commission as five percent of sales and then automatically adds a five percent bonus for those sales that exceed the quota. The *C5>D5* in Cell I5's formula does the trick. It is a *condition*. Like IF, it evaluates to 1 *if* the condition is true (sales exceed quota), or to 0 if it is false. Since the bonus is multiplied by this value, the bonus automatically is 0 if C5 does not exceed D5.

Using a condition alone is a shortcut to the IF function. It takes a lot more thought, but can save space in the worksheet file.

> Tip: If you need more than two alternatives, explore the use of Excel's CHOOSE function as listed in the appendix.

TABLE LOOKUPS—VLOOKUP AND HLOOKUP

Lookup tables are logical spreadsheet functions of the form VLOOKUP (lookup_value, table_array, col_index_num, . . .) or HLOOKUP (lookup_value, table_array, row_index_num . . .) both use a two-dimensional table to return values that fall within set intervals; VLOOKUP uses a vertical table, whereas HLOOKUP

SS168 SPREADSHEETS WITH MICROSOFT EXCEL 5.0

FIGURE SS3-10 ■ **THE IF FUNCTION**

(a) Logical operators. (b) IF examples

Symbol	Explanation	Example
<	Less than	A1<A2
>	Greater than	A1>A2
=	Equal to	A1=A2
>=	Greater than or equal to	A1>=A2
<=	Less than or equal to	A1<=A2
<>	Not equal to	A1<>A2
NOT	Logical NOT test	NOT(A1,A2)
AND	Logical AND test	AND(A1>A2,A2>A3)
OR	Logical OR text	OR(A1>A2,A2<A3)

(a)

Using the following spreadsheet, the IF function shown at the left will return the result displayed on the right:

	A	B	C
1	7	5	
2	5	Hello	
3			

IF Statement	Result
1. =IF(A1>A2,1,0)	1
2. =IF(A1=A2, "yes", "no")	no
3. =IF(A1<>B2,A1*5,A2*3)	35
4. =IF(B1, "Text OK", A2)	Test OK
5. =IF(AND(A1=7,B1>10), "OK", "—")	—
6. =IF(OR(A1=7,B1>B10), "OK", "A3")	OK
7. =IF(B2="Hello",A1,A2)	7
8. =IF(A1−5,SUM(A1:A2),0)	12
9. =IF(A3>A1, "YES",IF(B2="Hello",1,2))	1
10. =IF(A1>A2,IF(B1>A1, "YES", "NO"),0)	NO

(b)

Note: Examples 9 and 10 are nested IF statements.

CHAPTER 3 ADVANCED SPREADSHEETS **SS169**

FIGURE SS3-11 ■ AN IF APPLICATION TO PAYROLL

	A	B	C	D	E	F	G	H	I	J	K
1	Dryden Weekly Payroll and Commission Report									11-01-XX	
2											
3							SALARY			Adj.	
4	Employee	Q?	Sales	Quota	Hrs	Pay	Gross	OT	Comm	Gross	
5	Burstein		$ 1,100	$ 900	43	$5.65	$ 226.00	$ 25.43	$ 65.00	$ 316.43	
6	Laudon	-	1,000	1,200	35	4.00	140.00	-	50.00	190.00	
7	Martin	-	850	900	45	5.75	230.00	43.13	42.50	315.63	
8	Parker		1,275	1,000	25	6.75	168.75	-	77.50	246.25	
9	Williams		1,450	1,300	51	3.50	140.00	57.75	80.00	277.75	
10	Totals		$ 5,675	$5,300			$ 904.75	$126.30	$ 315.00	$ 1,346.05	
11											
12	Notes:		Cell	Formula or Function							
13			B5	=IF(C5>D5," ","-")							
14			G5	=IF(E5>40,F5*40,F5*E5)							
15			H5	=IF(E5>40,(E5-40)*F5*1.5,0)							
16			I5	=C5*0.05+(C5>D5)*(C5-D5)*0.05							
17											

---

uses a horizontal one. This exercise examines a VLOOKUP table that returns the amount of tax for a given income and category.

1.   **Close any open workbook**

2.   **Open the *TAX* workbook from your data disk**

3.   **If you do not have the *TAX* workbook (or if you want the practice), type it now, matching the data shown in Figure SS3-12a, and save it as *TAX***

To create a lookup, you should first name the lookup table range. Although you could type cell addresses, a range name makes the function more understandable.

4.   **Select the range A9:E12**

MOUSE APPROACH

5.   **Click *Insert, Name, Define* for its dialog box**

6.   **Type** `Tax` **and click *OK***

KEYBOARD APPROACH

5.   **Press** Alt + I , N , D **for the Define Name dialog box**

6.   **Type** `Tax` **and press** ↵

The entries in the first column of the table will be used for comparison; the remaining columns contain the values that will be returned.

7.   **In Cell C5, type** `=VLOOKUP(C3,TAX,C4+1)`

The "+1" in the VLOOKUP function, instructs Excel to look one cell to the right of the indicated column number. For instance, typing the number 2 in Cell C4 instructs Excel to look in Column C of the range.

SS170 SPREADSHEETS WITH MICROSOFT EXCEL 5.0

FIGURE SS3-12 ■ **LOOKUP TABLES**

(a) This is the TAX workbook. (b) The VLOOKUP function returns one of the cell values from the tax table.

	A	B	C	D	E	F
1	TAX TABLE EXAMPLE					
2						
3	Income:					
4	Category:					
5	Your TAX is:					
6						
7		Category				
8	Income	1	2	3	4	
9	$ 25,000	$ 7,250	$ 6,525	$ 5,870	$ 5,278	
10	25,500	7,413	6,671	5,999	5,376	
11	26,000	7,575	6,793	6,118	5,500	
12	26,500	7,685	6,901	6,217	5,599	
13						
14						

(a)

	A	B	C	D	E	F
1	TAX TABLE EXAMPLE					
2						
3	Income:		$ 25,625			
4	Category:		2			
5	Your TAX is:		$ 6,671			
6						
7		Category				
8	Income	1	2	3	4	
9	$ 25,000	$ 7,250	$ 6,525	$ 5,870	$ 5,278	
10	25,500	7,413	6,671	5,999	5,376	
11	26,000	7,575	6,793	6,118	5,500	
12	26,500	7,685	6,901	6,217	5,599	
13						
14						
15						

(b)

---

8. **Press** ↵

This lookup function compares the value in Cell C3 with each cell in the first column of the tax table. For this to work properly, values in the first column must be in ascending sequential order. When Excel finds a cell in the first column that is closest to the value in C3 *without exceeding it,* Excel moves across that row to the column specified by the value in Cell C4. (Currently, "#N/A" messages may appear in cells until you complete the remaining cells.)

9. **In Cell C3, enter an income of** 25625

10. **In Cell C4, enter an offset of** 2 **and then press** ↓

Your screen should now resemble Figure SS3-12b. The VLOOKUP function locates

CHAPTER 3   ADVANCED SPREADSHEETS   SS171

the row that contains a value close to, but not exceeding, 25625. It then uses the off-set value to locate the proper column and return the appropriate cell.

11. Save this workbook as TAX1 and then close it

Change the income and offset values in Cells C3 and C4 and examine the value returned in C5. Incomes that exceed the highest value in the table will use the last row of the table. Incomes that are less than the first value in the table will return an error message.

CHECKPOINT

✓ On a new workbook, type 10 numbers between zero and 100 in Column A.
✓ Create an IF function in Column B that will multiply each cell in Column A by two if the value exceeds 50, and otherwise return a zero in the Column B cell.
✓ Using the worksheet you just created, create a VLOOKUP table that will return a letter grade in Column C for each number in Column A as follows: "F" for 0–59, "D" for 60–69, "C" for 70–79, "B" for 80–89, and "A" for 90 and above.
✓ Create an HLOOKUP table that does the same task just outlined.
✓ What is the purpose of adding a "+1" to a Lookup argument?

MODULE 3: DATA MANAGEMENT

Although Excel is used primarily as a spreadsheet, any related data placed in rows and columns can also be treated as an Excel *database table*—an organized collection of data. As shown in Figure SS3-13, each worksheet row forms a *record,* and each column contains one *field*—a category of data common to each record. The entries in any field (column) must be consistent—either all values (including formulas) or all text, but not some of each.

FIGURE SS3-13 ■ THE SPREADSHEET AS A DATABASE

	A	B	C	D	E	F	G	H	I	J
1	STUDENT GRADES									
2								Grade		
3		STUDENT	TEST 1	TEST 2	AVERAGE	GRADE		Lookup		
4		Jerry	56	87	72	C		0	F	
5		Elissa	92	96	94	A		60	D	
6		Andrea	98	90	94	A		70	C	
7		Edward	56	80	68	D		80	B	
8		Charles	84	90	87	B		90	A	
9		Rita	85	93	89	B				
10		Lesley	72	85	79	C				
11										
12										
13										
14										

The top row of the database must contain *field names* that identify all the fields in the database. This row must be followed immediately by the first record—blank rows or separator lines cannot be used. More than one database can appear within the same worksheet as space permits.

The following exercises examine various database commands. In preparation for these exercises,

1. **Close any open worksheet and then open the *GRADES* workbook**

2. **If you do not have the *GRADES* workbook (or want the practice), type it now, matching the data shown in Figure SS3-13, and then save it as *GRADES***

   Note: If you create the worksheet yourself, *type* the letters in Column F even though they are generated by a VLOOKUP table in this example. You do not need the lookup table to use the database.

MODULE 3A: GENERATING A SEQUENCE OF NUMBERS

A useful data feature is Excel's *Fill* commands, which generate number sequences in a given range. For example, assume you want to give each student in the database a student number, starting *101* and increasing by one for each student on the list. You could type these numbers yourself, but it is easier to let Excel do it by either using the Fill submenu or the Fill handle.

1. **Open the *GRADES* workbook if needed**

2. **Move to Cell A4**

THE FILL SUBMENU.   To use the Fill submenu to generate a sequence of numbers beginning with *101* in Cell A4 and ending with *107* in Cell A10,

1. **Type** 101 **and press** ↵
2. **Select the fill range A4:A10**

MOUSE APPROACH	KEYBOARD APPROACH
3. **Click *Edit, Fill* for its submenu**	3. **Press** Alt + E , I **for the Fill submenu**

The Fill submenu contains commands to fill a range. The first five commands fill a range in the direction of the command. The Series command fills a range with a series of numbers or dates and the Justify command rearranges text to fill a range of cells.

MOUSE APPROACH	KEYBOARD APPROACH
4. **Click *Series* for its dialog box**	4. **Press** S **for the Series dialog box**

The Series dialog box should appear as Figure SS3-14a. At this point, you can change the default step value, stop value, type, or series in row or column. The step value is the value added to each number to generate the next number in the sequence. A type is the frequency with which a sequence number will appear.

At this point you can change the different series options. For now, to accept this range and other default settings,

CHAPTER 3   ADVANCED SPREADSHEETS   SS173

FIGURE SS3-14 ■ DATA FILL

(a) The Fill parameters have been set in the Fill dialog box. (b) This is the complete fill.

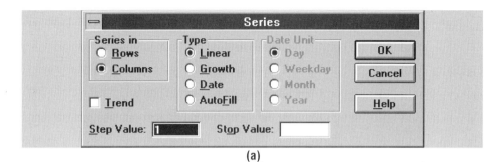

(a)

(b)

MOUSE APPROACH	KEYBOARD APPROACH
5. Click the *OK* button	5. Press ↵
6. Press ↑ to deselect and move to Cell A3	

The range is instantly filled with the proper values as if you had typed them (as shown in Figure SS3-14b).

7. Save this workbook as *GRADES1* and then close it

THE FILL HANDLE. The small square box at the bottom-right corner of Excel's cell pointer is called the **fill handle.** It is a feature that can be used to quickly fill a range with a sequence of numbers or other data by mouse. If only one number is placed in a cell of the fill range, the fill handle will copy that number to the empty cells in that range. Try this,

1. Open the workbook *GRADES*

2. Move to Cell A4

3. Type 101

4. Slowly point to the fill handle of the cell pointer until the mouse pointer turns into a (+) (see left margin)

SS174 SPREADSHEETS WITH MICROSOFT EXCEL 5.0

5. Drag the fill handle to Cell A10 and release your mouse

    Note that 101 has been copied to the range A5:A10. Now, do the following to generate a sequence of numbers using the fill handle.

6. Press Delete to remove the contains of the range A4:A10

7. In Cell A4, type 101 and press ↵

8. In Cell A5, type 102

9. Select Cells A4 and A5

10. Drag the fill handle to Cell A10 and then release your mouse

11. Press ↑ to move to Cell A3

Your worksheet should resemble Figure SS3-14b again.

12. Close the worksheet without saving

MODULE 3B: SORTING DATA

Data that are listed vertically in any range can also be *sorted,* or arranged in order. Data are normally sorted in ascending order (from lowest value to highest), but can also be sorted in descending, or reverse, order (highest to lowest). The following exercise sorts the test data in alphabetical order by student name.

> Note: Before you sort, it is usually good practice to save your worksheet. This way, if the sort does not work as expected, you can always open the worksheet and try again. The *Undo* feature will also return the worksheet to its "pre-sort" state.

IDENTIFYING THE DATA RANGE.   The first step in the sort process is to identify the data range to be sorted.

1. Open the *GRADES* workbook

2. Move to Cell B4

3. Select the range B4:F10

Notice (as shown in Figure SS3-15a) that the data range includes *all* columns of the records (rows) to be sorted, not just the student name column. Columns and rows that are left out of the data range *will not be sorted.* The top row of field names is purposely not included in the data range, or it too would be sorted.

SETTING KEYS.   The second step is to select key fields, or *keys,* to be used for the sort. As you will soon see, key fields are selected using drop-down boxes in the Sort dialog box (data menu).

MOUSE APPROACH	**KEYBOARD APPROACH**
1. Click *Data, Sort* for its dialog box	1. Press Alt + D , S for the Sort dialog box

The *Sort* dialog box should now appear as in Figure SS3-15b. You can select up to three sort key fields using this dialog box. The key field selected in the *Sort By* drop-

CHAPTER 3   ADVANCED SPREADSHEETS   **SS175**

down box will sort before the key field selected in the *Then By* drop-down box, and so on. You can also select the order of each key field's sort (ascending or descending).

Excel automatically selects the "STUDENT" as the *Sort By* key field and the default sort order—ascending. Although you can select another key or a different sort order, none is needed in this exercise.

PERFORMING THE SORT. The last step is to activate the sort.

MOUSE APPROACH	KEYBOARD APPROACH
1. Click the *OK* button	1. Press ↵

FIGURE SS3-15 ■ SORTING DATA

(a) The data range includes all fields and records but not field names. (b) This is the *Sort* dialog box.

	A	B	C	D	E	F	G	H	I	J
1	STUDENT GRADES									
2								Grade		
3		STUDENT	TEST 1	TEST 2	AVERAGE	GRADE		Lookup		
4		Jerry	56	87	72	C		0	F	
5		Elissa	92	96	94	A		60	D	
6		Andrea	98	90	94	A		70	C	
7		Edward	56	80	68	D		80	B	
8		Charles	84	90	87	B		90	A	
9		Rita	85	93	89	B				
10		Lesley	72	85	79	C				
11										
12										

(a)

(b)

(continued)

FIGURE SS3-15 ■ *(continued)*

(c) The entire data range has been sorted alphabetically.

	A	B	C	D	E	F	G	H	I	J
1	STUDENT GRADES									
2								Grade		
3		STUDENT	TEST 1	TEST 2	AVERAGE	GRADE		Lookup		
4		Andrea	98	90	94	A		0	F	
5		Charles	84	90	87	B		60	D	
6		Edward	56	80	68	D		70	C	
7		Elissa	92	96	94	A		80	B	
8		Jerry	56	87	72	C		90	A	
9		Lesley	72	85	79	C				
10		Rita	85	93	89	B				
11										
12										

(c)

2. Press ↑ to deselect, move to Cell B3
3. Save this workbook as *GRADES3*

Examine your screen and Figure SS3-15c. Notice that records within the data range have been sorted into alphabetical order according to the key field—STUDENT. All tests and averages have been moved as well since they were part of the data range. The title, field names, and grade lookup table were unaffected.

SORTING WITH TWO KEYS. This exercise demonstrates sorting with two keys—as the *average* as the *Sort By* key and *student* as the *Then By* key.

1. Select the range B4:F10

MOUSE APPROACH

2. Click *Data, Sort* for its dialog box

3. Click the ± button of the *Sort By* drop-down box
4. Click *AVERAGE* from the drop-down list
5. Click the *Descending* option button of the *Sort By* group

6. Click the ± button of the *Then By* drop-down box
7. Click *STUDENT* from the drop-down list

KEYBOARD APPROACH

2. Press Alt + D, S for the Sort dialog box
3. Press Alt + ↓ for the Sort By drop-down list
4. Press ↓ three times to select *AVERAGE*
5. Press Alt + D to select descending sort order
6. Press Alt + T for the Then By drop-down list
7. Press ↓ to select *STUDENT*

CHAPTER 3   ADVANCED SPREADSHEETS   SS177

Your Sort dialog box selections should resemble Figure SS3-16a. If not, redo Steps 3 through 7.

MOUSE APPROACH

8. Click *OK*

9. Press ↑ to deselect and move to Cell B3

KEYBOARD APPROACH

8. Press ↵

The completed sort appears in Figure SS3-16b. Note that the rows are ordered first according to the average test grade in decreasing order *(AVERAGE, descending order)*. Where primary fields are identical— as for Andrea and Elissa—the rows are further ordered in normal alphabetical order by name *(STUDENT, ascending order)*.

FIGURE SS3-16 ■ THE COMPLETED SORT

(a) This is the sort dialog box with two key field selections.
(b) These data have been sorted by AVERAGE GRADE and STUDENT name.

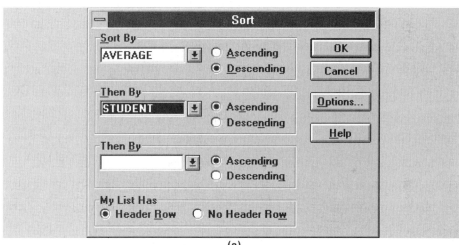

SS178 SPREADSHEETS WITH MICROSOFT EXCEL 5.0

10. Close the workbook without saving

> Tip: You can also sort a range by using the ascending or descending toolbar buttons.

MODULE 3C: CREATING A DATA DISTRIBUTION

Excel can also prepare a data distribution of values in a range. A **data distribution** (or *frequency distribution*) is a count of spreadsheet values (within a *values range*) that fall within specified numeric intervals (listed in a *bin range*). The following exercise creates a data distribution that determines how many test grades are less than or equal to 60, greater than 60 but less than 70, and so on, up to a grade of 100.

The first step is to select two unused adjacent columns where the distribution will appear. Use Columns H and I starting at Row 12, as shown in Figure SS3-17a. Column H will hold the upper limit of each interval or *bin;* the distribution will appear in Column I.

CREATING THE BINS. Increasing values can now be entered into the appropriate bins to create a specific interval for counting. The program interprets the contents of each bin you create as "less than or equal to this number." Thus, the first value of 60 will collect any value that is less than or equal to 60.

1. Open the *GRADES1* workbook

FIGURE SS3-17 ■ CREATING A DATA DISTRIBUTION

(a) Creating the bins.

	A	B	C	D	E	F	G	H	I	J
1	STUDENT GRADES									
2								Grade		
3		STUDENT	TEST 1	TEST 2	AVERAGE	GRADE		Lookup		
4	101	Jerry	56	87	72	C		0	F	
5	102	Elissa	92	96	94	A		60	D	
6	103	Andrea	98	90	94	A		70	C	
7	104	Edward	56	80	68	D		80	B	
8	105	Charles	84	90	87	B		90	A	
9	106	Rita	85	93	89	B				
10	107	Lesley	72	85	79	C		Distribution		
11								Up to		
12								60		
13								70		
14								80		
15								90		
16								100		
17										
18										

(a)

CHAPTER 3   ADVANCED SPREADSHEETS   SS179

Now place some identifying labels as follows:

2. **In Cell H10, type** Distribution

3. **In Cell H11, type** Up to

These two titles are simply reminders for future reference; they are not needed for the actual calculations.

4. **In Cells H12 through H16, enter the numbers as shown in Figure SS3-17a**

Your screen should resemble Figure SS3-17a, with 60, 70, 80, 90, and 100 appearing in Cells H12 through H16. If it does not, retype these cells now.

INVOKING THE DISTRIBUTION.   Once the bins have been created, you can invoke the command to calculate the distribution.

1. **Select the frequency-distribution-results range I12:I17 (the "I" in "I12" and "I17" stands for Column I—do not use "112" or "117")**

Note that this range includes one cell more (Cell I17) then the corresponding bin numbers.

2. **Type** =FREQUENCY(C4:D10,H12:H16) **but *DO NOT* press Enter**

The range C4:D10 is the *data-array range;* it includes all the data in the TEST1 and

---

FIGURE SS3-17 ■ *(continued)*

(b) The completed distribution of test grades.

	A	B	C	D	E	F	G	H	I	J
1	STUDENT GRADES									
2								Grade		
3		STUDENT	TEST 1	TEST 2	AVERAGE	GRADE		Lookup		
4	101	Jerry	56	87	72	C		0	F	
5	102	Elissa	92	96	94	A		60	D	
6	103	Andrea	98	90	94	A		70	C	
7	104	Edward	56	80	68	D		80	B	
8	105	Charles	84	90	87	B		90	A	
9	106	Rita	85	93	89	B				
10	107	Lesley	72	85	79	C		Distribution		
11								Up to		
12								60	2	
13								70	0	
14								80	2	
15								90	6	
16								100	4	
17									0	
18										

(b)

SS180 **SPREADSHEETS WITH MICROSOFT EXCEL 5.0**

TEST2 columns. The H12:H16 is the *bin-array range* and includes the distribution criteria. To produce the distribution shown in Figure SS3-17b,

3. Press `Ctrl` **+** `Shift` **+** `↵`

Step 3 copies the frequency function to each cell in the distribution-results range as an absolute formula, which is encased in brackets ({ }).

4. Press `↑` **to deselect and move to Cell I11**

Your worksheet should resemble Figure SS3-17b.

The results can be interpreted as follows: two tests were 60 or less; no tests were between 61 and 70; two tests were between 71 and 80; six tests were between 81 and 90; and finally, four tests were greater than 90 but less than or equal to 100. The final zero beneath the distribution shows that no tests were above the last bin limit. The sum of the counts shown in the distribution is 14—the number of tests in the values range.

5. Save this workbook as *GRADES2* and then close it

Since the distribution range contains frequency functions, changing a test score in the data-array range will automatically update the distribution results. You can calculate as many distributions as you want by changing the number of bin rows, their upper limits, or the data-array range to be counted once the FREQUENCY functions have been placed in the distributions results range.

MODULE 3D: INFORMATION RETRIEVAL—DATA QUERIES

A **database query** is a question asked of a database. Database query commands let you locate (and edit) records in a database table that meet certain criteria. Although database queries are more useful in large spreadsheets, the principles of creating and using queries can be learned more easily on a smaller scale.

To query an Excel database table, use the Filter commands that are accessed through the Data menu. **Filter** commands find and extract records in a database that match a specific criteria. **Criteria** are conditions that are used to find matching records in a database.

FILTERING DATA. Excel's *AutoFilter* command can be used to filter records based on criteria specified through drop-down list boxes. The results of the filtering process are displayed in place of the source database table. The table is not lost, but rather hidden, and may be redisplayed using the *Show All* command (Filter menu). Try this to filter the database to display information based on the criteria STUDENT=Jerry.

1. Open the *GRADES* workbook

2. Move to Cell B3, the first cell in the Field Names row

3. Save the workbook as *GRADES4*

MOUSE APPROACH	KEYBOARD APPROACH
4. Click *Data*, *Filter*, *AutoFilter* to turn on the AutoFilter feature and Filter mode	**4. Press** `Alt` **+** `D` **,** `F` **,** `F` **to turn on the AutoFilter feature and Filter mode**

Drop-down list buttons (`↓`) should appear at the right end of each field name cell as in Figure SS3-18a.

CHAPTER 3   ADVANCED SPREADSHEETS   SS181

MOUSE APPROACH	KEYBOARD APPROACH
5. Click the STUDENT drop-down list button ⬇	5. Press Alt + ↓ for the STUDENT drop-down list
6. Click *Jerry* from the drop-down list	6. Press ↓ as needed to select *Jerry* and then press ↵

Excel filtered the record meeting the criteria "STUDENT=Jerry" as in Figure SS3-18b.

By using the custom option of the filter drop-down list, you can filter students who match other search conditions. Try this,

MOUSE APPROACH	KEYBOARD APPROACH
7. Click *Data, Filter, Show All* to redisplay the entire database	7. Press Alt + D, F, S to redisplay the entire database
8. Click the ⬇ button of the TEST1 drop-down box (in Cell C3)	8. Move to Cell C3 and press Alt + ↓ for the TEST1 drop-down list

FIGURE SS3-18 ■ FILTERING RECORDS

(a) The AutoFilter command places drop-down list buttons at the right end of each field name's cell. (b) Setting a filtering criterion with a drop-down list will display only the result of the filter.

	A	B	C	D	E	F	G	H	I	J
1	STUDENT GRADES									
2								Grade		
3		STUDEN⬇	TEST⬇	TEST⬇	AVERAG⬇	GRAD⬇		Lookup		
4		Jerry	56	87	72	C		0	F	
5		Elissa	92	96	94	A		60	D	
6		Andrea	98	90	94	A		70	C	
7		Edward	56	80	68	D		80	B	
8		Charles	84	90	87	B		90	A	
9		Rita	85	93	89	B				
10		Lesley	72	85	79	C				
11										
12										

(a)

	A	B	C	D	E	F	G	H	I	J
1	STUDENT GRADES									
2								Grade		
3		STUDEN⬇	TEST⬇	TEST⬇	AVERAG⬇	GRAD⬇		Lookup		
4		Jerry	56	87	72	C		0	F	
11										
12										

(b)

FIGURE SS3-19 ■ CUSTOM DATA FILTERING

(a) This is the Custom AutoFilter dialog box.
(b) This screen shows filtered data.

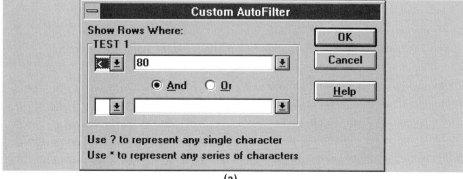

(a)

(b)

9. Click *(Custom...)* for the Custom AutoFilter dialog box
10. Type 80
11. Click the button of the operator drop-down box and click <

   Your dialog box should appear as Figure SS3-19a.

12. Click *OK*

9. Press ↓ as needed to select *(Custom...)* and then press ↵ for the Custom AutoFilter dialog box
10. Type in 80 and press Shift + Tab
11. Type <
12. Press ↵

Your worksheet should resemble Figure SS3-19b. If not, repeat Steps 6 through 11. Note that only the records that meet the criterion "TEST1<80" are displayed.

13. Close the workbook without saving

> Tip: The Form dialog box *(Data, Form)* can be used to find, change or delete records in a database.

USING MULTIPLE CRITERIA. More than one search criterion can be used at a time. These criteria can be identified using logical connectors—such as AND or OR. Logical connectors are available through the Custom AutoFilter dialog boxes.

CHAPTER 3   ADVANCED SPREADSHEETS   SS183

Multiple criteria can be set in a single field or in multiple fields using similar techniques. Try this multiple-criteria entry to find records whose average (single field) exceeds 59 *and* is also less than 70.

Note: An AND connector requires that all criteria be met for a record to be selected.

1. Open the *GRADES4* workbook

MOUSE APPROACH	KEYBOARD APPROACH
2. Click *Data*, *Filter*, *AutoFilter*	2. Press Alt + D , F , F
3. Click the *AVERAGE* drop-down list button	3. Move to Cell E3 and press Alt + ↓
4. Click *(Custom...)* for the Custom AutoFilter dialog box	4. Press ↓ until *(Custom...)* is selected and press ↵
5. Type 59	5. Type 59
6. Click the ▼ button of the first Operator drop-down box	6. Press Shift + Tab
7. Click >	7. Type >
8. Click the ▼ button of the second Operator drop-down box	8. Press Tab three times to move to the second Operator drop-down box
9. Click <	9. Type <
10. Click the second value drop-down box to place the insertion point	10. Press Tab
11. Type 70	11. Type 70
Your dialog box should appear as in Figure SS3-20a.	Your dialog box should resemble Figure SS3-20b.
12. Click *OK*	12. Press ↵

FIGURE SS3-20 ■ **MULTIPLE CRITERIA SEARCHES**

(a) Entering multiple-criteria information.

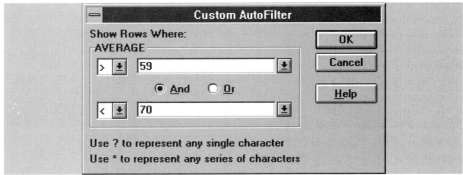

(a)

(continued)

SS184 **SPREADSHEETS WITH MICROSOFT EXCEL 5.0**

FIGURE SS3-20 ■ *(continued)*

(b) The results of the multiple-criteria search.

	A	B	C	D	E	F	G	H	I	J
1	STUDENT GRADES									
2								Grade		
3		STUDEN↓	TES↓	TES↓	AVERA↓	GRA↓		Lookup		
7		Edward	56	80	68	D		80	B	
11										
12										

(b)

The result of your multiple criteria search appears as in Figure SS3-20b.

13. Close the workbook without saving

ADVANCED FILTERING. As mentioned earlier, multiple criteria that pertain to different fields can also be set with an AND or OR connector. You can use the Auto-Filter drop-down list boxes to set criteria for more than one field, thereby creating an AND connector. OR connectors containing different fields require the use of the Advance Filter dialog box. The next exercise explores an OR connector entry using Excel's Advanced Filter feature.

1. Open the *GRADES4* workbook

2. Insert four new rows below Cell A2

3 In Cell B3, type `TEST 2` **(with a space between TEST and 2)**

4. In Cell B4, type `>=C8+10`

5. In Cell C3, type `AVERAGE`

6. In Cell C5, type `<90`

Placing criteria in different rows, as in Steps 4 and 5 above, invokes an OR connector. The above entries should agree with the corresponding cells at the top of Figure SS3-21a.

7. Move to Cell B7 (or any cell in the database table)

MOUSE APPROACH	**KEYBOARD APPROACH**
8. Click *Data, Filter, Advanced Filter*	**8. Press** `Alt` + `D`, `F`, `A`
9. Click the *Criteria Range* text box	**9. Press** `Alt` + `C` **for the Criteria Range text box**

10. Type `B3:C5`

Your dialog box should resemble Figure SS3-21b. Note that Excel places the List Range as long as the cell pointer is positioned in one of the cells in the database.

CHAPTER 3   ADVANCED SPREADSHEETS   **SS185**

FIGURE SS3-21 ■ **USING MULTIPLE CRITERIA**

	A	B	C	D	E	F	G	H	I	J
1	STUDENT GRADES									
2										
3		TEST 2	AVERAGE							
4		>=C8+10		─ Criteria						
5			<90							
6								Grade		
7		STUDENT	TEST 1	TEST 2	AVERAGE	GRADE		Lookup		
8		Jerry	56	87	72	C		0	F	
11		Edward	56	80	68	D		80	B	
12		Charles	84	90	87	B		90	A	
13		Rita	85	93	89	B				
14		Lesley	72	85	79	C				
15										
16										

(a)

(a) This screen shows the results of filtering. (b) The Advanced Filter dialog box can be used to filter data based on multiple criteria specified on a worksheet.

Advanced Filter

Action
- ● **F**ilter the List, in-place
- ○ C**o**py to Another Location

OK
Cancel
Help

List Range: $B$7:$F$14
Criteria Range: B3:C5
Copy to:

☐ Unique **R**ecords Only

(b)

MOUSE APPROACH	KEYBOARD APPROACH
11. Click *OK*	**11. Press** ↵

The results of your multiple criteria search should agree with those at the bottom of Figure SS3-21a.

12. Resave the workbook as *GRADES4*

CREATING A QUERY TABLE.   A filter list can also be copied to another location as a separate query table. This is done by selecting the *Copy to Another Location* option button of the Advanced Filter dialog box.

1.   **Open the** *GRADES4* **workbook, if needed**

2.   **Delete the content of range B3:C5 and move to Cell B3**

SS186 | **SPREADSHEETS WITH MICROSOFT EXCEL 5.0**

FIGURE SS3-22 ■ CREATING A QUERY TABLE

(a) The *Copy to Another Location* option at the Advanced Filter dialog box can be used to create a Query table.

Advanced Filter

Action
○ Filter the List, in-place
◉ Copy to Another Location

List Range: $B$7:$F$14
Criteria Range: B3:B4
Copy to: B16:F18

☐ Unique Records Only

[OK]
[Cancel]
[Help]

(a)

MOUSE APPROACH

3. Click *Data, Filter, Show All* to clear all previous filter settings

4. In Cell B3, type TEST 1

5. In Cell B4, type =85

6. Move to Cell B7

KEYBOARD APPROACH

3. Press Alt + D , F , S to clear all previous filter settings

MOUSE APPROACH

7. Click *Data, Filter, Advanced Filter*

8. Click the *Copy to Another Location* option button

9. Press Alt + C to highlight the content of the Criteria Range text box and press Delete to remove prior settings

10. Type B3:B4 and press Tab

11. Type B16:F18 in the Copy to text box

KEYBOARD APPROACH

7. Press Alt + D , F , A

8. Press Alt + O to select *Copy to Another Location*

Your dialog box should resemble Figure SS3-22a.

MOUSE APPROACH

12. Click *OK*

KEYBOARD APPROACH

12. Press ↵

Your worksheet should now resemble Figure SS3-22b. Filter commands can also be applied to the copied filter list.

13. Save this workbook as *GRADES5*

Now try creating another query table to contain the record of students who received A's as final grades.

1. Open the *GRADES5* workbook, if needed

FIGURE SS3-22 ■ *(continued)*

((b) This is a Query table containing the results of the filtering process.

	A	B	C	D	E	F	G	H	I	J
1	STUDENT GRADES									
2										
3			TEST 1	— Criteria						
4			85							
5										
6								Grade		
7		STUDENT	TEST 1	TEST 2	AVERAGE	GRADE		Lookup		
8		Jerry	56	87	72	C		0	F	
9		Elissa	92	96	94	A		60	D	
10	Data-	Andrea	98	90	94	A		70	C	
11	base —	Edward	56	80	68	D		80	B	
12	table	Charles	84	90	87	B		90	A	
13		Rita	85	93	89	B				
14		Lesley	72	85	79	C				
15										
16		STUDENT	TEST 1	TEST 2	AVERAGE	GRADE	— Query table			
17		Rita	85	93	89	B				
18										

(b)

2. In Cell D3, type GRADE
3. In Cell D4, type A
4. Move to Cell B7

MOUSE APPROACH

5. Click *Data*, *Filter*, *Advanced Filter*

6. Click the *Copy to Another Location* option button

KEYBOARD APPROACH

5. Press Alt + D , F , A

6. Press Alt + O to select *Copy to Another Location*

7. Press Alt + C to highlight the content of the Criteria Range text box and press Delete to remove prior settings

8. Type D3:D4 and press Tab

9. Type B19:F21 in the Copy to text box as in Figure SS3-23a

MOUSE APPROACH

10. Click the ↓ of the vertical scroll bar until the new query table is visible as in Figure SS3-23b

KEYBOARD APPROACH

10. Use arrow keys to view the new query table as in Figure SS3-23b

FIGURE SS3-23 ■ CREATING AN ADDITIONAL QUERY TABLE

(a) Enter the "Criteria Range" and "Copy to" range for the Query table in the Advanced Filter. (b) These are the second Query table results.

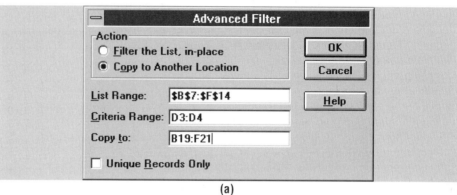

(a)

(b)

11. Save this workbook as GRADES6 and then close it

Now, only two records that match these criteria—*Elissa* and *Andrea*—are copied into the query table as shown in Figure SS3-23b.

MODULE 3E: USING DATA FUNCTIONS

Data functions, as listed in Figure SS3-24, combine the qualities of statistical functions with lookup and database concepts to include only selected records in a specific calculation. Data functions follow the form DFUNCTION *(input, offset, criteria).* In this format, the criteria range tells the program which records in the input range to

CHAPTER 3   ADVANCED SPREADSHEETS   SS189

FIGURE SS3-24 ■ DATABASE FUNCTIONS

@DAVERAGE	Averages the values in a database field based on certain criteria
@DCOUNTA	Counts the nonblank cells in a database field based on certain criteria
@DMIN	Finds the smallest value in a database field based on certain criteria
@DSTDEVP	Calculates the population standard deviation of the values in a database field based on certain criteria
@DSUM	Totals the field values in a database field based on certain criteria
@DVARP	Calculates the population variance of the values in a database field based on certain criteria

---

include in the calculation of the column listed in the *offset*. The following exercise demonstrates its use.

1. Open the *CHECKS* workbook

Your screen should resemble Figure SS3-25, which depicts a simple checkbook management system. (While you are in this spreadsheet, you may want to examine the use of Column B's DATE function or Column E's IF function.) Note that titles have already been entered and formats selected to help structure your results.

FIGURE SS3-25 ■ THE CHECKS WORKSHEET

	A	B	C	D	E	F	G
1	CHECKBOOK						
2							
3	NUMBER	DATE	TRANSACTION	AMOUNT	BALANCE		
4		07-Oct	Deposit	$ 1,000.00	$ 1,000.00		
5	101	07-Oct	Rent	415.00	585.00		
6	102	12-Oct	Utilities	66.75	518.25		
7	103	14-Oct	Phone	54.50	463.75		
8	104	21-Oct	Ed's Applicances	350.32	113.43		
9	105	30-Oct	Charlie's Record Shop	67.07	46.36		
10		01-Nov	Deposit	625.00	671.36		
11	106	03-Nov	Dryden Books	124.15	547.21		
12	107	03-Nov	Rent	415.00	132.21		
13	108	04-Nov	Phone	42.65	89.56		
14	109	08-Nov	Utilities	75.46	14.10		
15							
16			TRANSACTION				
17				Total:			
18				Average:			

CHECKS / Sheet2 / Sheet3 / Sheet4 / Sheet5 / Sheet

2. **Move to Cell E17**

At this point, you can either use Excel's Function Wizard to help you enter functions arguments or simply type them. The Steps 3 through 10 use the Function Wizard to enter the first function =DSUM(A3:E14,4,C16:C17). All other functions in this exercise are presented as type-in data.

MOUSE APPROACH	KEYBOARD APPROACH
3. Click *Insert, Function* for the Function Wizard	3. Press Shift + F3 for the Function Wizard
4. Click *Database* in the Function Category list box	4. Press Alt + C for the Function Category list box and use the arrow keys to select *Database*
5. Click *DSUM* in the Function Name list box	5. Press Alt + N for the Function Name list box and use the arrow keys to select *DSUM*
6. Click *Next>*	6. Press ↵ to move to the next step

7. Type A3:E14 in the database text box and press Tab
8. Type 4 in the field text box and press Tab
9. Type C16:C17 in the criteria text box

Your Function Wizard dialog box should resemble Figure SS3-26a.

MOUSE APPROACH	KEYBOARD APPROACH
10. Click *Finish*	10. Press ↵

FIGURE SS3-26 ■ **ENTERING DATABASE FUNCTIONS**

(a) The Function Wizard dialog box can be used to help enter a database function.

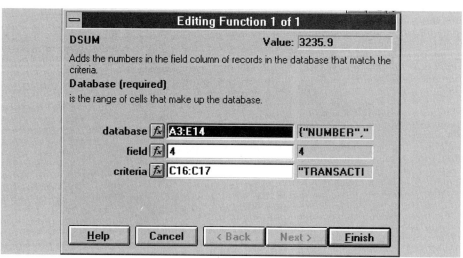

(a)

CHAPTER 3   ADVANCED SPREADSHEETS   SS191

This formula translates as "within the stated input range (A3:E14), total the fourth offset column (AMOUNT) for those records that match the criteria in cells C16:C17."

Since the criteria range is empty, all records are included—the function simply calculates the total of Column D.

11. **Format Cells E17 and E18 to the accounting-currency, two decimal format**

12. **In Cell C17, type** [Deposit] **and press** ↵

As shown in Figure SS3-26b, the total now reflects only those records whose TRANSACTION matches the label "Deposit."

13. **In Cell E18, type** [=DAVERAGE(A3:E14,4,C16:C17)] **and press** ↵

14. **In Cell E19, type** [=DCOUNTA(A3:E14,4,C16:C17)] **and press** ↵

These formulas average and count the deposits, respectively, as shown in Figure SS3-26c. When entering database functions, you can use named ranges for the input and criteria, or you can specify a cell address that contains a value for the offset.

15. **Save this workbook as** *CHECKS1*

16. **In Cell C17, type** [Rent] **and press** ↵

FIGURE SS3-26 ■ *(continued)*

(b) The DSUM in Cell C17 adds all records whose transactions show "Deposit."

	A	B	C	D	E	F	G
1	CHECKBOOK						
2							
3	NUMBER	DATE	TRANSACTION	AMOUNT	BALANCE		
4		07-Oct	Deposit	$ 1,000.00	$ 1,000.00		
5	101	07-Oct	Rent	415.00	585.00		
6	102	12-Oct	Utilities	66.75	518.25		
7	103	14-Oct	Phone	54.50	463.75		
8	104	21-Oct	Ed's Applicances	350.32	113.43		
9	105	30-Oct	Charlie's Record Shop	67.07	46.36		
10		01-Nov	Deposit	625.00	671.36		
11	106	03-Nov	Dryden Books	124.15	547.21		
12	107	03-Nov	Rent	415.00	132.21		
13	108	04-Nov	Phone	42.65	89.56		
14	109	08-Nov	Utilities	75.46	14.10		
15							
16			TRANSACTION				
17			Deposit	Total:	$ 1,625.00		
18				Average:			

(b)

(continued)

SS192 | SPREADSHEETS WITH MICROSOFT EXCEL 5.0

FIGURE SS3-26 ■ *(continued)*

(c) The DAVERAGE and DCOUNTA functions have been added. (d) Changing the criterion to "Rent" automatically changes the results of all database functions.

15					
16		TRANSACTION			
17		Deposit	Total:	$	1,625.00
18			Average:	$	812.50
19			Count:		2
20					

(c)

15					
16		TRANSACTION			
17		Rent	Total:	$	830.00
18			Average:	$	415.00
19			Count:		2
20					

(d)

As shown in Figure SS3-26d, all the database functions now reflect results for the new criterion—*Rent*. By redefining the criteria range, you can also specify multiple criteria as you did for data queries.

10. Close the workbook without saving

CHECKPOINT

✓ Open the GRADES workbook. Sort the data in Columns B through F by Test 2 scores from *highest* to *lowest*.

✓ Resort by NAME and TEST 1 score in normal order.

✓ Generate a sequence of numbers in Column J that starts with 50, counts by fives, and ends at 95.

✓ Using the GRADES workbook, create a database that finds all records whose TEST 1 *or* TEST 2 score exceeds 89.

✓ Extract the STUDENT and AVERAGE fields for these records into a range starting in Row 20.

MODULE 4: MACROS

A **macro** is a set of mouse actions, keystrokes, or command instructions for automating a task. Macros save time that you might normally spend performing repetitive tasks. The more mouse actions or keystrokes involved in a procedure, the more time is saved, and the more likely it is that you will want to automate it with a macro.

CHAPTER 3   ADVANCED SPREADSHEETS   SS193

CREATING A MACRO

Macros can be created by following a simple procedure: planning, recording, assigning, and saving. The following exercise will create a simple macro that automatically changes a column width to 12.

PLANNING A MACRO.   The first step in creating a macro is to identify all the steps required. An easy way to plan a macro is to perform the task while recording each keystroke on paper. For example,

1.   Open the *GRADES* workbook

2.   Delete Columns F, G, H, and I (select the range *F1:I1*, click *Edit*, *Delete*, Entire *Column*, and then *OK*)

3.   Delete Column A

These actions remove columns that are not needed in this exercise and provide some demonstration space. Get a piece of paper and a pen or pencil before continuing.

4.   Write each action on paper as you change Column A's width to 12

When you have finished, these actions should appear on your paper:

MOUSE APPROACH	KEYBOARD APPROACH
Format, *Column*, *Width*, 1 2 OK	Alt + O C W 1 2 ↵

5.   Save this workbook as *MACRO1*

A macro can now be created in four steps: assigning the macro a name and description in the Record New Macro dialog box, turning on the macro recorder, recording the actual macro mouse/keyboard actions in a **module sheet,** and turning off the macro recorder.

> Tip: Macro commands can also be created from scratch and entered directly into a workbook, menu, or shortcut keys. This technique requires knowledge of Visual Basic, a programming language. Refer to your on-line help for information on Visual Basic.

RECORDING A MACRO.   After a macro has been planned, you are ready to record the macro's mouse/keystroke actions.

MOUSE APPROACH	KEYBOARD APPROACH
1. Click *Tools*, *Record Macro*, *Record New Macro* for its dialog box	1. Press Alt + T , R , R for the Record New Macro dialog box

2.   Type COLUMN_WIDTH_12 in the Macro Name text box and press Tab

Note that you can use up to 256 characters for a macro name, however, it cannot have any blank spaces separating words.

3.   Type CHANGE THE COLUMN WIDTH TO 12 in the Description text box

Your Record New Macro dialog box should appear as in Figure SS3-27.

4.   Click *OK* to turn on the macro recorder

FIGURE SS3-27 ■ RECORDING A NEW MACRO

The Record New Macro dialog box is used to name, decribe and turn on the Macro recorded.

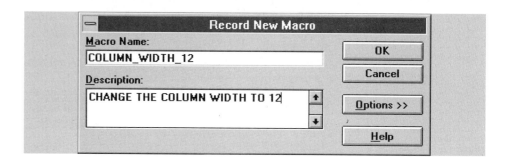

Excel uses *Visual Basic*, a programming language, for macro commands. When the macro recorder is turned on, Excel adds a new sheet called the **module** sheet to store your actions in Visual Basic code. Although not currently visible, this sheet is added behind Sheet 16 in the workbook. Methods to access the module sheet are discussed later.

MOUSE APPROACH

5. Click *Format*, *Column*, *Width*

6. Type `12` and click *OK*

7. Click the *Stop Macro* toolbar button or *Tools*, *Record Macro*, *Stop Recording* to turn off the macro recorder

8. Resave this workbook as *MACRO1*

KEYBOARD APPROACH

5. Press `Alt` + `O`, `C`, `W`

6. Type `12` and press `↵`

7. Press `Alt` + `T`, `R`, `S` to turn off the macro recorder

RUNNING A MACRO

Once macros have been created, they are available for use. They can be run using the Macro dialog box, a shortcut key, the Tools menu or a macro button. The latter three options first require the macro to be assigned to them and are discussed in the next section. Try this to run the macro using the Macro dialog box,

1. Open the *MACRO1* workbook, if needed

2. Move to Column B (any row)

MOUSE APPROACH

3. Click *Tools*, *Macro* for its dialog box

4. Click *COLUMN_WIDTH_12*

KEYBOARD APPROACH

3. Press `Alt` + `T`, `M` for the Macro dialog box

4. Press `Tab` and then use the arrow keys to select *COLUMN_WIDTH_12*

Your Macro dialog box should resemble Figure SS3-28a. Note that this dialog box lists all macros created and saved with a workbook. It also displays a description of the macro as entered when created.

CHAPTER 3   ADVANCED SPREADSHEETS   SS195

FIGURE SS3-28 ■ RUNNING A MACRO

(a) The Macro dialog box (Tools menu) can be used to run a macro using its name. (b) These are the results of running the macro in Column B to increase its width to 12.

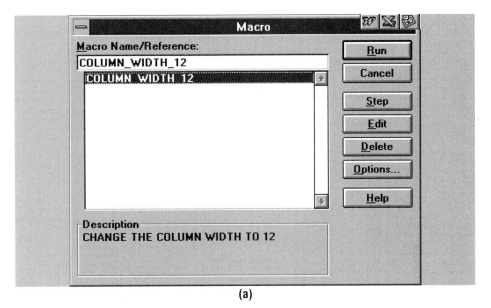

MOUSE APPROACH

5. Click *Run* to run the macro

KEYBOARD APPROACH

5. Press ↵ to run the macro

Column B's width has now been changed to 12 as in Figure SS3-28b.

ASSIGNING A MACRO

As mentioned earlier, a macro can also be run from shortcut keys, the Tools menu or a button. To do so requires first assigning the macro commands to one of these items.

ASSIGNING TO SHORTCUT KEYS. A macro can be assigned to shortcut keys either during its recording or after by using the Macro Options dialog box. This dialog box can be invoked from the Record New Macro dialog box when recording a macro, or from the Macro dialog box after a macro has been recorded. These macros will be referred to as *one-letter macros*. They generally involve the use of the **Ctrl** or **Ctrl** + **Shift** keys and one letter. The **Ctrl** or **Ctrl** + **Shift** keys are automatically selected by Excel when assigning a macro to shortcut keys. This is to prevent conflict with previously programmed Excel or user-defined shortcut keys.

To assign the macro *COLUMN_WIDTH_12* to the shortcut keys `Ctrl` + `Shift` + `W`,

> Tip: When assigning a macro to shortcut keys, try to use a letter that is easy for you to remember and relates to the macro's function.

MOUSE APPROACH

1. Click *Tools, Macro* for its dialog box

2. Click *COLUMN_WIDTH_12*

3. Click the *Options* button for the Macro Options dialog box

4. Click the *Shortcut Key* check box

5. Click the text box next to "Ctrl+"

6. Type `W` and note that "Ctrl+Shift" appears before it

7. Click *OK, Close*

KEYBOARD APPROACH

1. Press `Alt` + `T`, `M` for the Macro dialog box

2. Press `Tab` and then use the arrow keys to select *COLUMN_WIDTH_12*

3. Press `Alt` + `O` for the Macro Options dialog box

4. Press `Alt` + `K` to select the shortcut key check box

5. Press `Tab` to move to the text box next to "Ctrl+"

6. Type `W` and note that "Ctrl+Shift" appears before it

7. Press `↵`, `Alt` + `F4`

Now, try running the macro using its shortcut keys.

8. Move to Column D

9. Press `Ctrl` + `Shift` + `W`

Column D's width should now be 12.

10. Save the workbook as *MACRO2* and then close it

ASSIGNING TO THE TOOLS MENU. The procedures to assign a macro to the Tools menu is similar to assigning it to a shortcut key. Again, a macro can be assigned to the menu either during its recording or after by using the Macro Options dialog box. Try this,

1. Open the *MACRO1* workbook

MOUSE APPROACH

2. Click *Tools, Macro* for its dialog box

3. Click *COLUMN_WIDTH_12*

4. Click the *Options* button for the Macro Options dialog box

5. Click the *Menu Item on Tools Menu* check box

6. Click the *Menu Item on Tools Menu* text box

KEYBOARD APPROACH

2. Press `Alt` + `T`, `M` for the Macro dialog box

3. Press `Tab` and then use the arrow keys to select *COLUMN_WIDTH_12*

4. Press `Alt` + `O` for the Macro Options dialog box

5. Press `Alt` + `U` to select the Menu Item on Tools Menu check box

6. Press `Tab` to move to the text box

7. Type [Column WD12]   7. Type [Column WD12]
8. Click *OK, Close*   8. Press [↵], [Alt] + [F4]
9. Save the workbook as *MACRO3*

To run the macro using the Tools menu,

10. Move to Column D

MOUSE APPROACH   **KEYBOARD APPROACH**

11. Click *Tools*   11. Press [Alt] + [T] for the Tools menu
12. Click *Column WD12*   12. Press [↓] as needed to select
                                             COLUMN WD12 and then press [↵]

ASSIGNING TO A BUTTON. To assign a macro to a button on the current worksheet,

1. Click *View, Toolbars, Drawing* check box, *OK*

The Drawing toolbar should now appear in your Excel window. This toolbar can be used to create a button or other objects (pictures or symbols) in your worksheet.

2. If needed, drag the Drawing toolbar's title bar to move it away from Cell F3

3. Click the *Create Button* on the Drawing toolbar

Note that the mouse pointer changes to a "+."

4. Point to the top-left corner of Cell F3 (or any desired location for the position of the macro button)

5. Drag the mouse pointer down to the bottom-left corner of Cell F4 and then across its right cell wall to create a button filling the Cells F3 and F4

A button briefly will appear and then the Assign macro dialog box will appear.

6. Click *COLUMN_WIDTH_12* and then *OK*

7. Point before the "B" in Button 1 and then drag across to select it as in Figure SS3-29a

8. Press [Delete] to remove it

9. Type [COL W12] for the button's name

Your macro button should appear as Figure SS3-29b.

At this point, you can move to any cell not occupied by the button to turn off the button edit mode. Now use the macro button to change Column C's width to 12,

10. Click to Cell C1 or any cell in Column C

11. Click the *COL W12* macro button to change the column width to 12

12. Click *View, Toolbars, Drawing, OK*

Once a button is created you can select the button and turn on the edit mode by pointing to it, clicking the right button and pressing [Esc].

FIGURE SS3-29 ■ CREATING A MACRO BUTTON

(a) Dragging over a macro button's name selects it for editing. (b) Once selected, simply type in a desired macro-button name.

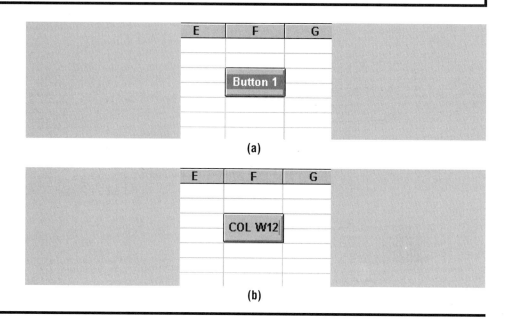

> Tip: You can also remove a toolbar by using the toolbar shortcut menu. Simply point to any toolbar, click the right mouse button, and then click the desired toolbar to turn it off/on. Clicking a toolbar's control-menu box will also close it.

13. Resave the workbook as *MACRO3*

ADDING ANOTHER MACRO

More than one macro can be created and saved within the same workbook. Now that you have learned how to create and invoke a simple macro, try applying these techniques to a more complicated macro. In the next exercise, you will create a print macro named *PRINT_COL_AB* on the MACRO3 workbook and assign it to the shortcut keys Ctrl+Shift+Print. This macro will print only Columns A and B.

1. Open the *MACRO3* workbook, if needed, and turn on your printer

   MOUSE APPROACH

   2. Click *Tools, Record Macro, Record New Macro* for its dialog box

   KEYBOARD APPROACH

   2. Press Alt + T, R, R for the Record New Macro dialog box

   3. Type PRINT_COL_AB in the Macro Name text box and press Tab

   4. Type PRINT ONLY COLUMNS A AND B in the Description text box

   MOUSE APPROACH

   5. Click the *Options* button

   KEYBOARD APPROACH

   5. Press Alt + O

6. Click the *Shortcut Key* check box and then press `Tab`
7. Type `P` (Use capital)
8. Click *OK* to turn on the macro recorder
9. Click *Edit*, *Go To*
10. Type `C1` and click *OK*
11. Select the range C1:D1
12. Click *Format*, *Column*, *Hide*
13. Click *File*, *Print*, *OK*

6. Press `Alt` + `U` to select the Shortcut Key check box and then press `Tab`
7. Type `P`
8. Press `↵` to turn on the macro recorder
9. Press `F5` for the Go To dialog box
10. Type `C1` and press `↵`
11. Select the range C1:D1
12. Press `Alt` + `O`, `C`, `H`
13. Press `Ctrl` + `P`, `↵`

The worksheet should print with only the STUDENT and TEST 1 columns. Now we'll return the worksheet display back to its original view.

MOUSE APPROACH

14. Click *Format*, *Column*, *Unhide*
15. Click the *Stop Macro* toolbar button or *Tools*, *Record Macro*, *Stop Recording* to turn off the macro recorder

16. Move to Cell A1
17. Press `Ctrl` + `Shift` + `P` to invoke the macro
18. Save the workbook as *MACRO4*

KEYBOARD APPROACH

14. Press `Alt` + `O`, `C`, `U`
15. Press `Alt` + `T`, `R`, `S` to turn off the macro recorder

EDITING A MACRO

Editing a macro requires knowledge of Visual Basic. As such, it is generally easier to delete a macro with a limited amount of statements and then rerecord it. Steps to delete a macro follow. (Do not perform these steps unless you want to delete a macro.)

1. Click *Tools*, *Macro* for the Macro dialog box
2. Click the macro to be deleted
3. Click the *Delete* button

For further information on editing a macro, see the appendix and Excel's on-line Help.

CHECKPOINT

✓ On a new worksheet, create a macro (with documentation) named ROW2 that will insert two rows at the current pointer position. Invoke it.
✓ Create a macro named *PAPER* that will print the range A1:C15 to the printer. Invoke it.
✓ Create a macro button for each of the two macros.
✓ Assign the ROW2 macro to a shortcut key. Invoke it.
✓ Assign the PAPER module to the Tools menu. Invoke it.

MODULE 5: USING MULTIPLE WORKBOOKS

You need not restrict your use of Excel to one workbook file at a time. Excel allows you to copy or move parts of a workbook or combine other workbooks with the current one. You can also create links between cells of *different* workbooks that will update values as if they were all part of one large spreadsheet.

In Excel, a workbook window is used to display a portion of a single workbook. Depending on your system's memory, you can create or open more than one workbook window in Excel's workspace at the same time. This makes manipulating data between multiple workbooks easier.

A new workbook initially has 16 sheets in its workspace. However, up to 255 sheets can be created and stored in a single workbook. Working with a workbook is similar to working with a book that contains 16 or more pages. An individual sheet is similar to a page in the book.

The exercises in this section first explore creating and manipulating multiple workbooks on your screen, and then manipulating their contents. As you work in this and the next module, remember that each workbook window contains only one workbook that may contain 16 or more sheets. Multiple sheets are discussed in Module 6.

SWITCHING BETWEEN WINDOWS

Since workbook windows are document windows (a window within an application window), standard Windows commands can be applied to manipulate them and their contents.

1. Close any open workbooks

2. Open the *SALES*, the *BOOKS*, and then the *TAPES* workbooks

As each additional file is opened, it is placed in its own window on top of the previously opened file. You can switch to another opened workbook window using the *Window* menu, shortcut keys, or control menu. Try this:

MOUSE APPROACH	**KEYBOARD APPROACH**
3. Click *Window* and then *3 SALES.XLS*	3. Press Ctrl + F6 twice to switch to the SALES window
4. Click the *control-menu* box of the SALES window for its control menu and then click *Next Window* to switch to the TAPES window	4. Press Ctrl + Tab to switch to the TAPES window

5. Use one of these switching techniques to switch to the BOOKS window

6. Close all worksheet windows without saving.

> Tip: You can select more than one workbook to be opened from the Open file dialog box by holding the Ctrl key while clicking each additional workbook.

ARRANGING WINDOWS

In the previous exercise, you viewed multiple workbook windows on separate screens. It is possible to display several files on one screen at the same time. The Arrange command (Window menu) opens to a dialog box that allows you to arrange your

CHAPTER 3   ADVANCED SPREADSHEETS   **SS201**

workbook windows in a Tile, Horizontal, Vertical or Cascade format. A sample of each window arrangement is shown in Figure SS3-30.

1. Open the *TAPES, SALES,* and *BOOKS* workbooks

MOUSE APPROACH

2. Click *Window, Arrange* for its dialog box

3. If an "x" appears in the *Windows of Active Workbook* check box, click it to remove it

4. Click *Tiled, OK* to tile windows as in Figure SS3-30a

5. Click *Window, Arrange*

6. Click *Horizontal, OK* to display the windows as in Figure SS3-30b

7. Click *Window, Arrange*

8. Click *Vertical, OK* to display the windows as in Figure SS3-30c

9. Click *Window, Arrange*

10. Click *Cascade, OK* to display the windows as in Figure SS3-30d

11. Double-click each workbook's *control menu* box to close it

KEYBOARD APPROACH

2. Press `Alt` + `W` , `A` for the Arrange dialog box

3. If an "x" appears in the *Windows of Active Workbook* check box, press `Alt` + `W` to remove it

4. Press `Alt` + `T` , `↵` to tile windows as in Figure SS3-30a

5. Press `Alt` + `W` , `A`

6. Press `Alt` + `O` , `↵` to display windows horizontally as in Figure SS3-30b.

7. Press `Alt` + `W` , `A`

8. Press `Alt` + `V` , `↵` to display the window as in Figure SS3-30c

9. Press `Alt` + `W` , `A`

10. Press `Alt` + `C` to display the windows as in Figure SS3-30d

11. Press `Ctrl` + `F4` three times to close the workbooks

FIGURE SS3-30 ■ **ARRANGING WORKBOOK WINDOWS**

The formats of workbook windows are (a) Tile

(a)

(continued)

SS202 SPREADSHEETS WITH MICROSOFT EXCEL 5.0

FIGURE SS3-30 ■ *(continued)*

(b) Horizontal (c) Vertical.

BOOKS.XLS

	A	B	C	D	E	F	G
1	Book Sales						
2		Book	Units	Total			
3	Book Title	Price	Sold	Sales			

BOOKS / Sheet2 / Sheet3 / Sheet4 / Sheet5 / Sheet6

SALES.XLS

	A	B	C	D	E	F	G	H
1	Total Sales							
2								
3	Item	Units	Sales					

SALES / Sheet2 / Sheet3 / Sheet4 / Sheet5 / Sheet6 / Sheet7 / Sheet8 / Sheet9 / Sheet10 / Sheet

TAPES.XLS

	A	B	C	D	E	F	G
1	Tape Sales						
2				Units	Total		
3	Tape	Type	Price	Sold	Sales		
4	The Rough-Faced Girl	Video	$ 22.95	97	$ 2,866.65		

TAPES / Sheet2 / Sheet3 / Sheet4 / Sheet5 / Sheet6 / Sheet7 / Sheet8 / Sheet9 / Sheet10 / Sheet

(b)

BOOKS.XLS

	A
1	Book Sales
2	
3	Book Title
4	The Rough-Faced Girl
5	Will's Mammoth
6	Foolish Rabbit's Mistake
7	The Hungry Tigress
8	Totals
9	
10	
11	
12	
13	
14	
15	
16	
17	

BOOKS

SALES.XLS

	A	B
1	Total Sales	
2		
3	Item	Units
4	Books	
5	Tapes	
6	Total:	-
7		
8		
9		
10		
11		
12		
13		
14		
15		
16		
17		

SALES / Sheet2 / Shee

TAPES.XLS

	A
1	Tape Sales
2	
3	Tape
4	The Rough-Faced Girl
5	Will's Mammoth
6	Three Little Pigs
7	The Wooly Mammoth
8	Japanese Ghost Stories
9	Foolish Rabbit's Mistake
10	Total Sales
11	
12	
13	
14	
15	
16	
17	

TAPES / Sheet2 / Shee

(c)

CHAPTER 3 ADVANCED SPREADSHEETS **SS203**

FIGURE SS3-30 ■ *(continued)*

(d) Cascade.

	TAPES.XLS						
	SALES.XLS						
	BOOKS.XLS						
	A	**B**	**C**	**D**	**E**	**F**	**G**
1	Book Sales						
2		Book	Units	Total			
3	Book Title	Price	Sold	Sales			
4	The Rough-Faced Girl	$ 16.95	25	$ 423.75			
5	Will's Mammoth	14.95	76	1,136.20			
6	Foolish Rabbit's Mistake	12.00	15	180.00			
7	The Hungry Tigress	16.00	67	1,072.00			
8	Totals		183	$ 2,811.95			
9							
10							
11							
12							
13							
14							
15							

BOOKS / Sheet2 / Sheet3 / Sheet4 / Sheet5 / Sh

(d)

Your Excel workspace should now be blank.

> Tip: To make a window active, simply click its title bar. To move a window by mouse, drag its title bar.

RESIZING WINDOWS

Any workbook window can be resized within Excel's workspace. Resizing is helpful when using multiple windows to display the desired content of each window. Standard Windows resizing commands include *Restore*—resize to a previous size or to a smaller window, *Minimize*—shrink to an icon, and *Maximize*—enlarge to maximum size. A window may also be resized to a custom size. When resizing with the keyboard, you must use the window's control menu.

> Tip: The following resizing techniques can also be used to resize an application window (for example, the Excel window).

STANDARD WINDOW RESIZING. Try the following to resize the BOOKS workbook window:

1. **Open the *BOOKS* workbook**

SS204 SPREADSHEETS WITH MICROSOFT EXCEL 5.0

If the BOOKS workbook is less than full size, *not* occupying Excel's entire workspace, do Step 2. Otherwise, go to Step 3.

MOUSE APPROACH	KEYBOARD APPROACH
2. **If needed, click the BOOKS window *maximize* button (located at the top right corner of window)**	2. **If needed, press** `Ctrl` + `F10` **to maximize the BOOKS window**
3. **Click the workbook window's *restore* button (located on the right side of the menu bar)**	3. **Press** `Ctrl` + `F5`

The BOOKS window should appear as a smaller window as in Figure SS3-31a. (The

---

FIGURE SS3-31 ■ **RESIZING A WORKSHEET WINDOW**

(a) The *Restore* command reduces the size of a maximized window.

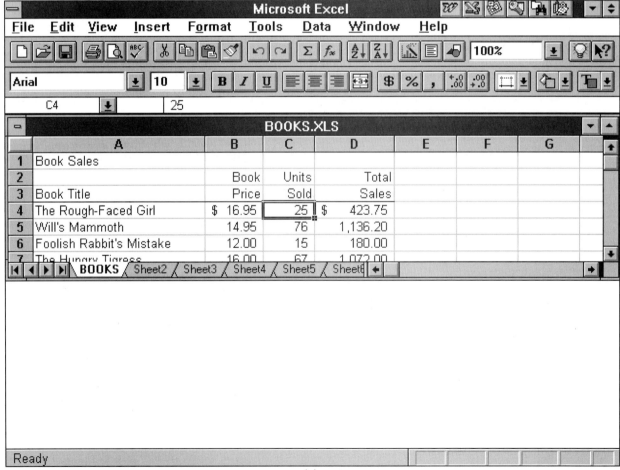

(a)

CHAPTER 3   ADVANCED SPREADSHEETS   SS205

size of your window may differ.) Note that it now has its own title bar and two resizing buttons (top right).

MOUSE APPROACH	KEYBOARD APPROACH
4. Click the workbook window's *minimize* button	4. Press Ctrl + F9

The BOOKS file should now appear as an icon at the bottom left of Excel's workspace as in Figure SS3-31b. To return the worksheet to its maximum size,

MOUSE APPROACH	KEYBOARD APPROACH
5. Click the *BOOKS.XLS* icon and then *Maximize*	5. Press Ctrl + F10

Tip: Double-clicking a workbook icon or a window's title bar will also resize it.

CUSTOM WINDOW RESIZING. Windows may be resized to a desired size. Try the following to custom-resize the BOOKS window as shown in Figure SS3-31c:

1. Open the *BOOKS* file, if needed

MOUSE APPROACH	KEYBOARD APPROACH
2. Click the workbook window's *restore* button to reduce the window's size (on the right side of menu bar)	2. Press Ctrl + F5 to reduce the window's size
3. Point slowly to the right window wall until the mouse pointer changes to a horizontal pointer with two arrows on each side	3. Press Ctrl + F8 for the cross-arrow pointer

FIGURE SS3-31 ■ *(continued)*

(b) The *Minimize* command reduces the window to an icon. (c) This is a custom-resized window.

(b)

(c)

4. Drag the right wall's outline to the left and stop just after the "S" in ".XLS" in the title bar

5. Drop (release mouse button) the right wall's outline to complete the resizing

4. Press → to move the cross arrow to the right wall (the pointer now changes its shape to a horizontal pointer with two arrows on each side)

5. Press ← until the right wall outline is just after the "S" in ".XLS" in the title bar and then press ↵ to complete the resizing

The BOOKS window should resemble Figure SS3-31c.

6. **Maximize the window and then close it without saving**

> Tip: To resize the entire window, slowly point to either bottom corner of the window until the pointer changes to a diagonal pointer with two arrows at each end. Then drag the corner in or out.

MANIPULATING DATA BETWEEN WORKBOOKS

Now that you have learned how to manipulate workbook windows on your screen, you are ready to perform data transfers between files. These transfers will include copying, moving, combining, and linking data from one workbook to another.

COPYING DATA. The commands to copy data from one workbook to another are similar to those for copying cell data from one range to another. The main difference is that the destination of the copied data is in another workbook. Try this to copy the NAME and then the GRADE columns of the GRADES file onto two new worksheet files:

1. Open the *GRADES* workbook

2. Move to Cell B3

3. Select the range B3:B10

MOUSE APPROACH	KEYBOARD APPROACH
4. Click *Edit*, *Copy* to copy the selected range to the Clipboard	4. Press Ctrl + C to copy
5. Click *File*, *New* for a new workbook window (file)	5. Press Ctrl + N for a new workbook window (file)
6. Click *Edit*, *Paste*	6. Press Ctrl + V to paste
7. Move to Cell B1	

> Tip: To move data from one file to another, replace Step 4 with Edit and Cut (or the Ctrl and X keys).

8. Save this workbook as *NAMES*

Your NAMES window should resemble Figure SS3-32a. Note that the GRADES window is currently hidden behind the NAMES1 workbook. To switch back to the GRADES window, copy the GRADES column, and then paste it to a new workbook,

CHAPTER 3   ADVANCED SPREADSHEETS   SS207

FIGURE SS3-32 ■ **COPYING DATA BETWEEN WORKBOOKS**

(a) The Copy and Paste commands (Edit menu) were used to copy this text to a new workbook. (b) The Values option of the Paste Special dialog box was used to copy the formulas from the GRADES workbook to Column B of the new workbook.

	A	B	C
1	STUDENT		
2	Jerry		
3	Elissa		
4	Andrea		
5	Edward		
6	Charles		
7	Rita		
8	Lesley		
9			
10			

(a)

	A	B	C
1	STUDENT	GRADE	
2	Jerry	C	
3	Elissa	A	
4	Andrea	A	
5	Edward	D	
6	Charles	B	
7	Rita	B	
8	Lesley	C	
9			
10			

(b)

MOUSE APPROACH	KEYBOARD APPROACH
9. Click *Window, 2 GRADES.XLS*	9. Press Ctrl + F6
10. Click *Cell F3*	10. Move to *Cell F3*
11. Select the range F3:F10	11. Select the range F3:F10
12. Click *Edit, Copy*	12. Press Ctrl + C to copy
13. Click *Window, 1 NAMES.XLS*	13. Press Ctrl + F6

Since the grades in the range F4:F10 were originally entered as formulas, they can be transferred to the new worksheet as formulas or values. To copy them as values,

MOUSE APPROACH	KEYBOARD APPROACH
14. Click *Edit, Paste Special* for its dialog box	14. Press Alt + E , S for the Paste Special dialog box
15. Click *Values, OK*	15. Press Alt + V then ↵
16. Move to Cell A1	
17. Save this workbook again as *NAMES*	

The NAMES file should resemble Figure SS3-32b.

SS208 SPREADSHEETS WITH MICROSOFT EXCEL 5.0

18. Close any open workbook

> **Tip:** Tiling the source and destination worksheet windows before copying may make the copy process visually easier.

LINKING FILES. Excel also allows you to link values *between* workbooks; that is, cells in other workbooks (called *server cells*) can be connected to cells in the current workbooks (called *client cells*). As shown in Figure SS3-33, when server cells are linked to client cells, changes in the server file will automatically be reflected in the client file when it is opened—a useful technique when consolidating data from a number of workbooks.

The process of linking cells is similar to copying; however, instead of selecting *Paste*, you select **Paste Link.** This command automatically places a *linking formula* that refers to the server cell (source) in the client cell. (Note: These formulas can also be typed in.) The following exercise creates links between two server files (BOOKS and TAPES) shown in Figure SS3-34 and then the consolidated client file (SALES).

1. Open the *BOOKS* workbook and maximize it if needed
2. Move to Cell C8
3. Select the range C8:D8

MOUSE APPROACH	KEYBOARD APPROACH
4. Click *Edit*, *Copy* to copy the range C8:D8 to the Clipboard	4. Press `Ctrl` + `C` to copy the range C8:D8 to the Clipboard

5. Open the *SALES* workbook
6. Change Column C's width to 12
7. Move to Cell B4

FIGURE SS3-33 ■ LINKING FILES

Changes in the server *cells* are automatically reflected in the client cells.

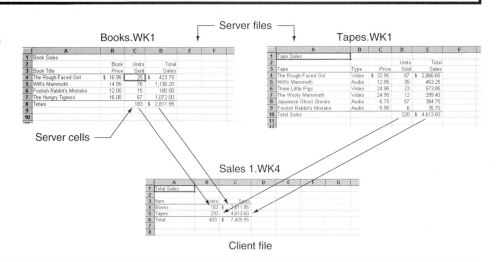

CHAPTER 3 ADVANCED SPREADSHEETS SS209

MOUSE APPROACH	KEYBOARD APPROACH
8. Click *Edit*, Paste *Special*, Paste *Link*	8. Press Alt + E , S , Alt + L

This links Cells C8 and D8 in the BOOKS file to Cells B4 and C4 in the SALES file by pasting linking formulas. As shown in Figure SS3-34a, the total for units and sales from the BOOKS file immediately appears.

9. Open the *TAPES* workbook
10. Move to Cell D10
11. Select the range D10:E10

MOUSE APPROACH	KEYBOARD APPROACH
12. Click *Edit*, *Copy*	12. Press Ctrl + C
13. Click *Window* and then *2 SALES.XLS* to switch to it	13. Press Ctrl + F6 to switch to the SALES window
14. Click Cell B5	14. Move to Cell B5
15. Click *Edit*, Paste *Special*, Paste *Link*	15. Press Alt + E , S , Alt + L

FIGURE SS3-34 ■ CREATING LINKS

(a) The link to the BOOKS file has been established in Cell B4 of the SALES file. (b) This is the completed file with all links.

B4   {=[BOOKS.XLS]BOOKS!$C$8:$D$8}

	A	B	C	D	E
1	Total Sales				
2					
3	Item	Units	Sales		
4	Books	183	2811.95		
5	Tapes				
6	Total:	183	$ 2,811.95		
7					
8					

(a)

C5   {=[TAPES.XLS]TAPES!$D$10:$E$10}

	A	B	C	D	E
1	Total Sales				
2					
3	Item	Units	Sales		
4	Books	183	$ 2,811.95		
5	Tapes	220	4,613.60		
6	Total:	403	$ 7,425.55		
7					
8					

(b)

SS210 **SPREADSHEETS WITH MICROSOFT EXCEL 5.0**

16. **Format Column C to resemble Figure SS3-34b (accounting-currency, two decimals in Cell C4 and accounting-comma, two decimals in Cell C5)**

As shown in Figure SS3-34b, these link formulas have brought data from the two server workbooks into the consolidation, where they are totaled and formatted.

17. **Move to Cell A1**

18. **Save this workbook as *SALES1***

To see the link effect, make the following change to the BOOKS worksheet:

19. **Switch to the *BOOKS* window**

Remember, use the *Window* menu or press the Ctrl and F6 keys.

20. **In Cell C4, type 86 and press ↵**

Your worksheet should resemble Figure SS3-35a.

21. **Resave the workbook as *BOOKS1***

22. **Switch to the *SALES1* window**

Your worksheet should resemble Figure SS3-35b, the linked cells in Row 4 reflect the changes in the BOOKS window.

FIGURE SS3-35 ■ LINKED WORKSHEET FILES

(a) Changes are made in the server worksheet. (b) These changes are automatically transferred to the client worksheet.

	A	B	C	D	E
1	Book Sales				
2		Book	Units	Total	
3	Book Title	Price	Sold	Sales	
4	The Rough-Faced Girl	$ 16.95	86	$ 1,457.70	
5	Will's Mammoth	14.95	76	1,136.20	
6	Foolish Rabbit's Mistake	12.00	15	180.00	
7	The Hungry Tigress	16.00	67	1,072.00	
8	Totals		244	$ 3,845.90	
9					
10					

(a)

	A	B	C	D	E
1	Total Sales				
2					
3	Item	Units	Sales		
4	Books	244	$ 3,845.90		
5	Tapes	220	4,613.60		
6	Total:	464	$ 8,459.50		
7					
8					

(b)

CHAPTER 3   ADVANCED SPREADSHEETS   SS211

22. **Close all the workbooks without saving**

> Tip: When working with more than one worksheet window, you may use the *Tile* or *Cascade* command to view the files more easily.

Objects (pictures) may also be linked among workbooks. In addition, Excel files may be linked to other application files. See the appendix for these operations.

CHECKPOINT

✓ Open any three workbooks and apply each Arrange command (Window menu).

✓ Open the TAPES workbook and resize it to an icon and back to a window.

✓ Use the GRADES workbook. Copy Column C to a workbook named TEST1.

✓ In the GRADES workbook, insert a column between TEST 2 and AVERAGE. Combine the TEST1 workbook into this Column. Do not save.

✓ Change the link formulas in the SALES1 workbook window to retrieve the appropriate numbers for WILL'S MAMMOTH only, not the totals from the server files. Do not save.

MODULE 6: USING MULTIPLE SHEETS

Until now, you have been working with only one sheet in a workbook. A *sheet,* as discussed earlier, may contain a worksheet, chart or other information. Sheets are similar to pages in a book. Each new workbook opens with 16 sheets. Excel allows you to create up to 239 more sheets (or 255 sheets in total) in a workbook.

Using multiple sheets in a single workbook lets you keep a set of related worksheets together. For example, a budget workbook may use 13 sheets: a summary sheet and one worksheet for each month.

To prepare for the exercises in this section,

1. **Close any open workbook**

2. **Open the *SHEET2* workbook (created in Chapter 1)**

USING SHEET TABS

Sheet tabs appear at the bottom of a workbook window, as in Figure SS3-36a. Sheet tabs can be used to switch to another sheet. They are used to identify a sheet and can be renamed.

Although a workbook opens with 16 sheets, only six sheet tabs (you can identify them on Sheets 1 through 6) are currently visible in the sheet-tab view area. To view other sheet tabs in a workbook, use the *tab-scrolling* buttons (left of the tab-viewing area). You can also enlarge the tab-viewing area by dragging the *tab-split* bar.

SWITCHING BETWEEN SHEETS.   Clicking a sheet tab will switch to that sheet and make it active. Try this,

MOUSE APPROACH	KEYBOARD APPROACH
1. **Click the *Sheet 3* tab**	1. **Press `Ctrl` + `PgDn` twice**

FIGURE SS3-36 ■ SHEET TABS

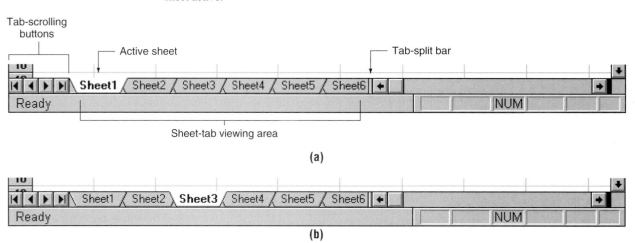

(a) Sheet tabs are located at the bottom of the workbook. (b) Clicking a sheet tab makes that sheet active.

Sheet 3 will appear on top as in Figure SS3-36b. Now to move back to Sheet 1.

MOUSE APPROACH	KEYBOARD APPROACH
2. Click the *Sheet 1* tab	2. Press Ctrl + PgUp twice

NAMING SHEET TABS. Each sheet can be assigned a name with up to 31 characters on its tab. To assign a name to a tab,

MOUSE APPROACH

1. Double-click *Sheet 1*'s tab
2. Type Total Regions and click OK
3. Double-click *Sheet 2*'s tab
4. Type Region A and click OK
5. Double-click *Sheet 3*'s tab

KEYBOARD APPROACH

1. Press Alt + O, H, R for the Rename Sheet dialog box
2. Type Total Regions
3. Press Ctrl + PgDn, Alt + O, H, R to move the Sheet 2 tab and rename it
4. Type Region A
5. Press Ctrl + PgDn, Alt + O, H, R to move the Sheet 3 tab and rename it

6. Type Region B and press ↵
7. Switch to the Total Regions Sheet and move to Cell A1
8. Save this workbook as *REGIONS1*

Your sheet tabs should now resemble those in Figure SS3-37.

CHAPTER 3   ADVANCED SPREADSHEETS   SS213

FIGURE SS3-37 ■ RENAMING SHEET TABS

Sheet tabs from Sheets 1 through 3 have been renamed using the Rename Sheet dialog box.

SHEET TAB SCROLLING. Tab-scrolling buttons are used to view tabs not currently visible in the sheet-tab viewing area. These buttons are accessible only by mouse. As indicated in Figure SS3-38a, there are four tab-scrolling buttons: First Tab, Previous Tab, Next Tab, and Last Tab. Try this to quickly view the last sheet tabs.

1. Click the *Last Tab* scroll button

Your tab-viewing area now displays Sheets 12 through 16, as in Figure SS3-38b. Note that the active sheet has not changed. To change the active sheet, click the desired sheet tab. For example,

2. Click *Sheet 15*'s tab to make it active

3. Now, click the *Previous Tab* button to one tab to the left

FIGURE SS3-38 ■ SHEET-TAB SCROLLING

(a) Tab-scrolling buttons can be used to view different sheet tabs in the sheet-tab viewing area.
(b) Clicking the Last Tab scroll button moves the view to the last tabs in the workbook.
(c) Clicking the Previous Tab scroll button moves the view one tab to the left.

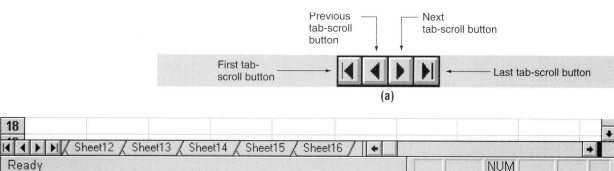

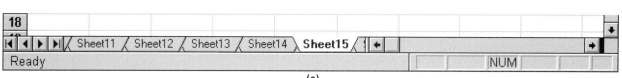

Your tab-viewing area should resemble Figure SS3-38c. To return to the Total Regions sheet (Sheet 1),

4. **Click the** *First Tab* **scroll button**

5. **Click** *Total Regions* **tab**

> Tip: The sheet-tab viewing area can also be enlarged by dragging the tab split bar to the right or reduced by dragging the bar to the left.

MANIPULATING DATA BETWEEN SHEETS

You can copy, move, or link data from one sheet to another just as from one worksheet file to another. In the following exercise, you will create the Region A and Region B sheets from the data in the Total Regions sheet and then link them.

COPYING DATA. To copy data from one sheet to another, you use the same commands as for copying data from one file to another. The only difference is the copied data's destination—another worksheet.

1. **Open the** *REGIONS1* **workbook if needed**
2. **Move to Cell A3**
3. **Select the range A3:B10**

FIGURE SS3-39 ■ **COPYING DATA FROM ONE WORKSHEET TO ANOTHER**

(a) Range A3:B10 has been copied from the Total Regions sheet to the A1:B8 range of the Region A sheet.

	A	B
1	Agent	Region A
2		
3	Michaels	500
4	Martin	200
5	Parker	300
6	Williams	50
7		
8	Totals	1050

Total Regions \ Region A / Re

(a)

CHAPTER 3   ADVANCED SPREADSHEETS   SS215

MOUSE APPROACH	KEYBOARD APPROACH

4. Click *Edit*, *Copy*

5. Click the *Region A* sheet tab

6. Click *Edit*, *Paste*

7. Move to Cell A1

4. Press Ctrl + C

5. Press Ctrl + PgDn to move to the Region A sheet

6. Press Ctrl + V

Your Region A sheet should resemble Figure SS3-39a. Now copy ranges A3:A10 and C3:C10 to the Region B sheet.

> Tip: To move data from one sheet to another, replace Step 4 with *Edit* and then *Cut* (or the Ctrl and X keys).

MOUSE APPROACH	KEYBOARD APPROACH

7. Click the *Total Regions* sheet tab

8. Select the range A3:A10

9. Click *Edit*, *Copy*

7. Press Ctrl + PgUp to return to the Total Regions sheet

8. Select the range A3:A10

9. Press Ctrl + C

FIGURE SS3-39 ■ *(continued)*

(b) Ranges A3:A10 and C3:C10 have been copied from the Total Regions worksheet to the A1:A8 and B1:B8 ranges of the Region B worksheet.

	A	B	C	D
1	Agent	Region B		
2				
3	Michaels	200		
4	Martin	450		
5	Parker	325		
6	Williams	125		
7				
8	Totals	1100		

Total Regions / Region A \ **Region B** /

(b)

10. Click the *Region B* sheet tab
11. Click *Edit, Paste*
12. Click the *Total Regions* sheet tab
13. Select the range C3:C10
14. Click *Edit, Copy*
15. Click the *Region B* sheet tab
16. Click *Cell B1*
17. Click *Edit, Paste*

10. Press Ctrl + PgDn twice to move to the Region B sheet
11. Press Ctrl + V to paste
12. Press Ctrl + PgUp twice to return to the Total Regions sheet
13. Select the range C3:C10
14. Press Ctrl + C
15. Press Ctrl + PgUp twice to move to the Region B sheet
16. Move to Cell B1
17. Press Ctrl + V to paste

18. Move to Cell B1
19. Resave this workbook as REGIONS1

The Agent and Region B data columns have now been copied to the Region B sheet as shown in Figure SS3-39b.

> Tip: To copy formulas as values, use the *Paste Special* command instead of the *Paste* command in Step 17.

LINKING SHEETS. The procedures to link values between sheet cells are similar to those for copying worksheet cells, except you use the *Paste Link* command instead of the *Paste* command. Remember, the *Paste Link* command connects cells in other sheets (called *server cells*) to the current sheet. Changes in the server sheet will automatically be reflected in the client sheet.

The next exercise uses the Region A and Region B sheets as servers and the Total Regions sheet as the client.

1. Move to the Total Regions sheet
2. Delete data in the range B5:C8
3. Move to Cell B5

The cells in range B5:C8 should now be empty, as shown in Figure SS3-40a. Also note that the totals show "0," because they are formulas that use the data in the range B5:C8.

4. Move to the Region A sheet
5. Move to Cell B3
6. Select the range B3:B6

MOUSE APPROACH

7. Click *Edit, Copy*
8. Click the *Total Regions* sheet tab

KEYBOARD APPROACH

7. Press Ctrl + C
8. Press Ctrl + Home to move back to the Total Regions sheet

CHAPTER 3   ADVANCED SPREADSHEETS   **SS217**

FIGURE SS3-40 ■ **LINKING SHEETS**

(a) The data in the range B5:C8 have been removed for the linking exercise.
(b) The range B3:B6 has been copied from the Region A sheet (server) to the B5:B8 range of the Total Regions sheet (client).

	A	B	C	D	E	F
1	Your Name				M/D/YY	
2						
3	Agent	Region A	Region B	Totals		
4						
5	Michaels			0		
6	Martin			0		
7	Parker			0		
8	Williams			0		
9						
10	Totals	0	0	0		
11						
12						
13						
14						
15						
16						
17						
18						

Total Regions / Region A / Region B / Sheet4 / Shee

(a)

B5   {='Region A'!$B$3:$B$6}

	A	B	C	D	E	F
1	Your Name				M/D/YY	
2						
3	Agent	Region A		Totals		
4						
5	Michaels	500		500		
6	Martin	200		200		
7	Parker	300		300		
8	Williams	50		50		
9						
10	Totals	1050	0	1050		
11						
12						
13						
14						
15						
16						
17						
18						

Total Regions / Region A / Region B / Sheet4 / Shee

(b)

(continued)

SS218 | SPREADSHEETS WITH MICROSOFT EXCEL 5.0

> **FIGURE SS3-40** ■ *(continued)*

(c) This is the complete linked client sheet.

	A	B	C	D	E	F
1	Your Name				M/D/YY	
2						
3	Agent	Region A	Region B	Totals		
4						
5	Michaels	500	200	700		
6	Martin	200	450	650		
7	Parker	300	325	625		
8	Williams	50	125	175		
9						
10	Totals	1050	1100	2150		
11						
12						
13						
14						
15						
16						
17						
18						

◄ ◄ ► ►◄ **Total Regions** / Region A / Region B / Sheet4 / Shee ◄

(c)

---

9. Click *Cell B5*	9. Move to Cell B5
10. Click *Edit, Paste Special, Paste Link*	10. Press **Alt** + **E** , **S** , **Alt** + **L** *Paste Link*

Your Total Regions sheet should resemble Figure SS3-40b. Note that the totals automatically update. Note also that the formula in Cell B5 (formula bar) has the sheet reference 'Region A'1 to indicate its linked source.

11. Using the same techniques, copy and paste link range B3:B6 of the Region B sheet to range C5:C8 of the Total Regions sheet

12. Move to Cell A1

Your final linked Total Region sheet should resemble Figure SS3-40c.

13. Save this workbook as *REGIONS2*

To see the linked effect, make the following changes to the Region B sheet,

14. Switch to the Region B sheet

15. In Cell B3, type 400 **and press** ↵

16. Switch to the Total Regions sheet

Your Total Regions sheet has been automatically updated as in Figure SS3-40d.

17. Save this workbook as REGIONS3 and then close it

CHAPTER 3　　ADVANCED SPREADSHEETS　　**SS219**

FIGURE SS3-40 ■ *(continued)*

(d) Changes in server sheet (Region B) is automatically reflected in the client sheet (Total Regions).

	A	B	C	D	E	F
1	Your Name				M/D/YY	
2						
3	Agent	Region A	Region B	Totals		
4						
5	Michaels	500	400	900		
6	Martin	200	450	650		
7	Parker	300	325	625		
8	Williams	50	125	175		
9						
10	Totals	1050	1300	2350		
11						
12						
13						
14						
15						
16						
17						
18						

Total Regions / Region A / Region B / Sheet4 / Shee

(d)

CHECKPOINT

✓ Open the GADGETS workbook, and then save it as BUDGET1.

✓ Name Sheet 1 "1st Quarter," Sheet 2 "January," Sheet 3 "February," and Sheet 4 "March."

✓ Copy the item name and corresponding monthly-sales data from the 1st Quarter worksheet into each respective month's worksheet. Save the workbook as *BUDGET2*.

✓ Delete the data in the range B4:D7 in the 1st Quarter sheet. Use the Paste Link command to insert linking formulas to place and link data from the January, February and March sheets into the 1st Quarter sheet. Save the workbook as *BUDGET3*.

✓ Change some of the data in the February sheet and switch to the 1st Quarter sheet to see the changes.

MODULE 7: PROTECTING THE SPREADSHEET

Computers follow your *instructions,* not your *intentions.* All too often, formulas or functions are mistakenly erased, replaced, or copied over. Lookup tables, macros, and databases (usually placed off-screen) are accidentally deleted or destroyed. Although the *Undo* feature allows you to cancel immediate mistakes, it is not useful for mistakes that go unnoticed—especially when other people use your spreadsheet. One way to prevent many of these mishaps is to "protect" cells.

Cells can be protected with a two-step process: (1) cells in which changes may occur must be marked unprotected, and then (2) the *Protection* feature must be turned on.

SETTING THE UNPROTECTED RANGE

Before you turn on the protection feature, you must specify which should remain unprotected. Unprotected cells allow changes after the protection feature is on. To designate the C4:D10 range of the GRADES worksheet to be unprotected,

1. Open the *GRADES* workbook
2. Move to Cell C4
3. Select the range C4:D10

MOUSE APPROACH	KEYBOARD APPROACH
4. Click *Format, Cells, Protection* tab	4. Press Ctrl + 1 , P , →
5. Click the *Locked* check box to remove the "X"	5. Press Alt + L to remove the "X" in the Locked check box

The Locked check box should be empty as in Figure SS3-41.

MOUSE APPROACH	KEYBOARD APPROACH
6. Click the *OK* button	6. Press ↵

FIGURE SS3-41 ■ PROTECTION TAB

The Protection tab is used to remove protection from specific ranges of cells after a sheet or workbook is protected.

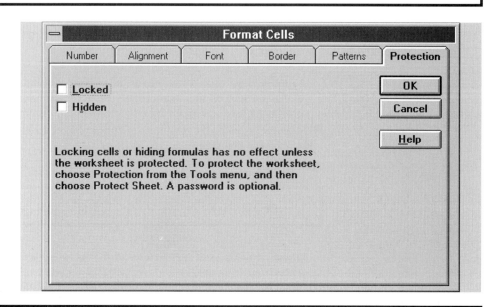

CHAPTER 3   ADVANCED SPREADSHEETS   SS221

7. Move to Cell B6

8. Save this workbook as *PROTECT1*

The unprotected cell range has now been set.

ACTIVATING THE PROTECTION FEATURE

Excel's **protection feature** can be activated on a sheet or workbook. When on, only cells that were specified as unprotected prior to its activation will be available for change. Try this,

1. Open the *PROTECT1* workbook, if needed

MOUSE APPROACH	KEYBOARD APPROACH
2. Click *Tools, Protection, Protect Sheet* for its dialog box	2. Press Alt + T , P , P for the *Protect* sheet dialog box

Your *Protect* sheet dialog box should resemble Figure SS3-42.

At this point, you may assign an optional password by typing it into the Password text box. You may also restrict the protection to just the Contents, Objects or Scenarios of the sheet or workbook by removing the "X" from the respective check boxes. For now, to close the dialog box without a password and turn on the protection feature,

MOUSE APPROACH	KEYBOARD APPROACH
3. Click the *OK* button	3. Press ↵

All cells except for the ones designated earlier as unprotected are protected.

4. Move to Cell B6—the ANDREA entry

5. Try typing Meryl

A dialog box with the message "Locked cells cannot be changed." will appear. A locked cell is a protected cell.

MOUSE APPROACH	KEYBOARD APPROACH
6. Click the *OK* button to remove the dialog box	6. Press ↵ to remove the dialog box

---

FIGURE SS3-42 ■ **THE PROTECTION FEATURE**

The Protection Sheet command (Protection Submenu, Tools menu) can be used to turn on the protection feature, assign a password, and restrict the protection.

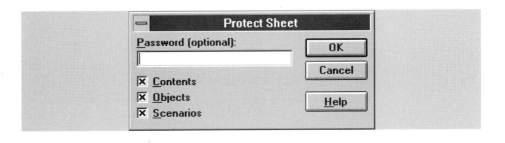

7. **Move to Cell D8**

8. **Type** `100` **and then press** `↵`

Note that AVERAGE and GRADE cells still automatically update. The protection feature protects the formulas in these cells from being altered. It does not affect their operations.

9. **Save this workbook as *PROTECT2* and then close it**

> **Tip: To make a change in a protected cell, you must first turn off the protection feature by selecting *Tools, Protection, Unprotect sheet* or *Unprotect Workbook*. Make the desired change and then turn on the protection feature again.**

A final word about protection: The *Protection* tab (format cells dialog box) simply allows you to identify those cells that are exempt from protection. The *Protect* sheet or Protect workbook dialog box (tools menu) allows you to protect the entire file except for those cells identified as unprotected with the *Protection* tab. Both commands are needed to invoke protection. Adding a password when invoking the protection feature may strengthen the protection form.

CHECKPOINT

✓ What does the protection feature do?
✓ How do you unprotect a range of cells?
✓ Open the GRADES workbook and unprotect the range of cells in C4:D10.
✓ Turn the *Protection* feature on and change a few grades in the unprotected range.
✓ Change "Rita" in Column A to "Karen" (you will have to disable the protection feature first, then enable it).

MODULE 8: SHARING DATA AMONG APPLICATIONS

You may want to move data from Excel to another software package, such as a database-management or word-processor program. Conversely, you may want to move data prepared in another program into Excel. Fortunately, there is a way to translate data into other software formats.

EXPORTING AND IMPORTING

Export and *import* commands facilitate data transfer by converting data into formats that can be read by other software packages. **Exporting** *saves* data in another format; **importing** *opens* data that have been saved in another format.

DIRECT CONVERSION. The easiest way to share data is to translate them into a form that another program can readily understand. For example, a spreadsheet can be converted directly into a database file, or vice versa. Some slight adjustments may have to be made, but those are usually minimal. Typically, direct conversions are offered for the most popular software packages.

CHAPTER 3 ADVANCED SPREADSHEETS **SS223**

ASCII—A COMMON DENOMINATOR. When direct conversion is not available, *ASCII* conversion may still allow data transfer. **ASCII** (pronounced "ask-key") stands for the "American Standard Code for Information Interchange." It is one of a few standard formats adopted by the computer industry for representing typed characters. ASCII eliminates the symbols unique to each software package, providing a common style for sharing data.

EXPORTING DATA FROM EXCEL

The following exercises export data from the BOOKS workbook into forms that can be read by a variety of word-processing and database applications.

1. **Start Excel and change the default drive to A**

2. **Open the *BOOKS* workbook**

Your screen should resemble Figure SS3-43.

EXPORTING AN ASCII FILE TO A WORD PROCESSOR. To save a worksheet as an ASCII file, the extension ".TXT" should be added to the file name when saving with the *Save As* dialog box. Spreadsheet data that are saved in ASCII format can be read directly by many word-processing programs. This exercise creates an ASCII file called BOOKS.TXT.

MOUSE APPROACH	KEYBOARD APPROACH
1. Click *File, Save As* for its dialog box	1. Press **F12** for the Save As dialog box.
2. Type BOOKS in the File Name text box	2. Type BOOKS in the File Name text box
3. Click the **↓** button of the *Save File as Type* drop-down box	3. Press **Alt** + **T** for the Save File as Type dialog box
4. Click *use the scroll bar* to scroll to *Text(OS/2 or MS-DOS)* and click it	4. Use the arrow keys to select *Text(OS/2 or MS-DOS)* and press **↵**

FIGURE SS3-43 ■ THE BOOKS WORKSHEET

	A	B	C	D	E
1	Book Sales				
2		Book	Units	Total	
3	Book Title	Price	Sold	Sales	
4	The Rough-Faced Girl	$ 16.95	25	$ 423.75	
5	Will's Mammoth	14.95	76	1,136.20	
6	Foolish Rabbit's Mistake	12.00	15	180.00	
7	The Hungry Tigress	16.00	67	1,072.00	
8	Totals		183	$ 2,811.95	
9					
10					

Note that the extension ".txt" is automatically added to the workbook name in the File Name text box.

MOUSE APPROACH	KEYBOARD APPROACH
5. Click *OK, OK*	5. Press ⏎ , ⏎
6. Close the workbook	

The BOOKS.TXT file has now been saved on your disk as an ASCII file. It can be read by WordPerfect or other word processing programs.

GENERAL EXPORTING TO A DATABASE.   Excel files can be exported to a variety of database file types using the Save File as Type drop-down box (Save As dialog box). In many cases, the data in the worksheet must first be placed into columnar form as discussed in the next section. Those database file types that are not available through the Save File as Type drop-down box, may require the file to be saved in ASCII format (Text).

DATA IN COLUMNAR FORM.   Before worksheets can be copied into ASCII files for database use, all numeric data must be free of dollar signs and commas.

1. Open the *BOOKS.XLS* workbook

2. Change Column B's format to "0.00-number, 2 decimals" (select the range B4:B7, then select *Format, Cells, Number* tab, *Number, 0.00*)

3. Change Column D's format to "number 2 decimals" (use the range D4:D7)

ASCII files intended for database use can contain only records. Titles, summary rows, and underlining must be omitted (or deleted) for the save range before the worksheet is saved in ASCII format. In this case, we'll save only Rows 4 through 7.

4. Delete Rows 1, 2 and 3

5. Delete Row 5

6. Remove the border line at the bottom of Cells A4:D4 (*Format, Cells, Border* tab, *Bottom, OK*)

7. Move to Cell A1

Your worksheet should resemble Figure SS3-44.

MOUSE APPROACH	KEYBOARD APPROACH
8. Click *File, Save As*	8. Press F12 for the Save As dialog box
9. Type BOOKS1	9. Type BOOKS1
10. Click the ⬇ button of the *Save File as Type* drop-down box	10. Press Alt + T for the Save File as Type drop-down box
11. Use the scroll bar to locate *Text (OS/2 or MS-DOS)* and then click it	11. Use the arrow keys to select *Text (OS/2 or MS-DOS)* and then press ⏎
12. Click *OK, OK* to save as an ASCII file	12. Press ⏎ , ⏎ to save as an ASCII file

CHAPTER 3   ADVANCED SPREADSHEETS   SS225

FIGURE SS3-44 ■ EXPORTING TO AN ASCII FILE

The title and total rows have been deleted to prepare the worksheet to be saved as an ASCII file.

	A	B	C	D	E
1	The Rough-Faced Girl	16.95	25	423.75	
2	Will's Mammoth	14.95	76	1136.20	
3	Foolish Rabbit's Mistake	12.00	15	180.00	
4	The Hungry Tigress	16.00	67	1072.00	
5					
6					
7					

This file includes only the four rows that contain data as in Figure SS3-44 (the titles, border lines, and summary rows are omitted from the file). This ASCII file is now available to be read into an existing database file.

13. Close the workbook without saving

DIRECT DATABASE EXPORTING.   An Excel file can also be directly exported into a variety of database file types that are available through the Save File as Type drop-down box. When preparing a spreadsheet for a direct database conversion, you can leave in one row of titles. Type this,

1.   Open the *BOOKS.XLS* workbook

2.   Format the cells in Columns B and D to number, 2 decimals (0.00)

3.   Delete Rows 1, 2, and then 6

4.   Remove the border line at the bottom of Cells A1:D1, A5:D5 (*F*o*rmat, C*e*lls, Border* tab, *B*ottom, OK)

5.   Move to Cell A1

FIGURE SS3-45 ■ DIRECT DATABASE CONVERSION

Direct database exporting in Excel allows you to retain a one-line title row.

	A	B	C	D	E
1	Book Title	Price	Sold	Sales	
2	The Rough-Faced Girl	16.95	25	423.75	
3	Will's Mammoth	14.95	76	1136.20	
4	Foolish Rabbit's Mistake	12.00	15	180.00	
5	The Hungry Tigress	16.00	67	1072.00	
6					
7					
8					

Your worksheet should resemble Figure SS3-45. Note that a row of column titles is included in the worksheet.

MOUSE APPROACH	KEYBOARD APPROACH
6. Click *File, Save As*	6. Press `F12` for the Save As dialog box
7. Type `BOOKS2`	7. Type `BOOKS2`
8. Click the `▼` button of the *Save File as Type* drop-down box	8. Press `Alt` + `T` for the Save File as Type drop-down box
9. Use the scroll bar to locate *dBASEIV* and then click it	9. Use the arrow keys to select *dBASEIV* and then press `↵`
10. Click *OK, OK* to save as a dBASEIV file	10. Press `↵`, `↵` to save as a dBASEIV

Any database format available in the Save File as Type drop-down box can be selected in Step 9 above, if desired.

11. **Close the workbook without saving**

IMPORTING DATA INTO EXCEL

The following exercises show you how to import data from database and ASCII files into Excel.

IMPORTING AN ASCII FILE. ASCII text files can be read by Excel using an Open command. However, they remain as rows of text—they do not contain mathematical formulas or separate cell entries.

The worksheets that result may require formatting, changing of column width, or separating the data into distinct columns. The following exercise imports the BOOKS.TXT file and then alters it into a more usable form. To prepare for this exercise,

1. **Start Excel if needed**

MOUSE APPROACH	KEYBOARD APPROACH
2. Click *File, Open* for its dialog box (and switch to the A drive, if needed)	2. Press `Ctrl` + `O` for the *Open File* dialog box

Note that the BOOKS.TXT file does not appear in the *File Name* list box; only files with the extension ".XLS" appear. To display files in the list box with extensions other than ".XLS," you must use the *List Files of Type* drop-down box. This will be demonstrated under the Mouse Approach.

MOUSE APPROACH	KEYBOARD APPROACH
3. Click the `▼` button of the *List files of Type* drop-down box and then *Text (*.prn; *.txt; *.csv)* (The *File Name* list box now displays all files with the extension ".TXT")	3. Type `A:\BOOKS.TXT`
	4. Press `↵`
4. Click *books.txt* in the File Name list box and then the *OK* button	

CHAPTER 3   ADVANCED SPREADSHEETS   **SS227**

The Text Import Wizard-Step 1 of 3 dialog box appears as in Figure SS3-46a to assist you in importing your ASCII (text) file.

MOUSE APPROACH	KEYBOARD APPROACH
5. Click *Next>* to accept the default Original type of data and move to the Step 2 of 3 dialog box as in Figure SS3-46b	5. Press ↵ to accept the default Original type of data and move to the Step 2 of 3 dialog box as in Figure SS3-46b
6. Click *Next>* to accept the default delimiter settings and move to the Step 3 of 3 dialog box as in Figure SS3-46c	6. Press ↵ to accept the default delimiter settings and move to the Step 3 of 3 dialog box as in Figure SS3-46c
7. Click *Finish* to accept the default conversion column and data format	7. Press ↵ to accept the default conversion column and data format

8. Change Column A's width to 25 and Column D's width to 12
9. Add bottom border lines to Rows 3 and 7
10. Format Cells B5:B7 and D5:D7 with accounting-comma format-2 decimals
11. Format Cells B4, D4 and D8 with accounting-currency format-2 decimals
12. Move to Cell A1

FIGURE SS3-46 ■ THE TEXT IMPORT WIZARD

The Text Import Wizard is used to import an ASCII or other text file into Excel. (a) Step 1 allows you to select the file type for importing.

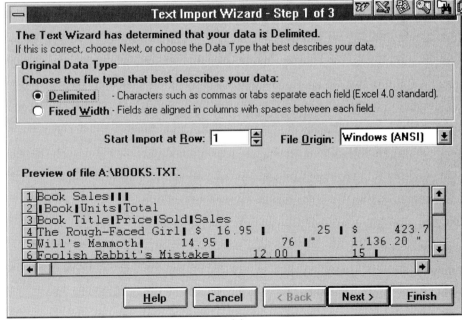

(a)

(continued)

| SS228 | **SPREADSHEETS WITH MICROSOFT EXCEL 5.0** |

FIGURE SS3-46 ■ *(continued)*

(b) Step 2 lets you specify the delimiters. (c) Step 3 allows you to select Column Data Format.

Text Import Wizard - Step 2 of 3

This screen lets you set the delimiters your data contains.
You can see how your text is affected in the preview below.

Delimiters
[X] Tab [ ] Semicolon [ ] Comma [ ] Treat consecutive delimiters as one
[ ] Space [ ] Other: [ ] Text Qualifier: ["]

Data Preview

Book Sales			
Book Title	Book Price	Units Sold	Total Sales
The Rough-Faced Girl	$ 16.95	25	$ 42
Will's Mammoth	14.95	76	1,13
Foolish Rabbit's Mistake	12.00	15	1

[Help] [Cancel] [< Back] [Next >] [Finish]

(b)

Text Import Wizard - Step 3 of 3

This screen lets you select each column and set the Data Format.

Column Data Format
(•) General
( ) Text
( ) Date: [MDY]
( ) Do Not Import Column (Skip)

'General' converts numeric values to numbers, date values to dates, and all remaining values to text.

Data Preview

General	General	General	General
Book Sales			
Book Title	Book Price	Units Sold	Total Sales
The Rough-Faced Girl	$ 16.95	25	$ 42
Will's Mammoth	14.95	76	1,13
Foolish Rabbit's Mistake	12.00	15	1

[Help] [Cancel] [< Back] [Next >] [Finish]

(c)

CHAPTER 3 ADVANCED SPREADSHEETS SS229

FIGURE SS3-47 ■ **THE IMPORTED DATABASE FILE**

	A	B	C	D	E
1	Book Sales				
2		Book	Units	Total	
3	Book Title	Price	Sold	Sales	
4	The Rough-Faced Girl	$ 16.95	25	$ 423.75	
5	Will's Mammoth	14.95	76	1,136.20	
6	Foolish Rabbit's Mistake	12.00	15	180.00	
7	The Hungry Tigress	16.00	67	1,072.00	
8	Totals		183	$ 2,811.95	
9					

---

13. Save the workbook as BOOKS3 (be sure the Save File as Type drop-down box indicates *Microsoft Excel Workbook* before saving)

Your worksheet should resemble Figure SS3-47.

14. Close the workbook and exit Excel

IMPORTING A DATABASE ".TXT" FILE. A ".TXT" file produced by a database program can be opened as any ASCII file. You may be able to use the worksheet as is, or you may have to use the Text Import Wizard to separate individual data columns or adjust formats and widths. You can try this technique with the BOOKS1.TXT file in the next Checkpoint exercise.

LINKING DATA FROM OTHER OFFICE APPLICATIONS

Typically, Excel is used in conjunction with other Microsoft Office applications, such as Word or Access. Office is known as a suite program—a set of separate applications that work together as if they were one large program. Some suite applications provide additional menus or toolbar buttons that let you easily transfer data to the other applications.

You have already learned some basic methods for sharing data among applications through ASCII files and file conversions. However, if you have other Office applications and a mouse, you can also use two additional techniques that allow you to combine data from different applications, namely, *linking* and *embedding*.

> Tip: Linking and embedding techniques will also work, for the most part, between any Windows programs.

OBJECT LINKING AND EMBEDDING. An **object** is a set of data. The term **OLE** (short for "Object Linking and Embedding") describes two options available for transferring data from one application to another.

Embedding copies objects from one application to another without changing the original. It is identical to copying except that it involves two applications. You might, for example, embed data from a Word document in an Excel worksheet.

Linking, on the other hand, establishes an ongoing connection between the application that provides the object (known as the *source*) and the one that receives it (the *destination*); and the destination is automatically updated. For example, if a Word object is linked with Excel, changes in the Word document will appear in the Excel worksheet.

> Note: Some programs perform linking or embedding through an approach known as DDE ("Dynamic Data Exchange").

Because you must have access to other Office programs to accomplish these tasks, a brief description of the process will be presented. You may want to try these techniques with the Word "EXWP3-6.DOC" file and any Excel workbook after you've learned how to use Word.

LINKING AN OBJECT. The following paragraphs describe how to link a block (selection) of data from the Word document "EXWP3-6.DOC" to an Excel workbook (named "EXCEL1"). The Excel workbook does not exist, but is used only for illustrative purposes. You can use a new workbook or any existing Excel file. The procedure assumes you have experience with Word. If so, you can perform the steps as outlined. If not, do not perform these steps for now, but use them as a guide in the future.

1. Start your computer and Windows and invoke the Microsoft Office icon so that its toolbar appears at the upper right of the title bar

   Note: You must start with the source document to create a link.

2. Start Word and open the EXWP3-6.DOC document (remember to first set your drive to A)

3. Identify the object (block of data) to be linked, such as the entire paragraph

4. Click *Edit, Copy*

The block of data is copied to the Windows' Clipboard and is available for linking.

5. Click the *Excel* button on the Office toolbar

6. If needed, open a new workbook

7. Position the cell pointer where you want the object to appear

8. Click *Edit, Paste Special*

9. In the dialog box, click *Paste Link* and then *OK*

10. Save the workbook as EXCEL1.XLS

The data block from the EXWP3-6.DOC document appears in the EXCEL1.XLS workbook and is dynamically linked to the original Word document. For example,

11. Double-click the linked object in Excel to switch to *Word*

> Tip: You can also click the *Word* button on the Office toolbar to switch back to Word.

12. Change some data within the selected block; for example, change Word to wordprocessor

13. Switch back to Excel, double-click the linked object and watch the data in the linked object change, as well

14. Switch to Word and exit without saving

If you make changes to the EXWP3-6.DOC document in the future and Excel was not currently active, the changes would appear the next time you opened the EXCEL1.XLS workbook for use.

EMBEDDING AN OBJECT. Embedding an object simply copies it into the other application, without creating a link between the two files.

1. Identify the object as you did in linking by following Steps 1 through 7 above

2. In Excel, click *Edit, Paste*

The data are copied, but will now remain static. Changes you make in EXWP3-6.DOC will not affect the EXCEL1.XLS workbook. Also note that the data is copied into a single cell in Excel that may contain a maximum of 255 characters. If the object you are copying is larger than 255 characters, the excess characters will not be copied.

3. Close the EXCEL1 workbook without saving

4. Switch to Word and exit without saving the document

CHECKPOINT

✓ Describe the difference between exporting and importing a file.
✓ Using Excel and the correct file extensions, export the GRADES.XLS workbook to an ASCII file named GRADES2.TXT for use by a database program.
✓ Import the BOOKS1.TXT file using the Text Import Wizard and save as a workbook named BOOKS4. Print the worksheet.
✓ What is object linking and embedding?
✓ How do you activate a linked object for editing?

SUMMARY

Specific mouse actions and keystrokes for the following commands can be reviewed in the chapter or in the appendix.

- Charts present information in picture form. Creating a chart includes selecting the chart data, invoking the *Chart* command (*Insert* menu), and selecting the chart's location.
- Chart enhancements include options such as titles, grids, and legends that can be customized.
- Conditional functions add decision-making capabilities to worksheets. The IF function takes one of two actions based on the condition's truth. The CHOOSE function returns a value in a list based on a calculated value. Table lookups—VLOOKUP and HLOOKUP—use a two-dimensional table to return values that correspond to specified intervals.
- Spreadsheet data can be treated as a database; rows are records and columns are fields. The top row of a database must identify field names.
- The *Fill* command generates an evenly spaced sequence of numbers.

- The FREQUENCY function creates a frequency distribution of numbers displaying how many values in a value range fall within specified numeric intervals listed in a bin range.

- The *Sort* command (Data menu) arranges any data range in ascending order (lowest to highest) or descending order (highest to lowest) based on a primary key and two optional keys.

- Data queries are questions asked of a database. The Filter command can be used to extract records from a database, based on specified criteria. The Form dialog box can be used to change or delete records in a database.

- Criteria are cell entries used as tests to select records. Multiple criteria can be placed in one cell or separate cells. Complexed criteria placed in one row are connected by an AND operator, whereas complexed criteria in two or more rows are connected by an OR operator.

- Data functions—like DSUM, DAVG, and DMAX—combine statistical functions with input and criteria ranges to limit calculations to selected records in the database.

- A macro is a set of mouse actions, keystrokes, or command instructions for automating a task. Macros must be planned, and must be named. Once named, a macro can be assigned to a shortcut key, the Tools menu or a macro button for invoking.

- Macros can be entered by using the *Record* command to record keystrokes or mouse actions, or by typing macro commands directly. The latter method requires knowledge of Visual Basic.

- Ranges can be copied into other workbooks or sheets or other application files.

- *Client* cells in the current worksheet or sheet can be linked to *server* cells in other workbooks or sheets with a linking formula (Paste Link command of the Paste Special dialog box, Edit menu). When server cells are changed, client cells are automatically updated.

- The protection feature prevents all cells from being edited or deleted except those cells unprotected by the *Protection* tab of the Format Cells dialog box (Format menu) before turning on the protection feature.

- *Import* and *Export* commands facilitate data transfer among programs.

- ASCII is one of a few standard formats adopted by the computer industry for representing typed characters.

- The Text Import Wizard dialog box separates data from an imported ASCII file into distinct columns.

KEY TERMS

Shown in parentheses are the page numbers on which key terms are boldfaced.

ASCII (SS223)	Fill handle (SS173)	Module sheet (SS193)
Chart (SS148)	Filter (SS180)	Object (SS229)
Column chart (SS148)	IF function (SS166)	OLE (SS229)
Criteria (SS180)	Importing (SS222)	Paste link (SS208)
Data distribution (SS178)	Line chart (SS160)	Pie chart (SS160)
Database query (SS180)	Linking (SS229)	Protection feature (SS221)
Embedding (SS229)	Lookup tables (SS167)	Selection handles (SS153)
Exporting (SS222)	Macro (SS192)	

CHAPTER 3   ADVANCED SPREADSHEETS   SS233

QUIZ

TRUE/FALSE

1. A chart may be inserted on a current sheet or on a new sheet.
2. A line chart is useful for showing trends over time.
3. An IF statement selects one of two possible actions.
4. Values that exceed the highest VLOOKUP table value return an error message.
5. A data distribution is also known as a frequency distribution.
6. An alphabetical list that runs from Z to A is sorted in descending order.
7. The Filter command and the Form dialog box can be used to query data.
8. Criteria may include field names and records to be searched.
9. Complexed criteria placed on adjacent rows (below each other) are linked by an OR logical connection.
10. Macros can record all keystrokes except function keys.

MULTIPLE CHOICE

11. The chart command can be invoked from which menu?
    a. Chart menu
    b. Insert menu
    c. Format menu
    d. Tools menu
12. Which chart option improves data estimation when reading a chart?
    a. Grid
    b. Title
    c. Color
    d. Legend
13. What result is returned by =IF(A1=5,"A","B") if Cell A1 = 0?
    a. A
    b. B
    c. 5
    d. 0
14. A column in a spreadsheet database corresponds to a:
    a. Record
    b. Cell
    c. Table
    d. Field
15. Which command creates a sequence of numbers separated at equal intervals?
    a. Frequency
    b. Fill
    c. Sort
    d. Key
16. Which rows should be included in a data-sort process?
    a. Field names and record row
    b. Field names only
    c. Record names only
    d. Primary key column only

17. Which command displays, in sequence records that match specified criteria?
    a. Filter
    b. Form
    c. Sort
    d. Fill
18. Which of these ranges does *not* include field names?
    a. Criteria range
    b. Sort range
    c. Query table
    d. Database table
19. Which Paste Special command creates a special connection between a source and destination copy?
    a. Cut link
    b. Copy link
    c. Paste
    d. Paste link
20. Which linking formula follows proper format?
    a. **A2**File
    b. +{{B3}}File
    c. {='Region B'!$B$3:$B$6}
    d. +[D7]in File

MATCHING

Select the lettered item from the figure below that best matches each phrase.

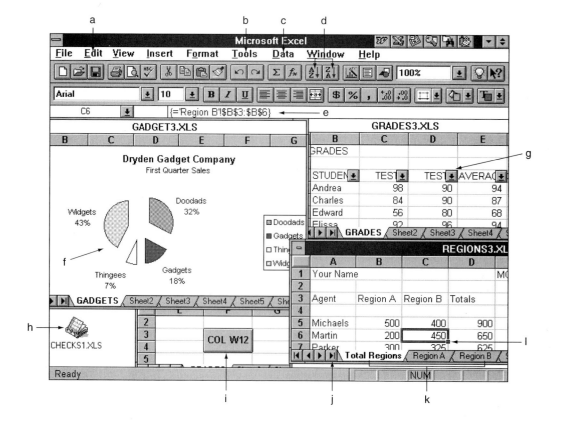

CHAPTER 3   ADVANCED SPREADSHEETS   **SS235**

21. Can be used to invoke a macro.
22. Can be dragged to fill a range of cells with a sequence of data or copies of the same data.
23. Used to identify and switch to different sheets in a workbook.
24. A pictorial representation of data.
25. The protection feature can be turned on/off using this menu.
26. This item can be used to scroll to the last sheet tab in the viewing area.
27. This menu can be used to invoke the Filter commands.
28. A workbook reduced to its minimum size.
29. Can be created by the Paste Link command.
30. Opens to a drop-down list for filtering a database.

ANSWERS

True/False: 1. T; 2. T; 3. T; 4. F; 5. T; 6. T; 7. T; 8. F; 9. T; 10. F
Multiple Choice: 11. b; 12. a; 13. b; 14. d; 15. b; 16. c; 17. a; 18. b; 19. d; 20. c
Matching: 21. i; 22. l; 23. k; 24. f; 25. b; 26. j; 27. c; 28. h; 29. e; 30. g

---

EXERCISES

I. OPERATIONS

Provide the Excel Mouse Approach and Keyboard Approach actions required to do each of the following operations.

1. Create a column chart.
2. Change the column chart to a pie-chart display.
3. Create an IF function that returns YES if A1>0, or NO if it does not.
4. Create an IF function that returns C1*5 if B1 = 2, or zero if it does not.
5. Fill a column with even numbers from 10 to 40 starting at Cell B6.
6. Create a data distribution of test grades in the range called EXAMS showing how many grades fall between each 10-point interval from zero to 100.
7. Sort cells D5:D20 in ascending order.
8. Use a criteria range to locate records whose NAME (in Column A) starts with an S and whose AGE (in Column B) exceeds 18. Assume the records start in Row 8.
9. Create a query table for the NAME and AGE of the records found in the previous exercise.
10. Create an average of grades (listed in Column D) for those cells in the input range B1:D20 whose grade (listed in Column C) is 12.
11. Create a macro to set the default format to fixed, two decimals.
12. Copy the formulas in B5:C12 to a file called "NEW."
13. In Cell L4, link Cell A25 in the "APRIL" file.
14. Protect the entire worksheet except for cells C4:C10.

II. COMMANDS

Describe fully, using as few words as possible, what command is initiated, or what is accomplished, in Excel by the following actions. Assume that Excel has already been invoked, and that each exercise is independent of any previous exercises. If the series of actions is not complete, indicate what action should be taken to finalize the command.

1. Double-clicking a chart's title
2. Typing =IF(A1<>1,"Error","OK")
3. Typing =IF(B1 = "Smith",5 + A1,A1)
4. Typing =VLOOKUP(C5,$MONEY,3)
5. Clicking *Window*, *Arrange*
6. Pressing the Ctrl + F6 keys
7. Clicking *Tools*, *Protection*, *Protect Sheet*
8. Clicking *Window*, *Cascade*
9. Typing =DAVG(A1:A10,2,D5:D6)
10. Typing {= 'Region A' !$B$3:$B$6}

III. APPLICATIONS

Perform the following operations and briefly describe how you accomplish each operation and its results.

APPLICATION 1: ADVANCE CLUB BUDGET

Save the workbook in this exercise as CLUB3 after each operation is completed (unless otherwise indicated) so that you can continue this exercise later if desired.

1. Open the CLUB2 workbook (created in the previous chapter).
2. Create a column chart showing the expense dollars by month. Add appropriate titles and resize the chart to adequately display its contents. Save the workbook as EXPENSE1. If a graphics printer is available, print the worksheet with the chart.
3. Create a pie chart that is formatted to display percentages for each slice. Save the workbook as EXPENSE2. Print only the pie chart, if a graphics printer is available.
4. Create a three-dimensional bar chart showing expenditures for each type of expense for individual months. Save the workbook as EXPENSE3. Print only the three-dimensional bar chart, if a graphics printer is available, and close the workbook.
5. Open the CLUB2 workbook. Sort the data in Cells A7 through H11 using Column A as the primary key (use ascending order). Save this workbook as CLUB3 and print it.
6. Select the range A6:I11 as the database table. Filter the database for only those records whose TOTAL data exceeds $500. Print and save this workbook.
7. Change the criteria in the previous exercise to filter records whose JUN data is less than 100 and whose TOTAL exceeds $500. Print and save.
8. Create a macro button in Column M that will print only the columns that display EXPENSES and TOTAL. (Hint: Your macro can hide the columns that you do not wish to print.) Print and save this workbook.
9. Unhide the columns that were hidden by the macro. Protect Cells B12:H12 and H7:H11.
10. In Cell H13, create a DAVERAGE function to calculate the average funds needed for a month. Save and print the workbook.
11. Exit the program.

APPLICATION 2: ADVANCED GPA

Save the workbook in this exercise as GPA3 after each operation is completed (unless otherwise indicated) so that you can continue this exercise later.

CHAPTER 3   ADVANCED SPREADSHEETS   **SS237**

1. Open the GPA2 workbook (created in the previous chapter).
2. Create a column chart showing the total points earned for each course taken. Add appropriate titles. Save the worksheet as GPA_B. Print the image if a graphics printer is available.
3. Create a pie chart showing the total points of each course. Save the workbook as GPA_P. Print the image if a graphics printer is available. Compare the percentages shown in the chart with the values in Column G.
4. Change the default width to 10. In Column H, add an IF function that will mark with two asterisks any course whose point value is four. Label and format as needed. Change the width of Column H to 2. Print the worksheet and save it.
5. Create this lookup table named CONVERT, starting in Cell J2 (the titles start in J2, the table begins in J3):

Grade	Points
F	0
D	1
C	2
B	3
A	4

   Replace the current entry in Cell E7 with a VLOOKUP function that compares the grade with that in this chart and returns the points automatically. Copy the function correctly into the remaining cells in the column. Print the worksheet and save it.
6. Sort the data in Cells A8:H13 using *only* COURSE as primary key (in ascending order). Print the spreadsheet. Now sort by TERM as primary key and COURSE as secondary key (both in ascending order). Print and save the workbook.
7. Create a data table for the range A5:F11. Use the Advanced Filter command to create a Query table in Cells A18:F22 that includes only those records from the data table whose GRADE is B. Print and save.
8. Change the criteria in the previous exercise to select records only if their TERM is 9301 *and* their GRADE is A. Create a Query table of these records. Print and save.
9. In Cell B24, create a DSUM function to calculate the total credits only for courses in business. (*Hint:* You may use a LEFT function.) Create a function below it to count the number of courses in this category. (Use Cells G22 and G23 for the criterion.) Title cells as needed.
10. Create a macro that will print only the columns that display courses and grades when invoked with **Ctrl** and **T** keys. (*Hint:* You may want to use a column hide and unhide routine.) Invoke the macro and then print the entire worksheet. Save the workbook.
11. Create a macro button that will print Columns A through F of the worksheet. Invoke the macro. Save the workbook.
12. Copy the COURSE and TERM columns to a new workbook called GPA3A. Open a new workbook. Copy GPA3A into this blank workbook starting in Cell A1. Print, but do not save.
13. Open the GPA3A workbook from the previous exercise (or create it if needed). Delete the rows that contain courses in ART or MUSIC. For the remaining rows, use the Paste-link command to link formulas in Column C that will open the grades from the GPA3 worksheet. Save as GPA3B and print.
14. Open GPA3. Protect all cells from change except the rows with data entry (from Column A to Column E). Save the workbook.
15. Exit the program.

SS238 SPREADSHEETS WITH MICROSOFT EXCEL 5.0

APPLICATION 3: ADVANCED CHECKBOOK
Save this workbook as CHECK3 after each operation is completed (unless otherwise indicated) so that you can continue this exercise later.

1. Open the CHECK2 workbook (created in the previous chapter).
2. Create a line chart showing the BALANCE during the time period from 01-Jan through 15-Jan. Add appropriate titles and resize the chart to adequately display its contents. Save the workbook as LCHECK. If a graphics printer is available, print the workbook with the chart. Close the workbook.
3. Open the CHECK2 workbook again. In Row 15, create a DMIN function to find the lowest BALANCE. Title the cells as needed.
4. Copy the DATE and BALANCE columns to Sheet 2. Rename Sheet 1, CHECKS, and Sheet 2 BALANCES. Save and print the entire workbook with all sheets.
5. Select the range A5:F11 as the database table. Filter only the deposits. Save and print the workbook.
6. Display the entire database table. Filter only the check payments. Save and print this workbook.
7. Display the entire database table. Create a macro that automatically adds the formula in the BALANCE column to the next cell below when invoked.
8. Assign the macro to the Tools menu.
9. Add the following data and invoke the BALANCE macro in the BALANCE column as needed.

DATE	CHECK#	PAYEE	PMT	DEP
20-Jan	109	M-Charge	340.00	
31-Jan		Deposit pay check		1,400.00

10. Reformat the worksheet as needed. Save and then print the workbook.
11. Protect Rows 4 and 5 and all data in the BALANCE column. Save the workbook and close it.
12. Open the CHECK2 workbook again. Format the worksheet as an ASCII file, save it as CHECKS.TXT, and then close it.
13. Use the Text Import Wizard to convert the CHECKS.TXT file into an Excel workbook.
14. Exit the program.

APPLICATION 4: ADVANCED INVESTMENTS
Save the workbook as INVEST3 after each operation is completed (unless otherwise indicated) so that you can continue this exercise later.

1. Open the INVEST2 workbook (created in the previous chapter).
2. Create a line chart for TOTAL SALES and TOTAL PURCH for each stock. Add appropriate titles and resize the chart to adequately display its contents. Print the chart if a graphics printer is available.
3. Change the default (standard) width to 11. In Column K, add an IF function to mark with an asterisk (*) any return on investment less than 5.00%. Change the width of Column K to 2. Save the workbook and then print it without the chart created in the previous step.
4. Sort the data in Cells A8:H12 by TYPE in ascending order. Print and save.

5. Sort the data in Cells A8:H12 by TYPE in ascending order and also by PROFIT/(LOSS) in descending order.
6. Select the range A7:H12 as the database table. Filter the database for those investments whose PROFIT is greater than $500.
7. Copy the TYPE, DATE SOLD, SELLING PRICE, QUANTITY, and TOTAL SALES columns to SHEET 2.
8. Copy the TYPE, DATE PURCH, PURCH PRICE, QUANTITY, and TOTAL PURCH columns to SHEET 3.
9. Rename Sheet 1's tab to TOTAL; Sheet 2's tab to SALES; and Sheet 3's tab to PURCHASES.
10. In the TOTAL sheet, delete the data in the range A8:H12. Create linking formulas in the cells of the deleted range to link to the appropriate information from the SALES and PURCHASES sheets. (*Hint:* Use the Paste Link command of the Special Paste dialog box.) Save the workbook.
11. Protect all of the data in the TOTAL sheet and the columns containing formulas in the SALES and PURCHASES sheets.
12. Change some of the data in the SALES and PURCHASES sheets and examine the results in the TOTAL sheet. Save the workbook.
13. Print the entire workbook (all sheets).
14. Exit the program.

APPLICATION 5: ADVANCED TAPES

1. Open the TAPES workbook. (If you do not have TAPES, enter the worksheet shown in the figure).
2. Create a column chart showing units sold for each title. Add appropriate titles. Save the workbook as CATALOG1 and then print the worksheet.
3. In Column F, add an IF function that will mark with a plus sign any title whose sales exceed $500. Format as needed. Print the worksheet and save it as CATALOG.

	A	B	C	D	E
1	Tape Sales				
2				Units	Total
3	Tape	Type	Price	Sold	Sales
4	The Rough-Faced Girl	Video	$ 32.95	87	$ 2,866.65
5	Will's Mammoth	Audio	12.95	35	453.25
6	Three Little Pigs	Video	24.95	23	573.85
7	The Wooly Mammoth	Video	24.95	12	299.40
8	Japanese Ghost Stories	Audio	6.75	57	384.75
9	Foolish Rabbit's Mistake	Audio	5.95	6	35.70
10	Total Sales			220	$ 4,613.60
11					

4. Create this lookup table named SHIPPING starting in Cell H4:

```
Price          Shipping
$0.00           $0.50
10.00           1.25
20.00           2.00
30.00           2.75
```

Title Column G "Shipping." Create a VLOOKUP function in Column G that compares the price with that in this chart and returns the shipping cost *multiplied by the units sold*. Format Column G as needed. Print the worksheet and save it.

5. Sort the data in Cells A4:G9 using *only* TYPE as the primary key and TAPE as the secondary key (use ascending order for both). Print the spreadsheet and save it.
6. Create a data table for the range A3:E9. Use the Advanced Filter command to create a Query table in Cells A18:E22 that includes only those records from the data table whose prices exceed $15. Print and save.
7. Change the criteria to select records only if their TYPE is "Video" *and* they sold more than 20 units. Create a Query table of these records. Print and save.
8. In Row 25, create a DSUM function to calculate the sum of SALES only for videos. Create a function below it to count the number of audio tapes. Title cells as needed.
9. Create a macro that will print only the tape TITLES when invoked with the Ctrl and T keys. Invoke the macro and print the entire worksheet. Save the worksheet.
10. Create a macro button that will print Columns A through E of the worksheet. Invoke the macro. Save the worksheet.
11. Copy the tape TITLE and TYPE to a new worksheet file called CATALOG2. Open a new worksheet. Combine CATALOG2 into this blank worksheet file starting in Cell A1. Print, but do not save.
12. Open the CATALOG2 worksheet from the previous exercise (or create one). Change Column A's width to 30. Delete the rows that contain audio tapes. For the three remaining rows, create linking formulas using the Paste Link command (Paste Special dialog box) in Column C that will open the units sold from the CATALOG worksheet. Save as CATALOG2 and print.
13. Open CATALOG. Protect all cells from change except the six rows with data entry (from Column A to Column D).
14. Save the workbook and exit the program.

APPLICATION 6: ADVANCED TICKETS

Save the workbook in this exercise as TICKET3 after each operation is completed so that you can continue this exercise later if desired.

1. Open the TICKET2 worksheet (created in the previous chapter).
2. Create a column chart showing the quantity of each seat type. Add appropriate titles and resize the chart to adequately display its contents. Save the workbook as TICK_B1. Add a second series of data for tickets sold and save it as TICK_B2. If a graphics printer is available, print the worksheet with the chart.
3. Remove the second set of data. Now, create a pie chart showing the *value* of each seat type. Save the workbook as TICK_P. Print the chart only if a graphics printer is available. Compare the percentages shown in the chart with the values in Column G.
4. Change the default width to 8. In Column H, add an IF function that will mark with an asterisk (*) any seat type whose value exceeds $5,000. Format as needed. Change the width of Column H to 2. Print the worksheet and save it as TICKET3.
5. Create this lookup table named HANDLING, starting in Cell J2 (the titles start in J2, the table begins in J3):

```
      Price          Shipping
      $10.00          $1.50
       30.00           2.00
       50.00           2.25
```

Format to match the sample. Title Column I HANDLING. Create a VLOOKUP function in Column I that compares the ticket price with those in this chart and returns the handling cost *multiplied by the number of tickets sold.* Extend the

CHAPTER 3   **ADVANCED SPREADSHEETS**   SS241

existing border lines to cover the added columns. Format the column to match Column F. Print the worksheet and save it.

6. Sort the data in Cells A7:I12 using *only* SEAT as primary key (in ascending order). Print the spreadsheet. Now sort by PRICE as primary key and SEAT as secondary key (both in descending order). Print and save the spreadsheet.

7. Create a data table for the range A6:F12. Use the Advanced Filter command to create a Query table in Cells A19:F23 that includes only those records from the data table whose SOLD data exceed 100. Print and save.

8. Change the criteria in the previous exercise to select records only if their EMPTY data are less than 100 seats *and* their VALUE exceeds $2,000. Create a Query table of these records. Print and save.

9. In Cell B23, create a DSUM function to calculate the sum of tickets sold only for seats that cost $50 or more. Create a function below it to total the number of available seats in this category. (Use Cells G22 and G23 for the criterion.) Title cells as needed.

10. Create a macro in Column M that will print only the columns that display seat types and number of empty seats when invoked with Ctrl and T keys. (*Hint:* You may want to use a column hide and unhide routine.) Invoke the macro and then print the entire worksheet. Save the workbook.

11. Create a macro button that will print Columns A through F of the worksheet. Invoke the macro. Save the workbook.

12. Copy the SEAT and PRICE columns to a new worksheet file called TICKET3A. Open a new workbook. Copy TICKET3A into this blank workbook, starting in Cell A1. Print, but do not save.

13. Open the TICKET3A workbook from the previous exercise (or create it if needed). Delete the rows that contain seats that sell for $50 or more. For the remaining rows, use the Paste-link command to insert linking formulas in Column C that will open the seats sold from the TICKET worksheet. Save as TICKET3B and print.

14. Open TICKET. Protect all cells from change except the rows with data entry (from Column A to Column F). Save the workbook.

15. Exit the program.

MASTERY CASES

The following Mastery Cases allow you to demonstrate how much you have learned about this software. Each case describes a fictitious problem or need that can be solved using the skills you have learned in this chapter. While minimum acceptable outcomes are specified, you are expected and encouraged to design your response (files, data, lists) in ways that display your personal mastery of the software. Feel free to show off your skills. Use "real" data from your own experience in your solution, although you may also fabricate data if needed.

These Mastery Cases allow you to display your ability to:

- Create charts
- Use conditional functions
- Create macros
- Use multiple workbooks

SS242 SPREADSHEETS WITH MICROSOFT EXCEL 5.0

- Use multiple sheets
- Protect cells in a workbook
- Share data among applications

CASE 1. ANALYZING YOUR EXAM GRADES: Open the exam grades workbook that you created for Mastery Case 1 of Chapter 2. Create a column chart showing your AVERAGE in each course. Print the workbook with the chart. Create a distribution of your final grades (AVERAGE column) assuming an A is 100-90, a B is 89-80, a C is 79-70, and so on. Copy the COURSE and AVERAGE columns to Sheet 2 of the workbook. Link the AVERAGE column between the sheets. Add data for two new classes to the workbook. Save and print the entire workbook (all sheets). Add other enhancements to make the workbook more attractive. Save the workbook and print Sheet 1.

CASE 2. ANALYZING YOUR HOLIDAY SHOPPING: Open the holiday-shopping workbook that you created for Mastery Case 2 of Chapter 2. Create a pie chart to show the ACTUAL amount that you spent for each person on your list. Print the worksheet with the chart. Sort your data in ascending order by ACTUAL amount spent on each person. Save and print the workbook. Create a Query table that displays only those records in which the ACTUAL amount spent is more than the BUDGET amount. Add other enhancements to make the workbook more attractive. Save and print your budget.

CASE 3. ANALYZING YOUR SALES REPORT: Open the sales report workbook that you created for Mastery Case 3 of Chapter 2. Create a pie chart to show the relative amount that each product has contributed to total sales. Print the worksheet with the chart. Create and execute a macro that will print only the PRODUCT and UNITS SOLD columns. Protect the PRODUCT and UNIT PRICE columns. Add other enhancements to make the workbook more attractive. Save and print your sales report.

MICROSOFT EXCEL VERSION 5.0
FEATURE AND OPERATION
REFERENCE

EXCEL MOUSE OPERATIONS

A mouse is an input device that allows you to control a mouse pointer (graphical image) on your screen. As you move your mouse on a flat surface, the mouse pointer moves on the screen in a similar fashion. See Figure SSA-1 for mouse-pointer forms and common mouse actions.

A summary of some Excel features that are accessible by mouse follows. Refer to Figure SSA-2 for the location of some of these features. Detailed applications of these features are incorporated within other sections of this appendix.

CANCEL BUTTON

Clicking the cancel button (X) (formula bar) will cancel the data being entered. The cancel button appears on the formula bar only when data are being entered into a cell.

ENTER BUTTON

Clicking the enter button (formula bar) will place data into the cell. The enter button appears on the formula bar only when data are being entered into a cell.

FUNCTION WIZARD BUTTON

Clicking the function Wizard button (formula bar) opens a Function Wizard.

CONTROL-MENU BOX

Double-clicking a control-menu box will quickly close a window. Clicking a control-menu box once will open the window's control menu.

The control-menu box is normally at the upper-left corner of a window. A maximized worksheet window's control-menu box, however, is located at the left end of the menu bar.

DRAGGING AND DROPPING

Excel's *Drag and Drop* feature offers a quick way to move a selection of cells or an object within the same worksheet. To drag a selection, point to it, and then press and hold the left mouse button while moving (dragging) the pointer and the selection to

MICROSOFT EXCEL VERSION 5.0

FIGURE SSA-1 ■ **MOUSE SYMBOLS AND MOUSE ACTIONS**

(a) Excel mouse pointer formats. (b) Mouse actions and explanations.

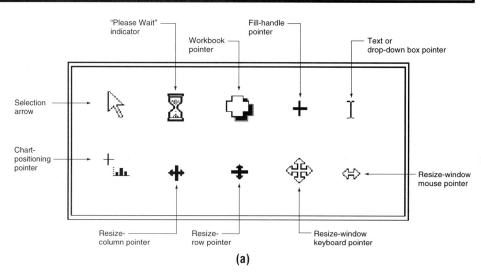

(a)

Mouse Actions	Explanations
Point	Move mouse, and thus mouse pointer, to desired item.
Click	Press and quickly release the left mouse button.
Double-click	Rapidly press and release the left mouse button twice.
Drag	Press and hold the left mouse button, move to the desired location and release the button to select.

(b)

a new location. Next, release your mouse button to place (drop) the selection in the next location.

MOVING THE CELL POINTER

Pointing to a desired location in a worksheet and clicking it will quickly move the cell pointer there.

SHORTCUT MENUS

Pointing to certain locations on the Excel window and clicking the right mouse button will open a Shortcut menu. Shortcut menus provide quick access to a variety of features. To select a Shortcut menu item by mouse, simply click it.

RESIZING BUTTONS

Clicking a resizing button is a quick way to change the size of a window. Standard resizing buttons include the following:

FIGURE SSA-2 ■ PARTS OF THE EXCEL WINDOW

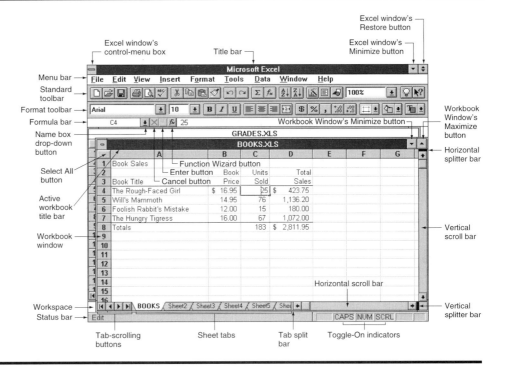

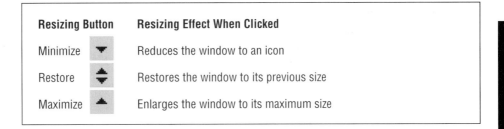

Two resizing buttons generally occupy the upper-right corner of a window. A maximized worksheet window, however, has only a restore button located at the right end of the menu bar.

MENU BAR

Clicking a menu-bar item opens its pull-down menu. Clicking a pull-down menu item selects that item.

SCROLLING

Clicking the arrow buttons at either end of a scroll bar or dragging the scroll box along a scroll bar will allow you to see areas of a worksheet or list not currently in the viewing area without moving the cell pointer/highlight. To move the pointer/highlight to a position or item in the current display area, simply point to it and click.

SELECTING A COLUMN

Clicking the letter of a column will select the entire column.

SELECTING A CHART

Clicking a chart's frame will select it. Double-clicking a selected chart puts it in chart Edit mode. Once in Edit mode, simply click the chart's part to select it. Note that a selected chart will have selection handles on its frame.

SELECTING A RANGE

A range is a selection of cells that resembles a highlighted rectangular area. Dragging the mouse pointer over desired cells will select them. A range of cells can also be selected by clicking the first cell of the desired range and then pressing and holding the Shift key while clicking the last cell of the range.

SELECTING A ROW

Clicking a row number will select the entire row.

SELECTING AN OBJECT

Clicking an object will select it by placing selection handles on its frame.

SELECTING MULTIPLE RANGES

To select multiple ranges, select the first range and then press and hold the **Ctrl** key while selecting each additional range.

SELECTING THE ENTIRE WORKSHEET

Clicking the worksheet identifier (top-left corner of worksheet) will select the entire worksheet.

SHEET TABS

Clicking a workbook's sheet tab allows you to switch to that sheet.

SPLITTING A WORKSHEET

To split a worksheet, drag the horizontal or vertical splitter bar to the desired split position in the worksheet and then release (drop) the splitter bar.

STATUS BAR

The status bar has a variety of indicators (messages) and selectors. To see a description of a toolbar button in the status bar, point to the button. To see a description of a menu item, open the menu and use the arrow keys to move the highlight to it.

APPENDIX   SS247

SWITCHING BETWEEN MULTIPLE WINDOWS

Clicking anywhere on a workbook window will make it the active window when multiple windows are in use.

TAB-SCROLLING BUTTONS

Clicking a Tab-scrolling button will move tabs into the sheet-tab-viewing area. Tab buttons include (left to right) the First Tab, Previous Tab, Next Tab, and Last Tab.

TITLE BAR

Double-clicking a window's title bar will resize the window.

EXCEL KEYS

Excel keys include both keystrokes that are common to most Windows applications and those that are unique to Excel.

COMMON WINDOWS KEYS

Common Windows keys concern basic menu and dialog-box operations, file management, window manipulation, and editing commands.

ALT

Pressed alone, the **Alt** key activates the selection highlight on Excel's (or any active application window's) menu bar. The highlight may then be moved to a menu-bar item using the arrow keys. If used in combination with other keys, the **Alt** key is held down when striking another key. The other key is usually a function key (**F1** through **F12**), the underlined letter of a menu item, button, or other option that has an underlined letter.

- **Alt** + **F4** exits Excel (or any Windows application) or any dialog box.
- **Alt** + **Backspace** or **Ctrl** + **Z** undoes the last action.
- **Alt** + **Spacebar** opens Excel window's (or any application window's) control menu.
- **Alt** + **– (Minus)** opens the control menu of a workbook (or document) window.
- **Alt** + **Tab** switches to the last application used when operating multiple applications. Pressing and holding the Alt key while tapping the Tab key scrolls through running applications.
- **Alt** + **Esc** switches to the next running application when operating multiple applications. An application can be running as a window or an icon.
- **Alt** + **Enter** switches a non-Windows application that was started in Windows between running in full screen and a window.
- **Alt** + **Print Screen** will copy an image of the active application window (or dialog box) to the Clipboard for future pasting.

ARROW KEYS

- Move the cell pointer one cell at a time in the direction of the arrow.
- Move the insertion point one character at a time in the direction of the arrow when editing data within a cell, text box, or drop-down box.
- Move the selection highlight in the direction of the arrow to each item on a menu or list (in a list box or drop-down box).

The arrow keys can also be used in conjunction with other keys to perform such tasks as resizing a window, moving a selection (data, chart, table, or object), or moving a drawing or editing tool.

BACKSPACE

Erases single characters to the left of the insertion point.

CAPS LOCK

Keeps the Shift key active so that all characters are typed in uppercase.

CTRL

The control key is used with another key to invoke a command.

- `Ctrl` + `Alt` + `Delete` exits the current application if it stops responding to the system.
- `Ctrl` + `B` turns on/off the bold feature.
- `Ctrl` + `C` or `Ctrl` + `Insert` copies a selection (data, chart, table, or object) to Windows Clipboard for future pasting.
- `Ctrl` + `Esc` opens the Task List dialog box.
- `Ctrl` + `F4` closes the active workbook (document) window.
- `Ctrl` + `F6` or `Ctrl` + `Tab` moves the highlight to another workbook (document) window or icon.
- `Ctrl` + `I` turns on/off the italic feature.
- `Ctrl` + `N` turns off the bold, italic, or underline feature.
- `Ctrl` + `O` opens a file.
- `Ctrl` + `P` prints the current worksheet (document) or range (selection).
- `Ctrl` + `S` saves the current workbook (document) to a file.
- `Ctrl` + `U` turns on/off the underline feature.
- `Ctrl` + `V` or `Shift` + `Insert` pastes the contents of Windows Clipboard to a desired location.
- `Ctrl` + `X` or `Shift` + `Delete` cuts (moves) a selection to Windows Clipboard for future pasting.
- `Ctrl` + `Z` or `Alt` + `Backspace` undoes the last action.

APPENDIX SS249

DELETE

The delete key will erase the following:

- Single characters to the right of the insertion point when editing data in a cell, text box, or drop-down box.
- A selection (individual cell, range, or object).

END

- Moves the insertion point to the end of a line when editing data in a cell, text box, or drop-down box.
- Moves the selection highlight to the last item in a menu, list box, or drop-down box.

ENTER

- Enters typed data into a cell (spreadsheet programs only).
- Invokes a command from a menu selection or dialog box.

ESC

- Cancels a menu or dialog box before a command is invoked.
- Returns a cell to its previous content before completing a new entry.

F1

Opens the Help window of any Windows application.

FUNCTION KEYS

Numbered **F1** through **F12** , the function keys are used alone, or in combination with the **Alt** , **Ctrl** , and **Shift** keys, to invoke an application's commands.

HOME

- Moves the insertion point to the beginning of a line of data in a cell, text box, or drop-down box.
- Moves the selection highlight to the beginning of a list in a menu, list box, or drop-down box.

INSERT

In certain situations, allows the insertion of characters at the insertion point when editing data in a cell, text box, or drop-down box.

NUMLOCK

Activates the numeric keypad that is on the right side of most keyboards. NumLock works as a toggle key; pressing it once activates the keypad, while pressing it again deactivates the keypad.

PG UP AND PG DN (PAGE UP AND PAGE DOWN)

Moves one screen page up or one down.

PRINT SCREEN (PRTSC)

Captures an image of a screen to the Clipboard.

SHIFT

Works like the **Shift** key on a typewriter; when it is held down and a letter or number is pressed, an uppercase letter or symbol assigned to the number key is produced. Other commands invoked when pressing the **Shift** key and another key include:

- **Shift** + → expands the selection highlight to the right.
- **Shift** + ← expands the selection highlight to the left.
- **Shift** + **Delete** or **Ctrl** + **X** cuts (moves) a selection to Windows Clipboard for future pasting.
- **Shift** + **Insert** or **Ctrl** + **V** pastes the content of the Windows Clipboard to a desired location.
- **Shift** + **Tab** will move the dotted selection rectangle to the previous option in a dialog box.

TAB

Moves the dotted selection rectangle to next option in a dialog box.

UNIQUE EXCEL KEYS

Unique Excel keys concern invoking commands that relate only to Excel features. The keys listed here assume that the transition check boxes in the Transition tab of the Options dialog box are empty. To check, select *Tools, Options, Transition* tab.

FUNCTION KEYS. Excel commands invoked by pressing a function key alone or with another key(s) are listed below.

- **F1** **(Help)**
  Invokes the Excel Help feature.
- **Shift** + **F1**
  Invokes context-sensitive Help.
- **F2** **(Edit)**
  Puts Excel in Edit mode, which displays the contents of the current cell in the Entry area of the formula bar for editing.
- **Shift** + **F2**
  Invokes the Note command (Insert menu).
- **Ctrl** + **F2**
  Opens the Info window.
- **F3**
  Pastes a name into a formula.
- **Shift** + **F3**
  Invokes the Function Wizard.

APPENDIX   SS251

- **Ctrl + F3**
Invokes the Define command (Insert menu, Name submenu).
- **Ctrl + Shift + F3**
Invokes the Create command (Insert menu, Name submenu).
- **F4**
Changes a cell or range from/to relative to absolute.
- **Ctrl + F4**
Closes the active workbook window.
- **Alt + F4**
Exits Microsoft Excel.
- **F5 (Goto)**
Moves cell pointer to a specified location.
- **Ctrl + F5**
Restores workbook window size.
- **F6 (Pane)**
Moves cell pointer between panes on a single sheet.
- **Shift + F6**
Moves to previous pane.
- **Ctrl + F6**
Moves to next workbook window.
- **Ctrl + Shift + F6**
Moves to previous workbook window.
- **F7**
Invokes spell-checker program.
- **Ctrl + F7**
Invokes the Move command (workbook window-Control menu).
- **F8**
Toggles Extend mode on/off.
- **Shift + F8**
Toggles Add mode on/off.
- **Ctrl + F8**
Invokes the Size command (workbook window-Control menu).
- **F9 (Calculate)** or **Ctrl + =**
Recalculates all workbook sheets.
- **Shift + F9**
Calculates only the active sheet.
- **Ctrl + F9**
Minimizes the workbook window.
- **F10** or **Alt (Menu)**
Activates the selection highlight on the menu bar.
- **Shift + F10**
Opens the shortcut menu.
- **Ctrl + F10**
Maximizes the workbook window.
- **F11**
Insert new chart sheet.
- **Shift + F11**
Inserts new sheet.

- **Ctrl** + **F11**
  Inserts new Microsoft Excel 4.0 macro sheet.
- **F12**
  Invokes Save As command (File menu).
- **Shift** + **F12**
  Invokes the Save command (File menu).
- **Ctrl** + **F12**
  Invokes the Open command (File menu).
- **Ctrl** + **Shift** + **F12**
  Invokes the Print command (File menu).

OTHER EXCEL KEYS. These Excel keys do not involve the use of function keys.

- **=**
  Starts a formula.
- **Alt** + **=**
  Places the AutoSum formula in the current cell address.
- **Alt** + **Page Up**
  Moves left one screen.
- **Alt** + **Page Down**
  Moves right one screen.
- **Alt** + **↵**
  Inserts a carriage return.
- **Ctrl** + **;** (semicolon)
  Enters the system date.
- **Ctrl** + **'** (apostrophe)
  Copies the formula from the cell above the current cell into the cell or formula bar.
- **Ctrl** + **`** (single left quotation mark)
  Switches between displaying values or formulas in cells.
- **Ctrl** + **0** (zero)
  Hides selected columns.
- **Ctrl** + **6**
  Switches between hiding objects, displaying objects, and displaying placeholders for objects.
- **Ctrl** + **7**
  Displays or hides the Standard toolbar.
- **Ctrl** + **8**
  Shows or hides the outline symbols.
- **Ctrl** + **9**
  Hides selected rows.
- **Ctrl** + **A**
  - Selects the entire worksheet.
  - Displays Step 2 of the Function Wizard, after a valid function name is entered in a formula.
- **Ctrl** + **Alt** + **Tab**
  Inserts a tab.
- **Ctrl** + **D**
  Fills a selection down.

APPENDIX   SS253

- **Ctrl** + **Delete**
Deletes data to the end of the line.
- **Ctrl** + **End**
Moves the cell pointer to the last cell in your worksheet (lower-right corner).
- **Ctrl** + **Home**
Moves the cell pointer to the beginning of the worksheet.
- **Ctrl** + **−** (minus sign)
Deletes the selection.
- **Ctrl** + **Page Up**
Moves the cell pointer to the previous sheet in the workbook.
- **Ctrl** + **Page Down**
Moves the cell pointer to the next sheet in the workbook.
- **Ctrl** + **R**
Fills a selection to the right.
- **Ctrl** + **Shift** + **:** (colon)
Enters the system time.
- **Ctrl** + **Shift** + **"**
Copies the value from the cell above the current cell into the cell or formula bar.
- **Ctrl** + **Shift** + **(**
Unhides selected rows.
- **Ctrl** + **Shift** + **)**
Unhides selected columns.
- **Ctrl** + **Shift** + **A**
Inserts the argument names and parentheses for the function after a valid function name is entered in the formula.
- **Ctrl** + **Shift** + **End**
Expands a selection to the last cell in a worksheet (lower-right corner).
- **Ctrl** + **Shift** + **Home**
Expands a selection to the beginning of the worksheet.
- **Ctrl** + **Shift** + **+**
Inserts blank cells at the cell pointer.
- **Ctrl** + **Shift** + **Spacebar**
Selects all objects on a sheet after the first one is selected.
- **Ctrl** + **Shift** + **↵**
Enters the formula as a range formula.
- **Ctrl** + **Spacebar**
Selects the entire column.
- **Ctrl** + **←** or **Ctrl** + **→**
Moves the cell pointer up or down to the edge of the current data region.
- **Ctrl** + **↑** or **Ctrl** + **↓**
Moves the cell pointer up or down to the edge of the current data region.
- **Ctrl** + **↵**
Fills a range of cells with the current entry.
- **End** , **Arrow** key
Moves the cell pointer by one block of data within a row or column.
- **End**
Turns on/off the End mode.
- **End** , **Shift** + **↵** *****
Expands a selection to the last cell in the current row.

- **End** , **↵** *****
  Moves the cell pointer to the last cell in the current row.
- **End** , **Shift** + **Arrow** key
  Expands a selection to the end of the data block in the direction of the arrow.
- **End** , **Shift** + **Home**
  Expands a selection to the last cell of a worksheet (lower-right corner).
- **End** , **Home**
  Moves the cell pointer to the last cell of a worksheet (lower-right corner).
- **Enter** (**↵**)
  Completes the cell entry.
- **Esc**
  Cancels an entry in a cell, formula bar, or menu.
- **Home**
  - Moves the cell pointer to the beginning of the row.
  - Moves the insertion point to the start of the line.
- **Page Up**
  Moves the cell pointer one screen up.
- **Page Down**
  Moves the cell pointer one screen down.
- **Scroll Lock**
  Turns on/off the scroll lock.
- **Shift** + **Arrow** key
  Expands a selection by one cell.
- **Shift** + **Backspace**
  Reduces the selection to the active cell.
- **Shift** + **Home**
  Expands a selection to the beginning of the row.
- **Shift** + **Page Up**
  Expands a selection one screen up.
- **Shift** + **Page Down**
  Expands a selection one screen down.
- **Shift** + **Spacebar**
  Selects the entire row.
- **Shift** + **Tab**
  Enters a cell entry and moves to the previous cell in the row or range.
- **Tab**
  - Moves the cell pointer among unlocked cells in a protected worksheet.
  - Enters a cell entry and moves to the next cell in the row or range.

DIALOG-BOX OPERATIONS

A dialog box is a window that requests or gives information. The following is a description of some of the parts of a dialog box. See Figure SSA-3 for each part's location.

To select a dialog-box part by mouse, simply click it. To select by keyboard, press the **Alt** key and then the underlined letter of the option.

APPENDIX SS255

FIGURE SSA-3 ■ PARTS OF A DIALOG BOX

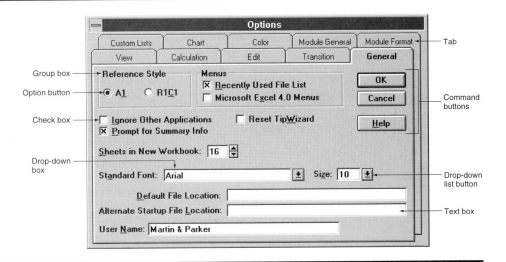

CHECK BOX

A check box with an "X" indicates that the option has been selected. More than one check box can be selected at a time.

COMMAND BUTTON

A command button can be used to invoke a command directly or to open another window or dialog box.

DROP-DOWN BOX, LIST, AND BUTTON

A drop-down box initially appears as a text box with a drop-down list ↓ button on its right. A drop-down list contains available options. Clicking the ↓ button (or pressing the Alt and ↓ arrow keys when the box is selected) will open its drop-down list.

GROUP BOX

A group box is an area of a dialog box containing related options.

INFORMATION BOX

An information box generally displays information about a current dialog box selection (not shown).

LIST BOX

A list box allows you to select from a list of available options (not shown).

OPTION BUTTON

An option button with a solid dot (●) indicates that the option has been selected. Only one option button can be selected in a group box.

TAB

A tab identifies a section of a dialog box. Clicking a tab will display that section's features.

TEXT BOX

A text box allows you to type in information to communicate with Excel.

SUMMARY OF COMMON EXCEL FEATURES

Following is a brief summary, with examples, showing how to use some of Excel's most popular features.

ALIGNING DATA

To align data after data have been placed into cells,

1. **Move to the cell containing the data or, if there are several cells, the first cell in the range**

2. **If desired, select the range of cells to be aligned**

MOUSE APPROACH	KEYBOARD APPROACH
3. **Click *Format*, *Cells*, Alignment tab**	3. **Press `Ctrl` + `1`, `A` for the Alignment tab**
4. **Click the desired *alignment option***	4. **Select the desired alignment by pressing `Alt` + the underlined letter of the option**
5. **Click the *OK* button**	5. **Press `↵`**

CANCELING

To cancel a pull-down or drop-down menu,

MOUSE APPROACH	KEYBOARD APPROACH
Click an open area outside the menu	**Press `Alt`**

To back up one menu level when using a submenu or to cancel a dialog box,

Press `Esc`

APPENDIX   SS257

To undo the effects of the last-issued command or action,

MOUSE APPROACH	KEYBOARD APPROACH
Click *Edit*, *Undo*	Press `Ctrl` + `Z`

CHANGING COLUMN WIDTH

To change the width of a specific column or range of columns,

1. Move the cell pointer to the column or select the desired range of columns whose width you wish to change

MOUSE APPROACH	KEYBOARD APPROACH
2. Click *Format*, *Column*, *Width* for its dialog box	2. Press `Alt` + `O` , `C` , `W` for the Column Width dialog box
3. Type in the new width in the Column Width text box	3. Type the new width in the Column Width text box
4. Click *OK*	4. Press `↵`

To change the default column width of all worksheets,

MOUSE APPROACH	KEYBOARD APPROACH
1. Click *Format*, *Column*, *Standard Width* for its dialog box	1. Press `Alt` + `O` , `C` , `S` for the Standard Width dialog box
2. Type in the new width in the *Standard Column Width* text box	2. Type the new column width in the *Standard Column Width* text box
3. Click *OK*	3. Press `↵`

CHANGING DIRECTORIES

To change the default directory that Excel uses to open or save files,

MOUSE APPROACH	KEYBOARD APPROACH
1. Click *Tools*, *Options* for its dialog box	1. Press `Alt` + `T` , `O` for the Options dialog box
2. Click the *General* tab	2. Press `G` for the General tab
3. Type in the identity of the new directory, for instance, A:\	3. Type in the identity of the new directory, for instance, A:\
4. Click *OK*	4. Press `↵`

To change the directory that Excel will default to in order to open or save files for the current work session only,

MOUSE APPROACH	KEYBOARD APPROACH
1. Click *File*, *Open* for the Open File dialog box or click *File*, *Save As* for the Save As dialog box	1. Press `Ctrl` + `O` for the Open File dialog box or press `F12` for the Save As dialog box

2. Click the desired directory in the Directories list box	2. Press **Alt** + **D** for the Directories list box and use the arrow keys to select the desired directory
3. Click *OK*	3. Press **↵**

Note that the *Drives* drop-down box and *Directories* list box of the *Open File* or *Save As* dialog box can be used to change the drive and directory for the current Excel session.

CREATING CHARTS3

To create a bar chart using a mouse and keyboard,

1. Select the data to be charted

MOUSE APPROACH	**KEYBOARD APPROACH**
2. Click *Insert, Chart, On This Sheet* for the chart pointer	2. Press **Alt** + **I** , **H** , **O** for the chart pointer

To place a chart on a new sheet instead of the current one, click *As New Sheet* in Step 2 instead of *On This Sheet.*

> Note: The chart pointer can be moved only by mouse.

3. Move the chart pointer to the position where you wish the upper-left corner of the chart to appear

4. Click the mouse to create a standard-size Excel chart or drag your pointer to create a custom range for the chart

To change the chart type,

1. Click the chart to select it, and then double-click it to turn on the Chart Edit mode

MOUSE APPROACH	**KEYBOARD APPROACH**
2. Click *Format, Chart Type* for its dialog box	2. Press **Alt** + **O** , **T** for the Chart Type dialog box
3. Click the desired chart type	3. Press **Alt** + **the underlined letter of the desired chart type**
4. Click *OK*	4. Press **↵**

CHARTING OPTIONS

To change chart headings, legends, or data labels; turn off grid lines; or change the chart's name,

1. Select the chart and then double-click it to put it in Chart Edit mode

MOUSE APPROACH	**KEYBOARD APPROACH**
2. Click *Insert* or *Format* for its menu	2. Press **Alt** + **I** or **O** for the Insert or Format menu

3. Click the desired option

4. Make the desired change

5. Click *OK*

3. Press the underlined letter of the desired option

4. Make the desired change

5. Press ↵

CLEARING (ERASING) CELL CONTENTS AND STYLES

The *Clear* submenu (*Edit* menu) can be used to erase All, Formats, cell contents, or Notes.

To erase the contents of one or more cells,

1. Move to the cell or select the range to be erased

MOUSE APPROACH

2. Click *Edit, Clear, Contents*

KEYBOARD APPROACH

2. Press Delete

To erase the format or both contents and format of one or more cells,

1. Move to the cell or select the range to be erased

MOUSE APPROACH

2. Click *Edit, Clear, Formats* or *All*

KEYBOARD APPROACH

2. Press Alt + E , A , F for formats or A for All

COPYING A SELECTION

A selection can consist of data, a table, a chart, or a graphic object. Copying a selection involves duplicating it from its source to a new location (destination). Copying requires invoking the *Copy* and *Paste* commands (*Edit* menu). The *Copy* command duplicates a selection to Windows Clipboard (a temporary holding application). The *Paste* command duplicates the contents of the Clipboard to a destination range.

To copy a selection from one part of a worksheet to another,

1. Select the source range of the data, table, chart, or graphic object to be copied

MOUSE APPROACH

2. Click *Edit, Copy* to copy the selection to Windows Clipboard

3. Select the destination range to copy to

4. Click *Edit, Paste* to paste from the Clipboard to the destination range

KEYBOARD APPROACH

2. Press Ctrl + C to copy the selection to Windows Clipboard

3. Select the destination range to copy to

4. Press Ctrl + V to paste from the Clipboard to the destination range

To copy a selection from one worksheet to another in a multiple-sheet file,

1. Select the source range of the data, table, chart, or graphic object to be copied

MOUSE APPROACH

2. Click *Edit, Copy*

KEYBOARD APPROACH

2. Press Ctrl + C to copy

3. Click the *Sheet tab* of the destination sheet

4. Select the destination range in the destination sheet

5. Click *Edit, Paste*

3. Press `Ctrl` + `PgDn` or `Ctrl` + `PgUp` until the destination sheet becomes the active sheet

4. Select the destination range in the destination sheet

5. Press `Ctrl` + `V` to paste

To copy a selection from the current workbook to another workbook file or Windows application file,

1. Select the range of the data, table, chart, or graphic object to be copied

MOUSE APPROACH

2. Click *Edit, Copy*

3. Open the destination workbook or application and file

4. Select the destination range

5. Click *Edit, Paste*

KEYBOARD APPROACH

2. Press `Ctrl` + `C` to copy

3. Open the destination or application and file

4. Select the destination range

5. Press `Ctrl` + `V` to paste

DATABASE TABLES

To create a database table, organize your worksheet data in rows and columns. Each worksheet row should form a record—a collection of related fields, and each column should contain one field—a category of data common to each record. The database table is the source in a database query operation.

DELETING ROWS, COLUMNS, OR SHEETS

The *Delete* dialog box (*Edit* menu) is used to delete a selection of rows or columns. Sheets can be deleted with the *Delete Sheet* command (Edit menu). To delete rows or columns,

1. Select the range to be deleted

MOUSE APPROACH

2. Click *Edit, Delete* for its dialog box

3. Click *Entire Row* or *Entire Column*

4. Click *OK*

KEYBOARD APPROACH

2. Press `Alt` + `E`, `D` for the *Delete* dialog box

3. Press `Alt` + `R` or `Alt` + `C` for row or column

4. Press `↵`

To delete a sheet, select *Delete sheet* from the Edit menu.

DISTRIBUTING DATA

To set up a frequency distribution that tallies the number of data values in a range that fall into each of several contiguous intervals (if data are already in a range, skip Step 1),

APPENDIX SS261

1. Place the data values to be tallied into a range

2. Set up a bin range (column), leaving the column to the right of the bin range empty

3. Select the frequency distribution results range (be sure to include one cell more than the corresponding bin numbers)

4. Type =FREQUENCY *(data array range,bin array range)* (but *DO NOT* press Enter)

5. Press Ctrl + Shift + ↵ to copy the frequency function to each cell in the distribution results range as an absolute formula, which is encased in brackets ({})

6. Press an arrow key to deselect

EDITING CELL DATA

To edit data in a cell,

1. Move the cell pointer to the cell containing the data to be edited

MOUSE APPROACH	KEYBOARD APPROACH
2. Double-click the cell to invoke the Edit mode	2. Press F2 to enter the *Edit* mode
3. Click that location to place the insertion point there	3. Move the insertion point to the place where you wish to make an edit
4. Make the edit	
5. Press ↵ to exit the *Edit* mode	

ENTERING DATA INTO A CELL

To enter data into a cell,

1. Move the cell pointer to the cell in which the data are to be entered

2. Type in the data

MOUSE APPROACH	KEYBOARD APPROACH
3. Click the *confirm* (✓) button to enter data or click the *cancel* (X) button to cancel the entry	3. Press ↵ to enter data or Esc to cancel the entry

If you want to enter data and move the cell pointer to another cell at the same time, replace Step 3 with the following:

MOUSE APPROACH	KEYBOARD APPROACH
3. Click the next desired cell	3. Press the arrow or tab key to move the cell pointer to the next desired cell

EXITING EXCEL

To exit by using the control-menu box or shortcut keys,

MOUSE APPROACH	KEYBOARD APPROACH
Double-click the *control-menu* box	Press Alt + F4

SS

To exit by using the control-menu,

MOUSE APPROACH

1. Click the *control-menu* box for the control-menu

2. Click *Close*

KEYBOARD APPROACH

1. Press `Alt` + `Spacebar`

2. Press `C` to close

To exit by using the menu bar,

MOUSE APPROACH

Click *File, Exit*

KEYBOARD APPROACH

Press `Alt` + `F`, `X`

FILTERING RECORDS

Before you can filter records that meet a specified condition, you need to organize your data into a database table. (Refer to the "Database Table" subsection.)
To filter records from a database table

1. Select the database table

MOUSE APPROACH

2. Click *Data, Filter, Auto Filter*

3. Use the *Field, Operator,* and *Value* drop-down boxes to set the criteria

4. Click *(Custom)* for its dialog box

5. Select the desired criteria

6. Click *OK* to filter records

KEYBOARD APPROACH

2. Press `Alt` + `D`, `F`, `F`

3. Move to the desired column heading and press `Alt` + `↓` for its drop-down list

4. Move to *(Custom)* and press `↵`

5. Press `↵` to filter records

FONT AND ATTRIBUTES

To change the font or attributes of a range,

1. Select the range

MOUSE APPROACH

2. Click *Format, Cells, Font* tab

3. Make the desired changes

4. Click *OK*

KEYBOARD APPROACH

2. Press `Ctrl` + `1`, `F` for the Font tab

3. Make the desired changes

4. Press `↵`

FORMATTING DATA

To change Excel's default format settings,

MOUSE APPROACH

1. Click *Format, Style* for its dialog box

KEYBOARD APPROACH

1. Press `Alt` + `F`, `S` for the Style dialog box

APPENDIX   SS263

2. Click *Modify* and make the desired
    format changes

3. Click *OK*

2. Press Alt + M and make the
    desired format changes

3. Press ⏎

To format data in a specific range of cells,

1. Select the desired range

MOUSE APPROACH

2. Click *Format, Cells* for the Format Cells
    dialog box

3. Click the desired format tab

4. Make the desired format changes

5. Click *OK*

KEYBOARD APPROACH

2. Press Ctrl + 1 for the Format
    Cells dialog box

3. Press the underlined letter of the
    desired format tab

4. Make the desired format changes

5. Press ⏎

FREEZING PANES

To freeze row titles, column titles, or both,

1. Move the cell pointer one row below the rows you wish to freeze

    or

    Move the cell pointer one column to the right of the columns you wish to freeze

    or

    Move the cell pointer one row below and one column to the right of the rows and columns
    you wish to freeze

MOUSE APPROACH

2. Click *Window, Freeze Pane*

3. Click *Window, UnFreeze Panes* to
    unfreeze

KEYBOARD APPROACH

2. Press Alt + W , F to the Freeze
    Panes

3. Press Alt + W , F to unfreeze
    panes

FUNCTION WIZARD

To use the Function Wizard to insert a function,

MOUSE APPROACH

1. Click *Insert, Function* for the Function
    Wizard dialog box

2. Click the desired Function Category in
    its list box

3. Click the desired function in the Function
    Name list box

KEYBOARD APPROACH

1. Press Alt + I , F for the
    Function Wizard dialog box

2. Press Alt + C and then use the
    arrow keys to select the desired
    Function Category and press ⏎

3. Press Alt + N and then use the
    arrow keys to select the desired function

4. **Click** *Next>* **for the Step 2 dialog box**

5. **Enter the function's arguments, pressing** `Tab` **to move to each text box**

6. **Click** *Finish*

4. **Press** `↵` **for the Step 2 dialog box**

5. **Enter the function's arguments, pressing** `Tab` **to move to each text box**

6. **Press** `↵`

HELP FEATURE

To invoke the *Help* feature,

MOUSE APPROACH

Click *Help*, *Content*

KEYBOARD APPROACH

Press `F1`

To get help on using a specific dialog box,

1. **Open the desired dialog box**

MOUSE APPROACH

2. **Click the** *Help* **button**

KEYBOARD APPROACH

2. **Press** `F1`

To use the *Help* search feature,

MOUSE APPROACH

1. **Click** *Help*, *Search for Help on* **for its dialog box**

2. **Type the desired topic**

3. **Click the** *Show Topics* **button to display options in the** *Select a Topic*, **then choose** *Go To* **list box**

4. **If needed, click the desired topic in that list box to move the highlight to it**

5. **Click the** *Go To* **button to get help on that topic**

KEYBOARD APPROACH

1. **Press** `Alt` + `H` , `S` **for the Search dialog box**

2. **Type the desired topic**

3. **Press** `Alt` + `S` **to show topics in the Select a Topic, then choose** *Go To* **list box**

4. **Press** `↓` **if needed to move the highlight to the desired topic**

5. **Press** `Alt` + `G` **get help on that topic**

To exit a Help window,

MOUSE APPROACH

6. **Double-click the Help window's control-menu box**

KEYBOARD APPROACH

6. **Press** `Alt` + `F4`

HIDE COLUMNS OR SHEETS

Hiding causes selected columns or sheets (worksheets) not to be displayed. The data or formulas contained in hidden columns or sheets are still active and can be redisplayed at any later time.

To hide columns,

1. **Select the range to be hidden**

APPENDIX   SS265

MOUSE APPROACH	KEYBOARD APPROACH
2. Click *Format, Column, Hide*	2. Press `Alt` + `O` , `C` , `H` to Hide columns

To redisplay previously hidden columns or sheets,

MOUSE APPROACH	KEYBOARD APPROACH
3. Click *Format, Column, Unhide*	3. Press `Alt` + `O` , `C` , `H`

To hide a sheet(s):

1.   **Select the Sheet or Sheets to be hidden**

MOUSE APPROACH	KEYBOARD APPROACH
2. Click *Format, Sheet, Hide* to hide sheet(s)	2. Press `Alt` + `O` , `H` , `H` to hide sheet(s)

To redisplay sheets previously hidden,

MOUSE APPROACH	KEYBOARD APPROACH
3. Click *Format, Sheet, Unhide*	3. Press `Ctrl` + `O` , `H` , `H`

INSERTING ROWS, COLUMNS, OR SHEETS

To insert rows, columns, or sheets (worksheets),

MOUSE APPROACH	KEYBOARD APPROACH
1. Click *Insert* for its menu	1. Press `Alt` + `I` for the Insert menu
2. Click *Rows, Columns* or *Worksheet*	2. Press `C` for columns, `R` for rows or `W` for sheet
3. Click *OK*	3. Press `↵`

LINKING A SELECTION

A selection can be a range of data, chart, table, or object. The *Link Paste* command (Paste Special dialog box-*Edit* menu) allows you to link a selection between workbooks.

To link a selection between workbooks,

1.   **Select the desired range, chart, table, or object to be linked in the source workbook**

MOUSE APPROACH	KEYBOARD APPROACH
2. Click *Edit, Copy* to copy the selection to the Clipboard	1. Press `Ctrl` + `C` to copy the selection to the Clipboard
3. Open the destination workbook	3. Open the destination workbook
4. Move to the place where you wish to place the link selection	4. Move to the place where you wish to place the link selection

5. Click *Edit, Paste Special, Paste Link* to paste the range with a link

5. Press `Alt` + `E` , `S` , `Alt` + `L` to paste the selection with a link

To link a selection between sheets,

1. **Select the range, chart, table, or object to be linked in the source sheet**

MOUSE APPROACH	KEYBOARD APPROACH
2. Click *Edit, Copy* to copy the selection to the Clipboard	2. Press `Ctrl` + `C` to copy the selection to the Clipboard
3. Click the destination sheet tab	3. Press `Ctrl` + `PgDn` to move to the next sheet
4. Move to the place where you wish to place the link selection	4. Move to the place where you wish to place the link selection
5. Click *Edit, Paste Special, Paste Link* to paste the selection with a link	5. Press `Alt` + `S` , `Alt` + `L` to paste the selection with a link

MACROS—CREATING AND ASSIGNING

Macros are stored mouse and keystroke sequences that you can invoke by holding down the `Ctrl` or `Ctrl` + `Shift` keys while pressing another (letter) key that, in effect, is the name of the macro. Macros can also be assigned to and invoked from the Tools menu or a macro button.

Macros can be created by using Excel's *Macro Recording* feature or written from scratch.

To create a macro using Excel's *Recording* feature,

MOUSE APPROACH	KEYBOARD APPROACH
1. Click *Tools, Records Macro, Record New Macro* for its dialog box	1. Press `Alt` + `T` , `R` , `R` for the Record New Macro dialog box

2. **Type a desired *MACRO NAME* in the Macro Name text box and press** `Tab`

Note that you can use up to 256 characters for a macro name; however, it cannot have any blank spaces separating words.

3. **Type a *DESCRIPTION* of the macro in the Description text box**

MOUSE APPROACH	KEYBOARD APPROACH
4. Click *OK* to turn on the macro recorder	4. Press `↵` to turn on the macro recorder

Excel uses **Visual Basic,** a programming language, for macro commands. When the macro recorder is turned on, Excel adds a new sheet called the *module sheet* to store your actions in Visual Basic code. Although not currently visible, this sheet is added behind Sheet 16 in the workbook.

5. **Perform desired mouse/keyboard actions**

MOUSE APPROACH	KEYBOARD APPROACH
6. Click *OK*	6. Press `↵`

APPENDIX   SS267

7. Click the *Stop Macro* toolbar button or *Tools*, *Record Macro*, *Stop Recording* to turn off the macro recorder

7. Press Alt + T , R , S to turn off the macro recorder

MACROS—ASSIGNING

A macro can be run using the Macro dialog box (Tools menu), shortcut keys, the Tools menu or a button. To run a macro using the latter three methods requires first assigning the macro commands to one of these items.

ASSIGNING TO SHORTCUT KEYS.   A macro can be assigned to shortcut keys either during its recording or after by using the Macro Options dialog box. This dialog box can be invoked from the Record New Macro dialog box when recording a macro, or from the Macro dialog box after a macro has been recorded. These macros will be referred to as *one-letter macros*. They generally involve the use of the Ctrl or Ctrl + Shift keys. These keys are automatically selected by Excel when assigning a macro to shortcut keys. This is to prevent conflict with previously programmed Excel or user-defined shortcut keys.

MOUSE APPROACH

1. Click *Tools*, *Macro* for its dialog box

2. Click *MACRO NAME* to be assigned

3. Click the *Options* button for the Macro Options dialog box

4. Click the *Shortcut Key* check box

5. Click the text box next to "Ctrl+"

6. Type the *ONE-LETTER* character for the macro

7. Click *OK, Close*

KEYBOARD APPROACH

1. Press Alt + T , M for the Macro dialog box

2. Press Tab and then use the arrow keys to select *MACRO NAME* to be assigned

3. Press Alt + O for the Macro Options dialog box

4. Press Alt + K to select the Shortcut Key check box

5. Press Tab to move to the text box next to "Ctrl+"

6. Type the *ONE-LETTER* character for the macro

7. Press ↵ , Alt + F4

ASSIGNING TO THE TOOLS MENU.   The procedures to assign a macro to the Tools menu is similar to assigning it to a shortcut key. Again, a macro can be assigned to the menu either during its recording or after by using the Macro Options dialog box.

MOUSE APPROACH

1. Click *Tools, Macro* for its dialog box

KEYBOARD APPROACH

1. Press Alt + T , M for the Macro dialog box

2. Click *MACRO NAME* to be assigned

3. Click the *Options* button for the Macro Options dialog box

4. Click the *Menu Item on Tools Menu* check box

5. Click the *Menu Item on Tools Menu* text box

6. Type a menu NAME for the macro

7. Click *OK, Close*

2. Press `Tab` and then use the arrow keys to select MACRO NAME to be assigned

3. Press `Alt` + `O` for the Macro Options dialog box

4. Press `Alt` + `U` to select the Menu Item on Tools menu check box

5. Press `Tab` to move to the text box

6. Type a menu NAME for the macro

7. Press `↵` , `Alt` + `F4`

ASSIGNING TO A BUTTON.   To assign a macro to a button on the current worksheet, try the following exercise.

1. Click *View, Toolbars*

2. Click the *Drawing* check box, *OK*

The Drawing toolbar should now appear in your Excel window. This toolbar can be used to create a button or other objects (pictures or symbols) in your worksheet.

3. Click the *Create Button* toolbar button

Note that the mouse pointer changes to a "+."

4. Point to the top-left corner of any desired location for the position of the macro button

Note that the mouse pointer changes to a "+."

5. Drag the mouse pointer down to create and size the button and then release

A button briefly appears and then the Assign macro dialog box will appear.

6. Click *MACRO NAME* to be assigned and then *OK*

7. Point before the "B" in Button 1 on the Button and then drag across to select it

8. Press `Delete` to remove it

9. Type a desired BUTTON NAME

At this point, you can move to any cell not occupied by the button to turn off the button edit mode.

10. Move to a different cell to exit the Button edit mode

MACROS—RUNNING

Once macros have been created, they are available for use. They can be run using the Macro dialog box, a shortcut key, the Tools menu or macro button. The latter three options first require the macro to be assigned to them.

To run a macro using the Macro dialog box,

APPENDIX   SS269

MOUSE APPROACH	KEYBOARD APPROACH
1. Click _Tools, Macro_ for its dialog box	1. Press **Alt** + **T** , **M** for the Macro dialog box
2. Click the desired macro	2. Press **Tab** and then use the arrow keys to select desired macro

The Macro dialog box lists all macros created and saved with a workbook. It also displays a description of the macro as entered when created.

MOUSE APPROACH	KEYBOARD APPROACH
3. Click _Run_ to run the macro	3. Press **↵** to run the macro

To invoke a one-letter macro,

1. Hold down the **Ctrl** key (or **Ctrl** + **Shift** keys) and then press the letter that corresponds to the name of the macro

To run the macro using the Tools menu,

MOUSE APPROACH	KEYBOARD APPROACH
1. Click _Tools_	1. Press **Alt** + **T** for the Tools menu
2. Click the desired _MACRO NAME_	2. Press **↓** as needed to select _MACRO NAME_ and then press **↵**

To invoke a macro from a button,

1. Click the desired _button_

MOVING A SELECTION

A selection can consist of a range, chart, table, or object. Moving involves removing a selection from its current location and placing it into a new location. The new location can be within the same worksheet or in another worksheet, worksheet file, or application. The _Cut_ command removes the selection from its current position and places it into the Windows Clipboard (a temporary holding application). The _Paste_ command copies the selection from the Clipboard into its new location.

To move a selection to a new location within the same worksheet,

MOUSE APPROACH	KEYBOARD APPROACH
1. Click _Edit, Cut_	1. Press **Ctrl** + **X** to cut
2. Move the cell pointer to the new location	2. Move the cell pointer to the new location
3. Click _Edit, Paste_	3. Press **Ctrl** + **V** to paste

To move a selection from one worksheet to another in a multiple-worksheet file,

1. Select the source range of the data, table, chart, or graphic object to be moved

MOUSE APPROACH	KEYBOARD APPROACH
2. Click _Edit, Cut_	2. Press **Ctrl** + **X** to cut

3. Click the *Sheet tab* of the destination Sheet

4. Select the destination range to move to in the destination sheet

5. Click *Edit, Paste*

---

3. Press `Ctrl` + `PgDn` or `Ctrl` + `PgUp` until the destination sheet becomes the active sheet

4. Select the destination range to move to in the destination sheet

5. Press `Ctrl` + `V` to paste

To move a selection from one workbook to another,

1. Open the source workbook

2. Select the range of data, table, chart, or graphic object to be moved

MOUSE APPROACH

3. Click *Edit, Cut*

4. Open the destination worksheet file

5. Select the destination range

6. Click *Edit, Paste*

KEYBOARD APPROACH

3. Press `Ctrl` + `X` to cut

4. Open the destination worksheet file

5. Select the destination range

6. Press `Ctrl` + `V` to paste

To move a selection from Excel to another Windows application,

1. Select the range of data, table, chart, or graphic object to be moved

MOUSE APPROACH

2. Click *Edit, Cut*

3. Open the destination application

4. Select the destination area

5. Click *Edit, Paste*

KEYBOARD APPROACH

1. Press `Ctrl` + `X` to cut

2. Open the destination application

4. Select the destination area

5. Press `Ctrl` + `V` to paste

OPENING FILES

To open a saved workbook,

MOUSE APPROACH

1. Click *File, Open* for the Open File dialog box

2. Type the file name or select it from the *File name* list box

3. Click *OK*

KEYBOARD APPROACH

1. Press `Ctrl` + `O` for the Open File dialog box

2. Type the file name or select it from the File Name list box

3. Press `⏎`

PAGE BREAKS

To create a page break in your worksheet,

1. Place the cell pointer in the leftmost column of the range you are printing, in the row where you want the new page to start

APPENDIX   SS271

MOUSE APPROACH

2.   Click *Insert, Page Break*

KEYBOARD APPROACH

2.   Press `Alt` + `I` , `B` for Page Break

PASSWORDS

To save a file with a password,

MOUSE APPROACH

1.   Click *File, Save As* for its dialog box

2.   Type the name of the file to be saved

3.   Click *Options* for its dialog box

4.   Type the password and then click *OK*

5.   Type the password again

6.   Click *OK*

KEYBOARD APPROACH

1.   Press `F2` for the Save As dialog box

2.   Type the name of the file to be saved

3.   Press `Alt` + `O` for the Options dialog box

4.   Type the password and then press `↵`

5.   Type the password again

6.   Press `↵`

PRINT PREVIEWING

To print preview the current workbook,

MOUSE APPROACH

1.   Click *File, Print Preview* for its window

KEYBOARD APPROACH

1.   Press `Alt` + `F` , `V` for the Print Preview window

To exit Print Preview,

MOUSE APPROACH

Click anywhere in the Print Preview window

KEYBOARD APPROACH

Press `Esc`

PRINTING

To print the current sheet, workbook, or a selected range,

1.   Select the print range if only printing a range

MOUSE APPROACH

2.   Click *File, Print* for its dialog box and go to Step 4 if printing the Selected Sheet

3.   If desired, click the *Entire Workbook* or *Selection* option

4.   Click *OK*

KEYBOARD APPROACH

2.   Press `Ctrl` + `P` for the Print dialog box and go to Step 4 if printing the Selected Sheet

3.   If desired, press `Alt` + `E` to select the Entire workbook option or `Alt` + `N` for a Selection

4.   Press `↵`

Note: The *Print* dialog box can also be used to set the range of pages and number of copies to print. Page setup and preview buttons are also available in this dialog box for quick access to their related dialog boxes.

PRINTING OPTIONS

A variety of printing options are available through the *Page Setup* dialog box. To open the *Page Setup* dialog box,

MOUSE APPROACH	KEYBOARD APPROACH
Click *File, Page Setup* for its dialog box	Press **Alt** + **F** , **U** for the Page Setup dialog box

To change the orientation from Portrait to Landscape,

1. Open the *Page Setup* dialog box

MOUSE APPROACH	KEYBOARD APPROACH
2. Click the *Landscape* option button 3. Click *OK*	2. Press **Alt** + **L** to select the Landscape option button 3. Press **↵**

COMPRESSED PRINTING. To control the compression of your worksheet, select either Adjust to (the default) or Fit to option button in the scaling group. The Adjust to option is preset to 100% and allows you to control the size of the printed data. To change it, you can either click the up or down triangle buttons to the right of the Adjust to text box or type in a desired size.

1. Open the *Page Setup* dialog box, select the *Page* tab

MOUSE APPROACH	KEYBOARD APPROACH
2. Click the **▼** or **▲** button of the Adjust to text box to reduce or increase the size 3. Click *OK*	2. Press **Alt** + **A** and then type in a desired size 3. Press **↵**

The *Fit to* option is helpful when you want to compress a large worksheet's width and/or length to that of a page or a desired number of pages. Like the *Adjust to* option, the Fit to option can be changed by either clicking the up or down triangle buttons to the right of its text boxes or you can type in a desired size.

PRINTING TITLES. The Print Titles group of the Sheet tab allows you to specify the range of rows to repeat at the top of a page and/or columns to repeat at the left of a page. To specify the rows as a print title:

1. Open the *Page Setup* dialog box, select the *Sheet* tab

MOUSE APPROACH	KEYBOARD APPROACH
2. Click the *Rows to Repeat at Top* or *Columns to Repeat at Left* text box 3. Type `FIRST ROW NUMBER:LAST ROW NUMBER` or `FIRST COLUMN LETTER:LAST COLUMN LETTER` to repeat 4. Click *OK*	2. Press **Alt** + **R** for the Rows to Repeat at Top or **Alt** + **C** for the Columns to Repeat at Left text box 3. Type `FIRST ROW NUMBER:LAST ROW NUMBER` or `FIRST COLUMN LETTER:LAST COLUMN LETTER` to repeat 4. Press **↵**

OTHER PRINT OPTIONS. The Sheet Tab (Page Dialog box) Print group provides print option check boxes that can be used to specify printing. The options are:

- Without grid lines—the default
- Print Notes—prints any cell notes defined in the worksheet
- Print in Draft Quality—no grid lines and less graphics
- Print in pure black and white
- Print with Row and Column headings—include row numbers and column letters.

Simply click the desired check box to either select (an "X" will appear in the check box) or deselect it. With the keyboard, press the **Alt** key and the underlined letter of the desired check box.

HEADERS/FOOTERS. To place a header or footer on a sheet,

1. Open the Page Setup dialog box (File menu), and select the *Header/Footer* tab

MOUSE APPROACH	KEYBOARD APPROACH
2. Click either *Custom Header* or *Custom Footer* for its dialog box	2. Press **Alt** + **C** for Custom Header dialog box or **Alt** + **U** for the Custom Footer dialog box
3. Enter the desired header or footer	3. Enter the desired header or footer
4. Click *OK, OK*	4. Press ↵ , ↵

PROTECTING (UNPROTECTING) CELLS

To protect a file from editing or erasure,

MOUSE APPROACH	KEYBOARD APPROACH
1. Click *Tools, Protection*	1. Press **Alt** + **T** , **P** for the Protection submenu
2. Click either *Protect Sheet* or *Protect Workbook*	2. Press either **P** for Protect Sheet or **W** for Protect Workbook
3. If desired, type a password, click *OK* and then type the password again; otherwise click the *OK* button	3. If desired, type a password, press ↵ , and then type the password again; otherwise, press ↵

To disable the *Protect* feature,

MOUSE APPROACH	KEYBOARD APPROACH
1. Click *Tools, Protection*	1. Press **Alt** + **T** , **P**
2. Click either *Unprotect Sheet* or *Unprotect Workbook*	2. Press **U** for Unprotect Sheet or **W** for Unprotect Workbook

To unprotect a range or ranges in a protected file,

1. Disable the *Protection* feature
2. Select the range to be unprotected

MOUSE APPROACH	KEYBOARD APPROACH
3. Click *Format, Cells, Protection* tab	3. Press **Ctrl** + **1** , **P** **P** for Protection tab

4. Click the _Locked_ check box to remove the "X"

5. Click _OK_

6. Repeat Steps 2 through 5 for each desired additional unprotected range

7. Turn on the Protection feature

4. Press `Alt` + `L` to remove the "X" from the Lock check box

5. Press `↵`

QUERY TABLES

A query table can be created by extracting records from a database table. To create a complex criteria range,

1. **In an area outside of the database table, type desired criteria labels (in the same row as each other) that identically correspond to those column labels (titles) that you want to analyze from the database table**

For example, to analyze the database column labeled _TEST 1,_ you must use that same label as a criteria label in the criteria range.

2. **Use one of the following guidelines to enter comparison criteria in the criteria range:**

- To find records that meet all criteria in a row, type the criteria in the same row in cells next to each other.
- To find records that meet more than one criterion for the same column, use the same column label in a new column.
- To find records that meet all criteria in the first row _or_ the second row, type the criteria in different rows.

3. **Select the database table range**

MOUSE APPROACH

4. Click _Data, Filter, Advanced Filter_ for its dialog box

5. Click _Copy to Another Location_ option button

6. Click the _Criteria Range:_ text box

7. Type in the Criteria Range

8. Press `Tab` and type in the Copy to range

9. Click _OK_

KEYBOARD APPROACH

4. Press `Alt` + `C` , `F` , `A` for the Advanced Filter dialog box

5. Press `Alt` + `O` to select the Copy to Another Location option button

6. Press `Alt` + `C` for the Criteria Range Text box

7. Type in the Criteria Range

8. Press `Tab` and type the Copy to range

9. Press `↵`

To just filter the database table instead of creating a new table, skip Steps 5 and 8 above.

RANGES

A range is a contiguous block of cells. Once a range is selected (marked), a variety of Excel commands can be applied to it. Ranges can also be selected after invoking many commands.

APPENDIX   SS275

To select a range by mouse before invoking a command,

Method 1

Drag the mouse pointer over the desired area

Method 2

1. **Click the upper-left cell in the desired range area**

2. **Press and hold** `Shift` **while clicking the bottom-right cell in the desired range area**

To select a range by keyboard before invoking a command,

Method 1

1. **Move the cell pointer to the upper-left cell in the desired range area**

2. **Press and hold** `Shift` **while pressing the arrow keys to highlight (select) the desired range**

Method 2

1. **Move the cell pointer to the upper-left cell in the desired range area**

2. **Press** `F8` **to "anchor" this cell**

3. **Press any of the arrow keys to highlight the desired range and then**

To select a range after invoking a command that uses a dialog box,

1. **Select the appropriate** *Range* **text box**

2. **Type the range**

To remove a range selection (highlight),

MOUSE APPROACH	**KEYBOARD APPROACH**
Click anywhere outside the range	**Press any arrow key**

To select a collection or group of ranges,

1. **Select the first range**

2. **Press and hold** `Ctrl` **while selecting each additional range**

To select the entire range of a worksheet,

Click the Select All button (see Figure SSA–2 for its location)

To select the entire range of a column,

Click the column's letter

To select the entire range of a row,

Click the *row's* **number**

REPEAT CHARACTERS

To repeat a character across a cell's space,

1. **Type the character and press** `↵`

MOUSE APPROACH	KEYBOARD APPROACH
2. Click *Format*, *Cells*, *Alignment* tab	2. Press `Ctrl` + `!` , `A` for the Alignment tab
3. Click *Fill*	3. Press `Alt` + `F` for Fill
4. Click *OK*	4. Press `↵`

SAVING WORKBOOKS

To save a workbook,

MOUSE APPROACH	KEYBOARD APPROACH
1. Click *File*, *Save As* for its dialog box	1. Press `F12` for the *Save As* dialog box
2. Type the name of the workbook if this is the first time it is being saved	2. Type the name of the workbook if this is the first time it is being saved
3. Click *OK*	3. Press `↵`
4. Click the *Yes* button if it is not the first time the workbook has been saved	4. Press `Alt` + `Y` to replace the workbook if this is not the first time it has been saved

To resave a workbook without confirmation,

MOUSE APPROACH	KEYBOARD APPROACH
Click *File*, *Save*	Press `Ctrl` + `S` to save

To save the entire workspace area,

MOUSE APPROACH	KEYBOARD APPROACH
1. Click *File*, *Save Workspace*	1. Press `Alt` + `F` , `W` for the Save Workspace dialog box
2. Type in a Workspace file name	2. Type in a Workspace file name
3. Click *OK*	3. Press `↵`

SELECTING

To *select* means to mark a range of cells, a chart, a table, or an object to make style (format) changes to it, to copy or move it, or to apply other programmed features to it. See the "Ranges" subsection to learn how to select a range of cells. These techniques also apply to tables.

To select a chart, any parts of a chart, or an object,

Click it

To deselect a chart or object,

MOUSE APPROACH	KEYBOARD APPROACH
Click outside the chart or object	Press `Esc` or any arrow key

SHORTCUT MENUS

Shortcut menus are available for quick mouse access to commands relating to certain areas of the Excel window. To open a Shortcut menu,

1. **Point to the desired area of the Excel Window**

2. **Click the right mouse button**

If a Shortcut menu is available, it will appear. To select a command from a Shortcut menu,

3. **Click it**

To exit a Shortcut menu without selecting a command,

Click an open area outside the Shortcut menu

SORTING DATA

Excel sorts data according to the "numbers first" collating sequence. This sequence is described by the following ordering:

1. **Blank cells**

2. **Data starting with numbers (in numerical order)**

3. **Data starting with letters (in alphabetical order)**

4. **Data starting with other characters**

5. **Numbers**

To sort a range,

1. **Select the range of data to be sorted**

MOUSE APPROACH

2. **Click *Data, Sort* for its dialog box**

3. **Use the *Sort By* drop-down box to set the first sorting key**

4. **Select the sorting order by either clicking the *Ascending* or *Descending* option button**

5. **If desired, use the *Then By* and *Then By* drop-down boxes to set second and third sorting keys**

6. **If Step 5 is performed, select the desired sorting order for each key (Ascending or Descending)**

7. **Click *OK* to sort**

KEYBOARD APPROACH

2. **Press `Alt` + `D`, `S` for the Sort dialog box**

3. **Use the *Sort By* drop-down box to set the first sorting key**

4. **Select the sorting order by either pressing `Alt` + `A` for Ascending or `Alt` + `D` for Descending**

5. **If desired, use the *Then By* and *Then By* drop-down boxes to set second and third sorting keys**

6. **If Step 5 is performed, select the desired sorting order for each key (Ascending or Descending)**

7. **Press `↵` to sort**

SPELL CHECKER

To use Excel's spell checker,

1. Move to Cell A1 (the beginning of the workbook)

MOUSE APPROACH	KEYBOARD APPROACH
2. Click *Tools, Spelling* for its dialog box	2. Press F7 for the Spelling dialog box
3. Click the desired option for each misspelled word	3. Select the desired option for each misspelled word
4. Click *OK* when the dialog box appears and reads, *finished spell checking entire sheet*	4. Press ↵ when the dialog box appears and reads, *finished spell checking entire sheet*

SPLITTING VIEWS

To split a worksheet into horizontal panes (parts),

1. Move the cell pointer to the row you wish to be the top edge of the second pane

MOUSE APPROACH	KEYBOARD APPROACH
2. Click <u>W</u>indow, <u>S</u>plit	2. Press Alt + W , S to Split

To split a worksheet into vertical panes,

1. Move the cell pointer to the column you wish to use as the left edge of the second pane

MOUSE APPROACH	KEYBOARD APPROACH
2. *Click <u>W</u>indow, <u>S</u>plit*	2. Press Alt + W , S to split

To move from one pane to another within the same worksheet or from one worksheet to another,

MOUSE APPROACH	KEYBOARD APPROACH
Click the pane or worksheet	Press F6

STARTING EXCEL

To start Excel from the Windows Program Manager,

1. Locate the Microsoft Office group or Microsoft Excel group

If it appears as a group icon, perform Step 2 to resize it to a window; otherwise go to Step 3

MOUSE APPROACH	KEYBOARD APPROACH
2. Double-click the *Microsoft Office* of *Microsoft Excel* group icon	2. Press Ctrl + F6 , if needed, to move the highlight to the Microsoft Office or Microsoft Excel group icon, and then press ↵

3. Point to the *Microsoft Excel* icon

4. Double-click the *Microsoft Excel* icon to start the program

3. Press `Ctrl` + `F6` , if needed, to move the highlight to the title bar of the Microsoft Office or Microsoft Excel window, and then use the arrow keys to move the highlight to the *Microsoft Excel* icon within the window

4. Press `↵` to start the program

TABLE LOOKUPS

To look up an entry in a specified column (vertical lookup) or row (horizontal lookup) in a table that corresponds to a value in a specific cell,

1. Move the cell pointer to the cell that will contain the result of the lookup

MOUSE APPROACH

2. Click *Insert, Function* for the Function Wizard dialog box

3. Click *Lookup & Reference* in the Function Category list box

4. Use the scroll bar of the *Function Name* list box to locate *VLOOKUP* or *HLOOKUP,* depending on whether you wish to do a vertical or horizontal lookup, and click it

5. Click *Next>* to move to Step 2 of the dialog box

KEYBOARD APPROACH

2. Press `Shift` + `F3` for the Function Wizard dialog box

3. Press `Alt` + `C` for the Function Category list box and then use the arrow keys to select *Lookup & Reference*

4. Press `Alt` + `N` to move to the Function Name list box, and then use the arrow keys to select either *VLOOKUP* or *HLOOKUP,* depending on whether you wish to do a vertical or horizontal lookup

5. Press `↵` to move to Step 2 of the dialog box

6. Enter the cell address of the data on which the search is to be based in the *lookup_value* text box and press `Tab`

7. Enter the range corresponding to the table to be searched in the *table_array* text box and press `Tab`

8. Type the offset, which is the number of columns (or rows) between the lookup column (or row) and the first table column (or row) in the *col_index_num* (or *row_index_num*) text box and press `↵`

TOOLBAR BUTTONS

Toolbar buttons provide quick access to Excel's commands by mouse. Toolbar buttons are grouped in sets and appear below the edit line of the Excel window.

To receive a description of a toolbar's function in the status bar,

1. Point to the desired toolbar button

To invoke a command using a toolbar button,

1. Point to the desired toolbar button

2. Click the toolbar button

To switch toolbar button sets,

1. Click _View, Toolbars_

2. Click the desired toolbar's check box

3. Click _OK_

To change the toolbar button's size,

1. Click _View, Toolbars_ for its dialog box

2. Click the _Large Buttons_ check box

3 Click _OK_

To customize a toolbar,

1. Click _View, Toolbars, Customize_ for its dialog box

2. Follow the directions of the dialog box to make your desired changes

3. Click _Close_

4. Click _OK_

TRANSPOSING DATA

To change the alignment of data in cells to vertical rather than horizontal or vice versa,

1. Select the vertical (or horizontal) range to be transposed

MOUSE APPROACH	KEYBOARD APPROACH
2. Click _Edit, Copy_	2. Press `Ctrl` + `C` to copy
3. Move to the cell address where you want the transposed range to begin	3. Move to the cell address where you want the transposed range to begin
4. Click _Paste Special, Transpose, OK_	4. Press `Alt` + `S` , `Alt` + `E` to select Transpose in the Paste Special dialog box, and press `↵`

UNDO

Undo cancels the most recent command or action you performed. To issue the _Undo_ command,

MOUSE APPROACH	KEYBOARD APPROACH
Click _Edit, Undo_	Press `Ctrl` + `Z`

APPENDIX   SS281

FUNCTIONS

Microsoft Excel version 5.0 offers more than 200 functions. To view a complete alphabetical on-line list and description of functions,

MOUSE APPROACH

1. Click *Insert, Function* for the Function Wizard dialog box

2. Click *All* in the Function Category list box

3. Locate the desired function in the Function Name list box (use the scroll bar if necessary)

4. Click the desired function in the Function Name list box

KEYBOARD APPROACH

1. Press `Shift` + `F3` for the Function Wiazrd dialog box

2. Press `Alt` + `C` for the Category list box and use the arrow keys to select *ALL*

3. Press `Alt` + `N` for the Function Name dialog box

4. Use the arrow keys to move to a desired button

Note that a description of the currently selected function appears below the Function Category list box.

To use a selected function,

MOUSE APPROACH

5. Click *Next>* for Step 2

6. Enter the arguments of the function

   Note: To move from one text box to another, use the `Tab` key.

7. Click *Finish*

KEYBOARD APPROACH

5. Press `↵` for Step 2

6. Enter the arguments of the function

7. Press `↵`

To exit the Function Wizard prior to completing an entry:

MOUSE APPROACH

8. Click *Cancel*

KEYBOARD APPROACH

8. Press `Esc`

Following is a list of the primary functions. If you need more advanced functions, use the Function Wizard to help you locate and use them. (Remember to type an `=` sign before entering a function.)

- **ABS(x)**
  Calculates the absolute (positive) value of the value x.
- **ACOS(x)**
  Calculates the arc cosine of the angle x, where x is expressed in radians.
- **ADDRESS (row_num, column_num, abs_num, a1, sheet_text)**
  Returns a cell reference as text to a single cell in a worksheet.
- **AND (logical1, logical2,...)**
  Return TRUE if all its arguments are TRUE.
- **AREAS (range)**
  Returns the number of areas in a range.

- **ASIN(x)**

  Calculates the arc sine of the angle x, where x is expressed in radians.

- **ATAN(x)**

  Calculates the arc tangent of the angle x, where x is expressed in radians.

- **ATAN2(x,y)**

  Calculates the radian angle whose tangent is y/x, where y and x are any values.

- **AVERAGE (range)**

  Averages values in a range.

- **CEILING (x, significance)**

  Calculates a number rounded to the nearest integer or the nearest multiple of significance.

- **CELL(attribute,range)**

  Returns information about a specified attribute for the first cell in a range. Some of the attributes for which information is provided are formatting, location, or contents.

- **CHAR(x)**

  Returns the character that corresponds to x (where x is between 1 and 255).

- **CHOOSE(index_num, value1, value2...)**

  Uses the offset (index_num) value to return the contents of one of the cells in the argument list. For instance, an offset of zero would return the contents of the first cell in the list.

- **CLEAN(text)**

  Removes nonprintable characters from text.

- **CODE(text)**

  Displays the number code that corresponds to the first character in a text string.

- **COLUMN (cell_reference)**

  Counts the column number of a cell reference.

- **COLUMNS(range)**

  Counts the number of columns in a range.

- **COS(x)**

  Calculates the cosine of the angle x, where x is expressed in radians.

- **COUNT (value1,value2,...)**

  Counts the numbers that are in the list of arguments.

- **COUNTA(value1,value2,...)**

  Counts the number of nonblank cells in a range.

- **COUNTBLANK (range)**

  Counts the number of blank cells in a range.

- **DATE(yy,mm,dd)**

  Calculates the date number for a given year/month/day combination.

- **DATEVALUE(date string)**

  Converts a date string (such as "5-Jan-95") into an equivalent date number.

- **DAVERAGE(database_range,field_offset,criteria_range)**

  Averages the values in a field of the database range that meet the criteria specified in the criteria range.

- **DAY(date_number)**

  Calculates a serial number that corresponds to the day in the date number.

- **DCOUNT (database_range,field, criteria_range)**

  Counts the number of cells containing numbers from a specified database and criteria.

- **DCOUNTA(database_range,field_offset,criteria_range)**
  Counts the number of nonblank cells in a field of the input range that meet the criteria specified in the criteria range.
- **DDB(initial cost,salvage value,useful life,period,factor)**
  Calculates the double-declining balance depreciation of an asset for one period, based on the asset's initial cost, salvage value, and useful life.
- **DMAX(database_range,field_offset,criteria_range)**
  Finds the largest value in a field of the database range that meets the criteria specified in the criteria range.
- **DMIN(database_range,field_offset,criteria_range)**
  Finds the smallest value in a field of the database range that meets the criteria specified in the criteria range.
- **DOLLAR(x, decimal)**
  Converts a number to text, using currency format.
- **DSTDEVP(database_range,field_offset,criteria_range)**
  Finds the population standard deviation of the values of a field in the database range that meet the criteria range.
- **DSUM(database_range,field_offset,criteria_range)**
  Finds the sum of the values of a field in the database range that meet the criteria specified in the criteria range.
- **DVAR(database_range,field_offset,criteria_range)**
  Finds the population variance of the values of a field in the database range that meet the criteria specified in the criteria range.
- **EVEN(x)**
  Rounds a number up to the nearest even integer.
- **EXACT(text_string1,text_string2)**
  Check to see that two text-string values are equivalent.
- **EXP(x)**
  Calculates the number e raised to the power x.
- **FALSE( )**
  Returns the value FALSE.
- **FIND(find_textstring,within_targettextstring,start number)**
  Locates the starting position of the find text string within the target text string. The start number is the first character of the search.
- **FREQUENCY (data_array, bin_array)**
  Returns a frequency distribution as a vertical display.
- **FV(rate, nperiod, payment, PV, type)**
  Calculates the future value of a series of equal payments made over a number of periods at a specified periodic interest rate.
- **HLOOKUP(lookup_value,table_array,row_index_num...)**
  Uses the lookup value x to look across the first row in the range (array) to find the value closest to but not larger than x; then it goes down that column the number of offset rows specified and selects the contents of the cell there.
- **HOUR(time_number)**
  Calculates the integer that corresponds to the hour in a time number.
- **IF(condition,result_if_true,result_if_false)**
  Returns one result if a condition is true, another if a condition is false.
- **INDEX(...)**
  Finds the value in the cell located at the specific row offset and column offset of the first cell in the range.

- **INT(x)**

  Truncates the value x to a whole number.
- **IRR(values, guess)**

  Calculates the internal rate of return of cash flows in a range. The estimate represents your initial guess of this rate.
- **ISERR(x)**

  A TRUE is returned if the value is any error value except #N/A.
- **ISNA(x)**

  Checks if an #N/A condition is present. If it is, a TRUE is returned.
- **ISNUMBER(x)**

  Tests whether a cell reference contains a number. Returns TRUE if it is a number.
- **LEFT(text_string,n)**

  Returns the first n characters of the text string.
- **LEN(text_string)**

  Counts the number of characters in a string.
- **LN(x)**

  Calculates the natural (base e) logarithm of the value x.
- **LOG(x)**

  Calculates the common (base 10) logarithm of the value x.
- **LOWER(text_string)**

  Converts all characters in a text string to lowercase characters.
- **MAX(number1,number2,...)**

  Finds the highest value in a range.
- **MID(text_string,start_number,n)**

  Extracts n contiguous characters from a text string, beginning at the start number. The start number corresponds to the first letter of the string.
- **MIN(number1,number2,...)**

  Finds the lowest value in a range.
- **MINUTE(time_number)**

  Calculates the integer that corresponds to the minute in a time number.
- **MOD(number,divisor)**

  Returns the remainder (modulus) that is produced when a number is divided by divisor.
- **MONTH(serial_number)**

  Calculates the serial number that corresponds to a month.
- **N(range)**

  Returns the value in the first cell of a range if the cell contains a text number.
- **NA( )**

  Returns the error value #N/A.
- **NOW( )**

  Returns a number that corresponds to the current time according to your computer's clock.
- **NPV(rate,value1,value2,...)**

  Calculates the net present value of the cash flows in a range, at a specified periodic interest rate.
- **PI**

  Returns the value of π (3.14159. . .).
- **PMT(rate,nper,pu,fv,type)**

  Calculates the payment made in each of a specified number of periods that, at a specified periodic interest rate, is equivalent to a present value (such as a loan).

APPENDIX SS285

- **PROPER(text_string)**
  Converts the first letter in each word of a text string to uppercase and converts the other letters to lowercase.
- **PV(rate,nper,pmt,fv,type)**
  Calculates the present value of a series of equal payments, at a specified periodic interest rate, over a specified number of periods.
- **RAND()**
  Generates a random value between 0 and 1.
- **RATE(nper,pmt,pv,fv,type,guess)**
  Calculates the periodic interest rate necessary for a present value to accrue to a future value, within a specified number of periods.
- **REPLACE(old_text_string,start_num,num_chars,new_text_string)**
  Replaces characters in the old text string with characters from the new string. The start number and length determine where replacement starts in the original text string and how many characters are to be replaced. The start number corresponds to the first letter in the original text string.
- **RIGHT(text_string,n)**
  Returns the last n characters of the text string.
- **ROUND(x,num_digits)**
  Rounds a value x to a specified number of decimal places.
- **ROWS(range)**
  Counts the number of rows in a range.
- **SECOND(time_number)**
  Calculates the serial number that corresponds to the second in a time number.
- **SIN(x)**
  Calculates the sine of the angle x, where x is expressed in radians.
- **SLN(initial_cost,salvage_value,useful_life)**
  Calculates the straight-line depreciation of an asset for each period, based on the asset's initial cost, salvage value, and useful life.
- **SQRT(x)**
  Calculates the square root of the value x.
- **STDEVP(range)**
  Calculates the population standard deviation of values in a range.
- **SUM(range)**
  Sums the values in a range.
- **SYD(initial_cost,salvage_value,useful_life,period)**
  Calculates the sum-of-the-year's-digits depreciation of an asset for one period, based on the asset's initial cost, salvage value, and useful life.
- **T(value)**
  Converts its argument to text.
- **TAN(x)**
  Calculates the tangent of the angle x, where x is expressed in radians.
- **TIME(hr,min,sec)**
  Calculates the time number for an hour/minute/second combination.
- **TIMEVALUE(time_string)**
  Converts a time string (such as "14:30:58") into an equivalent time number.
- **TRIM(text_string)**
  Removes leading, consecutive, and trailing blanks from a text string.
- **TRUE( )**
  Returns the value TRUE.

- **UPPER(string)**

  Converts all characters in a string to uppercase characters.

- **VALUE(text_string)**

  Converts a string that looks like a number into a value. For example, the text string 55.3 becomes the value 55.3.

- **VAR(range)**

  Calculates the population variance of values in a range.

- **VLOOKUP(lookup_value,table_array,col_index_num,...)**

  Uses the lookup value x to look down the first column in the range (array) to find the value closest to but not larger than x; then it goes across that row the number of offset columns specified and selects the contents of the cell there.

- **YEAR(date_number)**

  Calculates the year from a date number.

MICROSOFT EXCEL'S MENU SYSTEM

Microsoft Excel's menu bar provides a menu system that allows you to access its features by mouse or keyboard. Figure SSA-4 provides an overview of each menu-bar item's pull-down menu. To see a description of a pull-down menu item in the status bar, first open the related pull-down menu by clicking its menu-bar item or pressing the **Alt** key and the underlined letter of the item. Next, use the arrow keys to move the selection highlight to the desired menu item without pressing the **Enter** key.

MACRO COMMANDS

Macros are short programs consisting of mouse actions, keystrokes, and special functions called *macro commands*. Excel uses Visual Basic, a programming language, for its macros. Macros can be created by using the macro recorder (*Tools*, *Record Macro*, *Record New Macro*) or written directly into a Visual Basic module. A *module* is a sheet that Excel uses to store macro command statements. When on, the macro recorder automatically types the correct Visual Basic macro statement as you perform an action by mouse or keyboard on a module sheet.

Refer to the "Summary of Common Excel Features" section of this appendix for macro recording operations.

WRITING A MACRO

Writing a macro from scratch involves the use of Visual Basic codes. Although these codes are complicated, Excel provides an on-line help with Example Codes for many common commands. These codes can be copied from the help window into a module sheet. To insert a module sheet (or switch to an existing one) and then copy a Visual Basic macro code:

Note: The procedures below can also be used for editing a macro.

APPENDIX SS287

FIGURE SSA-4 ■ MICROSOFT EXCEL'S MENU SYSTEM

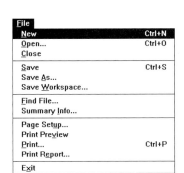

MOUSE APPROACH

1. Click *Insert, Macro, Module* for a new module sheet or click an existing module sheet tab.

2. Click *Help, Content, Programming with Visual Basic*

3. Click *Search* for its dialog box

4. Use the scroll bar to locate the desired code, click it, *Show Topics*

5. Click the desired topic in Select a Topic, choose Go To list box, and click *Go To*

6. Click *Example* for the Visual Basic Reference Example window

KEYBOARD APPROACH

1. Press Alt + I , M , M for a new module sheet or press Ctrl + PgDn or Ctrl + PgUp to move to an existing module sheet tab

2. Press Alt + H , C and then press Tab until *Programming with Visual Basic* is selected and press ↵

3. Press Alt + S for the Search dialog box

4. Press Tab and then use the arrow keys to select the desired code, and then press Alt + S

5. Use the arrow keys to select the desired topic and press Alt + G

6. Press Tab to select *Example* and press ↵ for the Visual Basic Reference Example window

7. Click the *Copy* button for the copy dialog box

8. Select the code and other information to copy

9. Click the *Copy* button to copy to the Clipboard

7. Press Tab until the Copy button is selected and then press ↵ for the Copy dialog box

8. Select the code and other information to be copied

9. Press Alt + C to copy to the Clipboard

At this point, you can switch to the module sheet and paste the codes and then switch back to the on-line help and copy another code or exit help. To switch to the module sheet and paste without closing help,

MOUSE APPROACH

10. Click the module sheet and move the insertion point to the desired paste location

11. Click *Edit, Paste*

12. Press Alt + Tab to switch to Help windows not needed and close them (for example, the windows that relate to the last code copied)

13. Switch to the Search window.

14. Repeat Steps 4 through 13 as desired

15. Close the Help windows

16. Resave the workbook with the new macro commands

17. Run the Macro to see it operate

KEYBOARD APPROACH

10. Press Alt + Tab until the module sheet is active and move to the insertion point to the desired paste location

11. Press Ctrl + V to paste

THE STEP FEATURE

Macros work so quickly that it is often difficult to locate errors when a macro does not work as expected. The Step feature helps locate errors by allowing a macro to be run one instruction at a time. This feature can be used in conjunction with the Steps in the "Writing a Macro" section to edit a macro.

MOUSE APPROACH

1. Click *View, Toolbars, Visual Basic, OK* for its toolbar

2. Click *Tools, Macro*

3. Click the MACRO to be edited

4. Click the *Step* button to turn on the Step mode

KEYBOARD APPROACH

1. Press Alt + T , M

2. Press Tab

3. Use arrow keys to select the *MACRO* to be edited

4. Press Alt + S to turn on the Step mode

If you are using the Keyboard Approach, the Visual Basic toolbar will not appear on your screen. The macro's current command sequence appears in a rectangular box. Although you can invoke the *Step Into* and *Step Over* commands from the Run menu, it is much easier to use toolbar buttons or shortcut keys. The Step Into command invokes the next macro command statement. The Step Over command skips the next command statement.

APPENDIX SS289

MOUSE APPROACH	KEYBOARD APPROACH
5. Click the *Step Into* toolbar button	5. Press F8

Each time you invoke the Step Into command, the program performs the next macro command in the sequence. You can then examine the effect of each command and locate the error. See your Excel manual for further information regarding Visual Basic codes. Keep repeating Step 5 to continue the process, and then make editing changes, or do the following to end it.

MOUSE APPROACH	KEYBOARD APPROACH
6. Click *Run, End*	6. Press Alt + R , E

7. If needed, turn off the Visual Basic toolbar (click its control-menu box)
8. Resave the workbook

Note: To quickly go to and edit a macro's module sheet, select *Edit* in the Macro dialog box. Note that the *Run* menu-bar item also appears when you display a module sheet.

TOOLBARS

Toolbars provide quick mouse access to Excel's feature buttons or drop-down boxes. As in Figure SSA-2, Excel opens with Standard and Format toolbars below its menu bar. Some toolbars automatically appear when a related command is invoked. For

FIGURE SSA-5 ■ TOOLBARS

Standard toolbar

1 2 3 4 5 6 7 8 9 10 11 12 13 14 15 16 17 18 19 20 21 22

Format toolbar

23 24 25 26 27 28 29 30 31 32 33 34 35 36 37 38 39

40 41 42 43 44 45 46 47

53 54 55 56 57 58 59 60 61 62 63 64

65 66 67 68 69 70 71 72 73

48 49 50 51 52

(continued)

FIGURE SSA-5 ■ *(continued)*

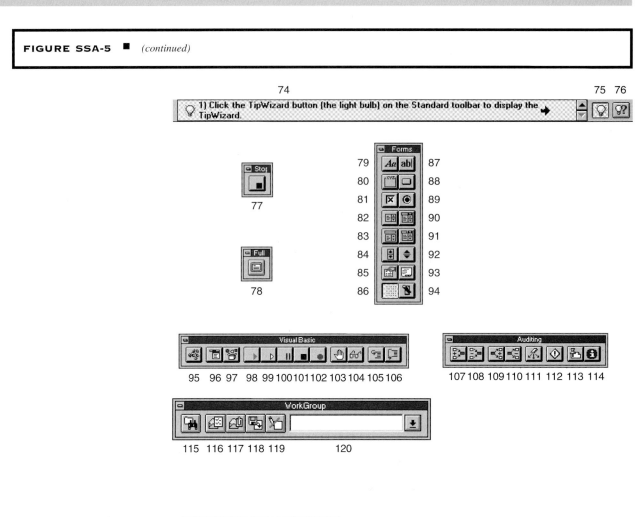

example, the Chart toolbar will appear when you invoke the Chart command or place an existing chart in edit mode.

Excel comes with 13 preset toolbars, which are displayed in Figure SSA-5. These toolbars can be turned on/off using the toolbars command of the View menu. You can also turn on/off a toolbar using its shortcut menu.

A toolbar can be moved by dragging its background or title bar. It can also be resized when not attached to the Excel window. Toolbars in this state are called *floating* toolbars and have their own title bar and control box. To resize a floating toolbar, drag one of its walls or corners.

Existing toolbars can also be customized and new toolbars can be created. Use Excel's on-line help to guide you through these operations.

The following chart's toolbar button numbers correspond to Figure SSA-5.

Toolbar

Button #	Description
	Standard Toolbar
1	Opens a new workbook
2	Opens a saved workbook
3	Saves the current workbook
4	Prints the current sheet, selection or entire workbook
5	Print Previews the current sheet
6	Starts the Spell Checker
7	Cuts a selection to Windows Clipboard
8	Copies a selection to Windows Clipboard
9	Pastes a selection from Windows Clipboard
10	Starts the Format Painter
11	Undoes the last action
12	Repeats the last action
13	Sums values in a range or above the cell pointer
14	Starts the Function WIzard
15	Sorts a range in ascending order
16	Sorts a range in descending order
17	Starts the Chart Wizard
18	Creates a text box
19	Turns on/off the Drawing toolbar
20	Zooms workbook view
21	Turns on/off the Tip Wizard toolbar
22	Offers context-sensitive help
	Format Toolbar
23	Changes the font
24	Changes font size
25	Turns on/off the boldface feature

26	Turns on/off the italicize feature
27	Turns on/off the underline feature
28	Left-aligns data in a cell
29	Center-aligns data in a cell
30	Right-aligns data in a cell
31	Center-aligns data across columns
32	Formats numbers (and formula results) in accounting currency-style format
33	Formats numbers (and formula results) in percenrage-style format
34	Format numbers (and formula results) in accounting comma-style format
35	Increases decimal place by one
36	Decreases decimal place by one
37	Places border(s) in cell or a range
38	Changes cell background color
39	Changes font color

Query and Pivot Toolbar

40	Starts the Pivot Table Wizard
41	Edits Pivot Table Field
42	Ungroups
43	Groups
44	Hides Detail
45	Shows Detail
46	Shows Pages
47	Refreshes data

Chart Toolbar

48	Changes chart type
49	Sets to default chart type
50	Offers Chart Wizard
51	Turns on/off horizontal gridlines
52	Edits legends

APPENDIX   SS293

Drawing Toolbar

53   Draws a line

54   Draws a rectangular shape

55   Draws an ellipse

56   Draws an arc

57   Draws free-form object

58   Creates a text box

59   Draws an arrow

60   Draws free hand

61   Draws a filled rectangle

62   Draws a filled ellipse

63   Draws a filled arc

64   Draws a filled free-form object

65   Creates a button

66   Selects an object

67   Moves selected object to the front

68   Moves selected object to the back

69   Groups objects

70   Ungroups objects

71   Reshapes objects

72   Creates a drop shadow

73   Creates a pattern

Tip Wizard Toolbar

74   Offers Tip Wizard box

75   Changes Tip

76   Helps

Stop Toolbar

77   Stops Macro Recording

Full Toolbar

78 Switches to/from full-screen display

Form Toolbar

79 Creates a label

80 Creates a group box

81 Creates a check box

82 Creates a list box

83 Edits a combination list

84 Creates a scroll bar

85 Controls properties

86 Switches toggle grid on/off

87 Edits box

88 Creates a button

89 Creates an option button

90 Creates a drop-down control

91 Edits a combination drop-down control

92 Creates a spinner control

93 Moves to object macro or creates a new one

94 Runs current dialog

Visual Basic

95 Inserts a new Visual Basic module sheet

96 Edits menus

97 Shows procedures, objects, methods, and properties

98 Runs a macro

99 Steps through macro command

100 Resumes macro after pause command is invoked

101 Stops macro recording or the execution of a running macro

102 Starts the macro recorder

103 Turns on/off breakpoint at insertion point

104	Shows the value of a mathematical expression
105	Executes next macro statement stepping into procedure
106	Executes next macro statement stepping over procedure

Auditing

107	Traces and displays cells that the current cell refers to (precedents)
108	Removes one level of tracer precedent arrows
109	Displays formulas that use the current cell (dependents)
110	Removes one level of tracer dependent arrows
111	Removes all tracer arrows
112	Traces and displays cells causing error in the selected cell
113	Creates and attaches a note to the current cell
114	Displays info window

Work Group

115	Searches for user-specified files
116	Attaches a routing slip to the current workbook
117	Sends electronic mail
118	Revises a read-only file to include the last update
119	Toggles a workbook from read-only to read-write status
120	Adds, displays, or edits scenarios

Microsoft Toolbar

121	Starts Microsoft Word
122	Starts Microsoft PowerPoint
123	Starts Microsoft Access
124	Starts Microsoft Fox Pro
125	Starts Microsoft Project
126	Starts Microsoft Schedule+
127	Starts Microsoft Mail

GLOSSARY

Absolute reference A cell address reference that always refers to the same cell regardless of where it is copied (SS116).

Alignment The position of data in a cell—either left, right, or centered (SS72).

ASCII (American Standard Code for Information Interchange) One of a few standard formats for transferring data among software programs (SS223).

Automatic recalculation A spreadsheet program feature that automatically recalculates formulas when values in related cells are changed (SS40).

Cell The intersection of a column and a row in a spreadsheet (SS13).

Cell address The column and row coordinates of a cell (SS13).

Cell pointer A rectangular box the size of one cell used in the worksheet to point to cells, thereby making them active (SS13).

Chart A pictorial representation of data (SS148).

Circular reference A condition that occurs in a spreadsheet when a cell formula refers to itself either directly or indirectly (SS118).

Closing This command (File menu) removes a workbook (and its window) from Excel's workspace (SS31).

Column A vertical group of contiguous single cells extending down the entire length of a spreadsheet (SS13).

Column (Bar) chart A chart that displays numeric data as a set of evenly spaced bars whose relative heights indicate values in the range being graphed (SS148).

Command buttons A series of pictures or symbols that represents a command.

They are mouse shortcuts to access a command. Clicking or double-clicking a command button invokes the command it represents. Many of Excel's command buttons are located on toolbars and are called toolbar buttons (SS12).

Constant values Data directly entered into a cell. They may be text or numeric values (SS34).

Copying Replicating the contents of a cell in another cell, while adjusting relative references to reflect the new position of the cell in the spreadsheet (SS82).

Criteria Cell entries placed in a criteria range that are used as tests by Excel to find matching records in a database (SS180).

Current cell The spreadsheet cell that will receive the next data entered or be affected by the next command (SS13).

Cut This command erases the contents of the source range and places it in Windows Clipboard for future pasting (SS88).

Database query A question asked of a database table (SS180).

Data distribution A frequency distribution, or count, of spreadsheet values that fall within specified numeric intervals (SS178).

Default changes Settings that Excel uses for the entire worksheet—Excel screens, or files (SS95).

Destination range The new location of a selection (data, chart, table, or object) in a copy or move operation, or the location of a new chart, table, object, or query result from data in a source range (SS83).

Drop-down box It first appears as a one-line rectangular box with a ⬇ but-

ton at its right side. Clicking that button opens the box to a drop-down list. Some drop-down boxes allow you to enter text into them (SS12).

Embedding This is used to copy objects from one application to another without changing the original (SS229).

Entry area Located on the right side of the formula bar, the entry area displays the content of the current cell. It can also be used to enter or edit data in the current cell (SS18).

Exporting The process of saving a file in a format other than the software's default format so that it can be read by other programs (SS222).

Fill handle A small square box at the bottom right corner of Excel's cell pointer, it can be used to quickly fill a range with a sequence of numbers or other data by mouse (SS173).

Filter A set of commands that can be used to find and extract records in a database to match a specific criteria (SS180).

Font A typeface style (SS70).

Format The way in which Excel displays a number in a cell (SS83).

Formula A value entry or function in a spreadsheet that directs the program to perform a mathematical operation on numeric constants and/or values in other cells (SS35).

Formula bar Located below Excel's toolbars, the formula bar displays information about data entered into a worksheet (SS12).

Freeze panes Rows or columns that are locked in place at the top or left of the spreadsheet (SS125).

SS296

GLOSSARY SS297

Function A predetermined formula built into the spreadsheet package (SS35).

IF function A logical spreadsheet function of the form IF (c,a,b) that returns one of two options (a or b) to the spreadsheet cell based on the truth of the stated condition (c) (SS166).

Importing The process of retrieving a file that was saved in a format other than the default format for the current program (SS222).

Line chart A chart that displays numerical data as a set of points along a line (SS160).

Linking This is an ongoing connection between the application that provides the object (known as the *source*) and the one that receives it (the *destination*). The destination is automatically updated (SS229).

Lookup tables A logical spreadsheet function of the form VLOOKUP (X, range, column-offset) or HLOOKUP (X, range, row-offset), which uses a two-dimensional table to return values that fall within set intervals (SS167).

Macro A set of mouse actions, keystrokes, or command instructions for automating an Excel task (SS192).

Mathematical operator A character used in a formula that tells the program to perform a certain calculation (SS38).

Mixed reference A cell address reference that is part absolute and part relative (SS118).

Module sheet A sheet used to record and edit macro commands (SS193).

Name box Located on the left side of the formula bar, the name box displays information about the current cell address (SS18).

New This command opens a new blank workbook in Excel's workspace (SS31).

Numeric value A value entry in a spreadsheet consisting of only numbers, which may be preceded by a negative symbol or include a decimal point (SS34).

Object A set of data (SS229).

OLE (Object Linking and Embedding) Describes the two options (see Linking and Embedding) used in transferring data from one application to another (SS229).

Open A command that can be used to open a file (SS32).

Panes A split in the worksheet screen, either horizontally or vertically, that allows you to view two parts of a worksheet at the same time (SS133).

Paste An Edit menu command that places the contents of the Windows Clipboard into a desired location (SS85).

Paste link An Edit menu Paste Special command that pastes a selection (data, chart, table, or object) from the Windows Clipboard into another worksheet or application's document with a link (SS208).

Pie chart A chart that displays data as parts of a whole circle, where each data "slice" corresponds to a percentage of the total (SS160).

Protection feature A feature that can be activated on a sheet or workbook. When on, only cells that were specified as unprotected prior to its activation will be available for change (SS221).

Pull-down menus Menus accessed from the menu bar that contain commands to activate Excel's features (SS12).

Range A rectangular grouping of one or more cells in a spreadsheet (SS44).

Range name A name used to identify a range on a worksheet (SS90).

Relative reference A cell address reference that, when copied, is automatically adjusted to reflect its new position in the worksheet (SS116).

Save This command will resave a workbook under its original name (SS29).

Save As A command that is used to save a new file or resave an existing file with confirmation (SS29).

Scroll A process by which a program automatically repositions the data on the screen to display the current work area (SS14).

Scroll bars Many appear on the right or bottom of any window or list box whose size does not permit its entire contents to be visible. They provide mouse access to scrolling (moving) through a window or list box's contents (SS15).

Selection handles Selection markers that appear on the borders of a chart (or its components), table, or object when selected (SS153).

Sheet A page in a workbook (SS11).

Shortcut menus Menus that are available by pointing to certain areas of the Excel screen and clicking the right mouse button (SS24).

Source range The selected data to be edited, copied, moved, or used to create a chart, table, or object or in a query operation (SS83).

Split A command (View menu) that splits a single worksheet into two panes (screens) either horizontally or vertically to allow you to view both parts at the same time (SS127).

Spreadsheet The electronic equivalent of multicolumned paper, used to display data in columnar (column and row) form (also known as a worksheet) (SS4).

Status bar Located at the bottom of the Excel window, the status bar displays information about the mode of operation and toggle switches (SS13).

Toolbar A series of command buttons and drop-down boxes usually located below Excel's menu bar that provide mouse shortcuts to Excel's features (SS12).

Transpose A range command that copies cell contents while changing the positions of columns and rows (SS89).

Undo A command that cancels the most recent operation (SS53).

Workbook A document file in Excel whose contents are viewed through a workbook window. It may contain a worksheet, chart or other information (SS11).

Worksheet The electronic equivalent of multicolumned paper, used to display data in columnar (column and row) form (also called a spreadsheet) (SS4).

INDEX

ABS(x), SS279
Absolute reference, SS116–SS118
Accounting number format, SS76–SS82
ACOS(x), SS279
ADDRESS, SS279
Adjust to option, SS131–SS132, SS270
Advanced Filter dialog box, SS184–SS185
Alignment, default, SS98–SS99
Alt key, SS245
American Standard Code for Information
        Interchange (ASCII), SS223
AND, SS279
AND connector, SS184
Apostrophe ('), SS35
Applications, sharing data among,
        SS222–SS231
Application window, SS5
AREAS, SS279
Arguments, SS121
Arrow keys, SS246
ASCII, SS223
ASCII file
    exporting to word processor, SS223–SS224
    importing, SS226–SS229
ASIN(x), SS279
ATAN(x), SS279
ATAN2(x,y), SS279
AutoFilter command, SS180
Autoformat dialog box, SS163
Automatic-number formatting, SS78
Automatic recalculation, SS40
AVERAGE, SS279

Background color, changing, SS111
Backspace key, SS246
Bar chart, SS148
Bin-array range, SS180
Bins, creating, SS178–SS179
Bold, SS110
Bold Italic, SS110
Brackets ( ), SS34
Buttons, assigning macros to, SS197–SS198,
        SS266

Cancel button, SS241
Canceling, SS254–SS255
Caps Lock key, SS246
CEILING, SS279
Cell, SS13
    aligning data within, SS73–SS74
    client, SS208
    copying, SS82–SS87
    editing, SS259
    entering data into, SS259
    erasing contents, SS257
    moving, SS87–SS89
    protecting, SS271–SS272
    replacing contents, SS51–SS53
    server, SS208, SS216
    transposing, SS89–SS90
CELL, SS279
Cell address, SS13
Cell pointer, SS13
    moving, SS241
Cell references, SS115–SS120
    absolute, SS116–SS118
    circular, SS118–SS120
    mixed, SS118
    relative, SS116–SS118
CHAR(x), SS279
Character color, changing, SS111
Chart command, SS148, SS287
Charting options, SS256–SS257
Charts, SS148–SS166
    adding subtitles, SS157–SS158
    changing subtypes, SS162–SS163
    copying, SS156
    creating, SS149–SS153, SS256
    editing parts, SS157–SS158
    gridlines, SS158
    line, SS160
    manipulating, SS154–SS156
    moving, SS155–SS156
    pie, SS160
        exploding, SS163–SS164
    printing, SS166
    resizing, SS154
    resizing components, SS165–SS166

SS298

resizing frame, SS155
selecting, SS244
types, SS158–SS163
Chart toolbar, SS287
Chart Type dialog box, SS160, SS162
ChartWizard, creating charts with,
    SS149–SS153
Check box, SS253
CHOOSE, SS279
Circular reference, SS118–SS120
CLEAN, SS280
Clear command, SS53
Clicking, SS8
Client cell, SS208
Clipboard, SS84, SS257, SS267
Close command, SS31
Closing
    Help window, SS19–SS20
    menu, SS20–SS21
    workbook, SS31
CODE, SS280
Color, changing, SS111
Column chart, SS148
    stacked, SS163
COLUMN, SS280
Columns, SS13
    center-aligning data across, SS74–SS75
    deleting, SS56, SS258
    hiding, SS104–SS105, SS262–SS263
    inserting, SS55–SS56, SS263
    selecting, SS244
    titles, repeating, SS132–SS133
    unhiding, SS105
COLUMNS, SS280
Column width
    adjusting, SS100–SS106
    changing, SS255
    changing in column range, SS104
    changing individual, SS101–SS103
    default changes, SS99–SS100
    dragging and dropping, SS102–SS103
    resetting to default width, SS103–SS104
Column Width dialog box, SS101–SS102
Command buttons, SS12, SS18–SS19, SS253
    operating, SS24–SS27
Commands
    AutoFilter, SS180
    Chart, SS148, SS287
    Clear, SS53
    Close, SS31
    Copy, SS83, SS84, SS86, SS88, SS115,
        SS257
    Cut, SS87–SS88, SS267
    Delete Sheet, SS258

Fill, SS172
Filter, SS180
Freeze Panes, SS125–SS127
Link Paste, SS263
macro, SS284–SS287
Maximize, SS203
Minimize, SS203
New, SS31
Open, SS32
Paste, SS85–SS88, SS115, SS216, SS257,
    SS267
Paste Link, SS208, SS216
Print, SS92
Print Preview, SS92
Protection Sheet, SS221
Restore, SS203
Rows, SS53
Save, SS29–SS30
Save As, SS29–SS30
Series, SS172
Show All, SS180
Split, SS127–SS129
Step Into, SS286
Step Over, SS286
Undo, SS53, SS86, SS219, SS278
using ranges in, SS70–SS95
Compressed printing, SS270
Conditional functions, SS166–SS171
Conditions, SS167
Constant values, SS34–SS35
    distinguishing from formulas, SS35–SS36
    entering, SS36–SS40
Control menu, SS23–SS24
Control-menu box, SS241
Copy command, SS83, SS84, SS86, SS88,
    SS115, SS257
Copy dialog box, SS147
Copying, SS82–SS83, SS257–SS258
    cells, SS82–SS87
    charts, SS156
    data between sheets, SS214–SS216
    data between workbooks, SS206–SS208
Copying and pasting, SS84
Copy to Another Location option,
    SS185–SS186
COS(x), SS280
COUNT, SS280
COUNTA, SS280
COUNTBLANK, SS280
Creating
    bins, SS178–SS179
    charts, SS149–SS153, SS256
    lines, SS112–SS113
    macros, SS193–SS194, SS264–SS265

new workbooks, SS31
outlines, SS114
page breaks, SS268–SS269
query tables, SS185–SS188
range names, SS91
worksheets, SS34–0043
Criteria, SS180
multiple, SS182–SS184
Ctrl key, SS246
Current cell, SS13
Custom AutoFilter dialog box, SS182
Cut command, SS87–SS88, SS267

Data
aligning, SS72–SS75, SS254
columnar, exporting, SS224–SS225
copying between sheets, SS214–SS216
copying between workbooks,
   SS206–SS208
entering, SS28–SS29
entering into cell, SS259
exporting from Microsoft Excel,
   SS223–SS226
filtering, SS180–SS182
formatting, SS260–SS261
importing into Microsoft Excel,
   SS226–SS229
management, SS171–SS192
manipulating between sheets,
   SS214–SS219
manipulating between workbooks,
   SS206–SS211
sharing among applications, SS222–SS231
sorting, SS174–SS178, SS276
transposing, SS278
Data-array range, SS179
Database ".TXT" file, importing, SS229
Database exporting
direct, SS225–SS226
general, SS224
Database functions, SS188–SS192
Database queries, SS180–SS188
Database tables, SS171, SS258
Data distribution, SS178–SS180,
   SS258–SS259
DATE, SS280
DATEVALUE, SS280
DAVERAGE, SS280
DAY, SS280
DCOUNT, SS280
DCOUNTA, SS280
DDB, SS280
Decimal places, changing, SS81–SS82
Default changes, SS95
Default drive, setting, SS27–SS28

Delete dialog box, SS56, SS258
Delete key, SS246–SS247
Delete Sheet command, SS258
Deleting
columns, SS56
range names, SS93–SS95
rows, SS56
Destination range, SS83
DFUNCTION, SS188
Dialog box, SS5, SS258
Advanced Filter, SS184–SS185
Autoformat, SS163
Chart Type, SS160, SS162
Column Width, SS101–SS102
Copy, SS147
Custom AutoFilter, SS182
Delete, SS56
features, SS29
Format Cells, SS72, SS73, SS78, SS79
FunctionWizard, SS190
Go To, SS91, SS92
Gridlines, SS158
Insert, SS55
Macro, SS195, SS266
Macro Options, SS195, SS196, SS265
Open File, SS32
operations, SS252–SS254
Options, SS71
Page Setup, SS130–SS131, SS133
parts, SS253
Print, SS130
Print Preview, SS130
Record New Macro, SS194, SS195, SS265
Save As, SS27–SS28
Series, SS172
Sort, SS174, SS177
Standard Width, SS99, SS100
Style, SS96, SS97
Direct conversion, SS222
Directories, changing, SS255–SS256
Disk drive, using, SS5
Display versus contents, SS81, SS82
DMAX, SS280
DMIN, SS280
Document window, SS5
DOLLAR, SS280
Double-clicking, SS8
Dragging, selecting range by, SS47
Dragging and dropping, SS8, SS243
column width, SS102–SS103
Drop-down box, SS12, SS253
Drop-down button, SS253
Drop-down list, SS253
Drop shadow, SS114
DSTDEVP, SS280

INDEX **SS301**

DSUM, SS280
DVAR, SS281

Editing
    cell data, SS259
    chart parts, SS157–SS158
    macros, SS199
    worksheets, SS51–SS56
Ellipsis (...), SS22
Embedding, SS229
    objects, SS231
End key, SS247
Enter box button, SS25
Enter button, SS241
Entering, constant values and formulas,
    SS36–SS40
Enter key, SS247
Entry area, SS18
Equal sign (=), SS35
Esc key, SS247
EVEN, SS281
EXACT, SS281
Excel. *See* Microsoft Excel
Exiting, Microsoft Excel, SS259–SS260
EXP(x), SS281
Exporting, SS222–SS223
    columnar data, SS224–SS225
    to database, SS224
    data from Microsoft Excel, SS223–SS226
    direct database, SS225–SS226

F1 key, SS247
FALSE, SS281
Field names, SS172
Fields, SS171
File Manager, SS146
Files
    linking, SS208–SS211
    opening, SS268
Fill command, SS172
Fill handle, SS173–SS174
Fill submenu, SS172–SS173
Filter commands, SS180
Filtering
    advanced, SS184–SS185
    data, SS180–SS182
    records, SS181, SS260
FIND, SS281
Fit to option, SS131–SS132, SS270
Font, SS107
    changing, SS260
Font face, changing, SS107–SS109
Font size, changing, SS109–SS110
Font style, changing, SS110–SS111
Font tab, SS110

Format. *See also* Number format
    default, SS96–SS98
Format Cells dialog box, SS72, SS73, SS78,
    SS79
Format codes, SS76
Formatting data, SS260–SS261
Format toolbar, SS25
Formula bar, SS12, SS18–SS19
Formulas, SS35
    distinguishing constant values from,
    SS35–SS36
    entering, SS38–SS40
    using, SS74
Freeze Panes command, SS125–SS127
FREQUENCY, SS281
Frequency distribution, SS178
Function keys, SS8, SS247, SS248–SS250
Functions, SS35, SS120–SS125,
    SS278–SS283
    conditional, SS166–SS171
    database, SS188–SS192
    HLOOKUP, SS167, SS281
    IF, SS166–SS167, SS168, SS169
    pointing to range for, SS46
    SUM, SS40
    typing range for, SS44–SS46
    VLOOKUP, SS167–SS171
Function Wizard, SS261–SS262, SS279
    using, SS121–SS125
Function Wizard button, SS241
Function Wizard dialog box, SS190
FV, SS281

General format, SS76
Go To dialog box, SS91, SS92
Graphical user interface (GUI), SS4
Gridlines, SS158
Gridlines dialog box, SS158
Group box, SS253
GUI. *See* Graphical user interface

Hard-disk drive, using, SS5
Header/footer tab, SS131
Headers/footers, SS271
Help feature, SS19–SS20, SS262
Hiding
    columns, SS104–SS105, SS262–SS263
    sheets, SS262–SS263
Hierarchy of operations, SS42
HLOOKUP function, SS167, SS281
Home key, SS247
HOUR, SS281

Icons, SS4
    program-item, SS9

IF, SS281
IF function, SS166–SS167, SS168, SS169
Importing, SS222–SS223
INDEX, SS281
Information box, SS253
Information retrieval, SS180–SS188
Insert dialog box, SS55
Inserting
    columns, SS55–SS56, SS263
    rows, SS53–SS55, SS263
    sheets, SS263
Insertion point, SS18
Insert key, SS247
INT(x), SS281
IRR, SS281
ISERR, SS281
ISNA(x), SS281
ISNUMBER(x), SS281
Italic, SS110

Keyboard
    scrolling by, SS14–SS15
    using, SS8
Keyboard approach, SS4
    activating protection feature, SS221–SS222
    adding macros, SS198–SS199
    advanced filtering, SS184–SS185
    aligning data, SS254
    aligning data within cell, SS73–SS74
    arranging workbook windows, SS201
    assigning macros to shorcut keys, SS265
    assigning macros to shortcut keys, SS196
    assigning macros to Tools menu,
        SS196–SS197, SS265–SS266
    canceling, SS254–SS255
    center-aligning data across columns, SS75
    changing background color, SS111
    changing character color, SS111
    changing chart subtype, SS162–SS163
    changing chart type, SS160–SS162
    changing column width, SS255
    changing default alignment, SS98–SS99
    changing default column width, SS99
    changing default format, SS97–SS98
    changing directories, SS255–SS256
    changing font and attributes, SS260
    changing font face, SS108–SS109
    changing font size, SS110
    changing font style, SS110
    changing individual column width, SS102
    changing line color, SS113
    changing number formats, SS78–SS79
    changing width in column range, SS104
    charting options, SS256–SS257
    clearing cell contents, SS257

closing workbook, SS31, SS36
compressed printing, SS270
copying data between sheets,
    SS215–SS216
copying data between workbooks,
    SS206–SS208
copying one cell, SS84–SS86
copying range of cells, SS86
copying selections, SS257–SS258
creating charts, SS150–SS153, SS256
creating lines, SS113
creating macros, SS264–SS265
creating new workbook, SS31
creating page breaks, SS269
creating query tables, SS186–SS187,
    SS272
creating range names, SS91
cutting and pasting, SS88–SS89
deleting, SS258
deleting range names, SS93–SS95
deleting rows or columns, SS56
direct database exporting, SS226
editing cell data, SS259
entering constant values and formulas,
    SS36
entering data into cell, SS259
entering text constant values, SS37
exiting Microsoft Excel, SS33,
    SS259–SS260
exiting Microsoft Windows, SS33
exploding pie chart, SS163–SS164
exporting ASCII file to word processor,
    SS223–SS224
exporting columnar data, SS224–SS225
filtering data, SS180–SS182
filtering records, SS260
fixing circular references, SS120
formatting data, SS260–SS261
freezing panes, SS126, SS261
functions, SS278–SS279
headers/footers, SS271
hiding columns, SS105
hiding columns and sheets, SS263
identifying menu item functions, SS21
importing ASCII files, SS226–SS229
inserting columns, SS55–SS56
inserting rows, SS54–SS55
inserting rows, columns, or sheets, SS263
linking files, SS208–SS211
linking selections, SS263–SS264
linking sheets, SS216–SS218
menu indicators, SS22–SS23
moving around worksheet, SS13
moving selection, SS267–SS268
multiple criteria search, SS183

naming sheet tabs, SS212
opening/closing Help window, SS19–SS20
opening/closing menus, SS20–SS21
opening files, SS268
passwords, SS269
performing sort, SS175–SS176
planning macros, SS193
pointing to range for function, SS46
printing, SS269
printing charts, SS166
printing options, SS270
printing to printer, SS49
printing to screen, SS48
printing selected range, SS50
printing titles, SS270
print previewing, SS269
protecting cells, SS271–SS272
ranges, SS273
recording macros, SS193–SS194
removing the split, SS129
repeating characters, SS273–SS274
repeating column or row titles, SS132
replacing cell contents, SS52–SS53
resetting column width to default width, SS104
resizing workbook window, SS17, SS18
resizing worksheet window, SS204–SS206
reviewing or modifying range names, SS91
running macros, SS194–SS195, SS267
saving workbooks, SS29–SS30, SS274
scaling page data, SS131–SS132
selecting, SS274
selecting menu item, SS21
selecting workbook from list, SS33
setting default drive, SS27–SS28
setting page breaks, SS130
setting panes, SS128
setting unprotected range, SS220
sorting data, SS276
sorting with two keys, SS176–SS177
splitting views, SS276–SS277
starting Microsoft Excel, SS9–SS11, SS277
switching panes, SS129
switching between sheets, SS211–SS212
switching between windows, SS200
table lookups, SS277–SS278
transition features, SS71–SS72
transposing cells, SS89
transposing data, SS278
typing workbook name, SS32
Undo command, SS278
unfreezing panes, SS127
unhiding columns, SS105
using data functions, SS190–SS191
using File Manager, SS146–SS148

using Fill submenu, SS172–SS173
using Function Wizard, SS123–125, SS261–SS262
using Help feature, SS262
using print options, SS133
using range names, SS92–SS93
using Step feature, SS286–SS287
using VLOOKUP, SS169
writing macros, SS284–SS286
Keys, SS245–SS252
sorting, SS174–SS178

LEFT, SS281
LEN, SS281
Line chart, SS160
Lines
changing color, SS113–SS114
creating, SS112–SS113
Linking, SS229–SS230, SS263–SS264
files, SS208–SS211
formulas, SS208
objects, SS230–SS231
sheets, SS216–SS219
Link Paste command, SS263
List box, SS253
LN(x), SS281
LOG(x), SS282
Lookup tables, SS167–SS171
Lotus 1–2-3, SS9, SS71
LOWER, SS282

Macro commands, SS284–SS287
Macro dialog box, SS195, SS266
Macro Options dialog box, SS195, SS196, SS265
Macros, SS192–SS199
adding, SS198–SS199
assigning, SS195–SS198, SS265–SS266
creating, SS193–SS194, SS264–SS265
editing, SS199
one-letter, SS195, SS265
running, SS194–SS195, SS266–SS267
Step feature, SS286–SS287
writing, SS284–SS286
Margin tab, SS131
Mathematical operators, SS38–SS40, SS42–SS43
MAX, SS282
Maximize button, SS25, SS242
Maximize command, SS203
Maximized window, SS25
Maximizing, SS17
Menu, SS284, SS285
control, SS23–SS24
opening and closing, SS20–SS21

operating, SS20–SS24
pull-down, SS12, SS21
shortcut, SS24, SS242, SS275
Menu bar, SS12, SS243
selections, SS22
using, SS20–SS22
Menu commands, selecting range for, SS46–SS47
Menu indicators, SS22–SS23
Menu item
identifying function, SS21
selecting, SS21
Microsoft Excel
exiting, SS33, SS259–SS260
exporting data from, SS223–SS226
importing data into, SS226–SS229
keys, SS245–SS252
menu system, SS284, SS285
starting, SS9–SS11, SS277
window, SS10, SS12–SS13
MID, SS282
MIN, SS282
Minimize button, SS25, SS242
Minimize command, SS203
MINUTE, SS282
Mixed reference, SS118
MOD(x,y), SS282
Module sheet, SS193, SS194, SS264, SS284
MONTH, SS282
Mouse
operations, SS241–SS245
scrolling by, SS15–SS16
symbols and actions, SS7, SS242
using, SS6–SS8
Mouse approach, SS4
activating protection feature, SS221–SS222
adding macros, SS198–SS199
advanced filtering, SS184–SS185
aligning data, SS254
aligning data within cell, SS73–SS74
arranging workbook windows, SS201
assigning macros to shortcut keys, SS196, SS265
assigning macros to Tools menu, SS196–SS197, SS265–SS266
canceling, SS254–SS255
center-aligning data across columns, SS75
changing background color, SS111
changing character color, SS111
changing chart subtypes, SS162–SS163
changing chart types, SS160–SS162
changing column width, SS255
changing default alignment, SS98–SS99
changing default column width, SS99
changing default format, SS97–SS98

changing directories, SS255–SS256
changing font and attributes, SS260
changing font face, SS108–SS109
changing font size, SS110
changing font style, SS110
changing individual column width, SS102
changing line color, SS113
changing number formats, SS78–SS79
changing width in column range, SS104
charting options, SS256–SS257
clearing cell contents, SS257
closing workbook, SS31, SS36
compressed printing, SS270
copying data between sheets, SS215–SS216
copying data between workbooks, SS206–SS208
copying one cell, SS84–SS86
copying range of cells, SS86
copying selections, SS257–SS258
creating charts, SS150–SS153, SS256
creating lines, SS113
creating macros, SS264–SS265
creating new workbooks, SS31
creating page breaks, SS269
creating query tables, SS186–SS187, SS272
creating range names, SS91
cutting and pasting, SS88–SS89
deleting, SS258
deleting range names, SS93–SS95
deleting rows or columns, SS56
direct database exporting, SS226
editing cell data, SS259
entering constant values and formulas, SS36
entering data into cell, SS259
entering text constant values, SS37
exiting Microsoft Excel, SS33, SS259–SS260
exiting Microsoft Windows, SS33
exploding pie chart, SS163–SS164
exporting ASCII file to word processor, SS223–SS224
exporting columnar data, SS224–SS225
filtering data, SS180–SS182
filtering records, SS260
fixing circular references, SS120
formatting data, SS260–SS261
freezing panes, SS126, SS261
functions, SS278–SS279
headers/footers, SS271
hiding columns, SS105
hiding columns and sheets, SS263
identifying menu item functions, SS21

INDEX   SS305

importing ASCII files, SS226–SS229
inserting columns, SS55–SS56
inserting rows, SS54–SS55
inserting rows, columns, or sheets, SS263
linking files, SS208–SS211
linking selections, SS263–SS264
linking sheets, SS216–SS218
menu indicators, SS22–SS23
moving around worksheet, SS13
moving selection, SS267–SS268
multiple criteria search, SS183
naming sheet tabs, SS212
opening/closing Help window, SS19–SS20
opening/closing menus, SS20–SS21
opening files, SS268
passwords, SS269
performing sort, SS175–SS176
planning macros, SS193
pointing to range for function, SS46
printing, SS269
printing charts, SS166
printing options, SS270
printing to printer, SS49
printing to screen, SS48
printing selected range, SS50
printing titles, SS270
print previewing, SS269
protecting cells, SS271–SS272
ranges, SS273
recording macros, SS193–SS194
removing the split, SS129
repeating characters, SS273–SS274
repeating column or row titles, SS132
replacing cell contents, SS52–SS53
resetting column width to default width, SS104
resizing workbook window, SS17, SS18
resizing worksheet window, SS204–SS206
reviewing or modifying range names, SS91
running macros, SS194–SS195, SS267
saving workbooks, SS29–SS30, SS274
scaling page data, SS131–SS132
selecting, SS274
selecting menu items, SS21
selecting workbook from list, SS33
setting default drive, SS27–SS28
setting page breaks, SS130
setting panes, SS128
setting unprotected range, SS220
sorting data, SS276
sorting with two keys, SS176–SS177
splitting views, SS276–SS277
starting Microsoft Excel, SS9–SS11, SS277
switching between sheets, SS211–SS212
switching between windows, SS200

switching panes, SS129
table lookups, SS277–SS278
transition features, SS71–SS72
transposing cells, SS89
transposing data, SS278
typing workbook name, SS32
Undo command, SS278
unfreezing panes, SS127
unhiding columns, SS105
using data functions, SS190–SS191
using File Manager, SS146–SS148
using Fill submenu, SS172–SS173
using Function Wizard, SS123–125, SS261–SS262
using Help feature, SS262
using print options, SS133
using range names, SS92–SS93
using Step feature, SS286–SS287
using VLOOKUP, SS169
writing macros, SS284–SS286
Mouse pointer, SS6–SS7
Moving, cells, SS87–SS89
Multiple criteria search, SS182–SS184

N, SS282
NA, SS282
Name box, SS18
Network, using, SS5
New command, SS31
NOW, SS282
NPV, SS282
Number format
    accounting, SS76–SS82
    adjusting, SS75–SS82
    changing, SS80
    general, SS76
Number tab, SS79, SS82
Numeric values, SS34
    entering, SS38
Numlock key, SS247

Object, SS229
    embedding, SS231
    linking, SS230–SS231
    selecting, SS244
Object linking and embedding (OLE), SS229–SS230
Offset, SS189
OLE. *See* Object linking and embedding
One-letter macros, SS195, SS265
Open command, SS32
Open File dialog box, SS32
Opening
    files, SS268
    Help window, SS19–SS20

menu, SS20–SS21
workbook, SS32–SS33
Operating menus, SS20–SS24
Option button, SS254
Options dialog box, SS71
OR connector, SS184
Outline, creating, SS114

Page breaks, SS129–SS130, SS268–SS269
Page data, scaling, SS131–SS132
Page Down key, SS248
Page Setup dialog box, SS130–SS131, SS133
Page Setup options, SS130–SS134
Page tab, SS130, SS131
Page Up key, SS248
Panes
    freezing, SS125–SS127, SS261
    setting, SS127–SS129
    switching, SS129
    unfreezing, SS127
Passwords, SS269
Paste command, SS85–SS88, SS115, SS216,
    SS257, SS267
Paste Link command, SS208, SS216
PI, SS282
Pie chart, SS160
    exploding, SS163–SS164
Plus (+) operator, SS38
PMT, SS282
Pointer, SS13
Pointer movement keys, SS15
Print command, SS92
Print dialog box, SS130
Printer, printing to, SS48–SS49
Printing, SS129–SS134, SS269
    charts, SS166
    compressed, SS270
    options, SS270
    titles, SS270
    worksheet, SS48–SS51
Print Preview command, SS92
Print Preview dialog box, SS130
Print previewing, SS269
Print Preview window, SS49
Print Screen key, SS248
Print titles, SS132–SS133
Program groups, SS6
Program-item icons, SS9
Program-items, SS6
Program Manager, SS6
PROPER, SS282
Protection feature, SS221, SS271–SS272
    activating, SS221–SS222
Protection Sheet command, SS221
Protection tab, SS220, SS222

Pull-down menu, SS12, SS21
PV, SS282

Query tables, creating, SS185–SS188, SS272

RAND, SS282
Range, SS43–SS48, SS272–273
    bin-array, SS180
    data-array, SS179
    destination, SS83
    multiple, selecting, SS244
    pointing to for a function, SS46
    printing selected, SS50–SS51
    selecting, SS244
    selecting by dragging, SS47
    selecting for toolbar or menu commands,
        SS46–SS47
    selecting by using shift key, SS47
    source, SS83
    typing for function, SS44–SS46
    unprotected, setting, SS220–SS221
    using in commands, SS70–SS95
Range names, SS90–SS95
    creating, SS91
    deleting, SS93–SS95
    reviewing or modifying, SS91
    using, SS92–SS93
RATE, SS282
Recalculation feature, SS40–SS42
Record New Macro dialog box, SS194,
    SS195, SS265
Records, SS171
    filtering, SS181, SS260
Relative reference, SS116–SS118
Repeat characters, SS273–SS274
REPLACE, SS282
Resizing buttons, SS25, SS242–SS243
Restore button, SS25, SS242
Restore command, SS203
RIGHT, SS283
ROUND, SS283
Row
    deleting, SS56, SS258
    inserting, SS53–SS55, SS263
    selecting, SS244
    titles, repeating, SS132–SS133
ROWS, SS283
Rows command, SS53

Save As command, SS29–SS30
Save As dialog box, SS27–SS28
Save command, SS29–SS30
Saving, workbooks, SS29–SS30, SS274
Scaling, page data, SS131–SS132
Screen, printing to, SS48

INDEX   SS307

Scroll bar, SS15
Scrolling, SS243
    by keyboard, SS14–SS15
    by mouse, SS15–SS16
    sheet-tab, SS213–SS214
Scrolling buttons, SS245
SECOND, SS283
Selecting, SS274
    menu item, SS21
    range for toolbar or menu commands,
        SS46–SS47
Selection handles, SS153
Series command, SS172
Series dialog box, SS172
Server cells, SS208, SS216
Sheets, SS11
    deleting, SS258
    hiding, SS262–SS263
    inserting, SS263
    linking, SS216–SS219
    manipulating data between, SS214–SS219
    switching between, SS211–SS212
    using multiple, SS211–SS219
Sheet tabs, SS18, SS131, SS132, SS244,
        SS270, SS271
    naming, SS212
    renaming, SS213
    scrolling, SS213–SS214
    using, SS211–SS214
Shift key, SS248
    selecting range using, SS47
Shortcut keys, SS4, SS8
    assigning macros to, SS195–SS196, SS265
Shortcut menus, SS24, SS242, SS275
Show All command, SS180
SIN(x), SS283
SLN, SS283
Sort dialog box, SS174, SS177
Sorting, data, SS174–SS178, SS276
Source range, SS83
Split bar, SS18
Split command, SS127–SS129
Splitting, SS127–SS129, SS244,
        SS276–SS277
Spreadsheet, SS4
    entering data, SS28–SS29
    managing large, SS125–SS129
    protecting, SS219–SS222
    recalculation feature, SS40–SS42
SQRT(x), SS283
Stacked column chart, SS163
Standard toolbar, SS25
Standard Width dialog box, SS99, SS100
Status bar, SS13, SS244
STDEVP, SS283

Step feature, SS286–SS287
Step Into command, SS286
Step Over command, SS286
Style dialog box, SS96, SS97
SUM function, SS40, SS283
SYD, SS283

T, SS283
Tab, SS254
Tab key, SS248
Table lookups, SS277–SS278
Tables
    database, SS171, SS258
    lookup, SS167–SS171
    query, SS185–SS188, SS272
Tab-scroll buttons, SS18, SS211, SS213
Tab-split bar, SS211
TAN(x), SS283
Text box, SS254
Text constant values, entering, SS36–SS37
Text Import Wizard, SS227–SS228
TIME, SS283
TIMEVALUE, SS283
Title bar, SS12, SS245
Titles, printing, SS270
Toolbar buttons, SS275
    using, SS26–SS27
Toolbar commands, selecting range for,
        SS46–SS47
Toolbars, SS12, SS25–SS27, SS287–SS293
    identifying function, SS25–SS26
Tools menu, assigning macros to,
        SS196–SS197, SS265–SS266
Transition tab, SS71
Transposing
    cells, SS89–SS90
    data, SS278
Triangle pointer, SS22
TRIM, SS283
TRUE, SS283

Undo command, SS53, SS86, SS219, SS278
Unhiding, columns, SS105
UPPER, SS283

VALUE, SS283
Values
    constant, SS34–SS35
        distinguishing from formulas,
            SS35–SS36
        entering, SS36–SS40
    numeric, SS34
        entering, SS38
VAR, SS283
VisiCalc, SS4

SS

Visual Basic, SS194, SS199, SS264, SS284, SS286
VLOOKUP function, SS167–SS171, SS283

Window. *See also* Workbook window
  maximized, SS25
  minimized, SS25
  Print Preview, SS49
Windows, SS5, SS10, SS12–SS13
  exiting, SS33
  starting, SS5–SS6
Word processor, exporting ASCII file to, SS223–SS224
Workbooks, SS11
  closing, SS31
  creating new, SS31
  manipulating data between, SS206–SS211
  opening, SS32–SS33
  saving, SS29–SS30, SS274
  selecting from list, SS32–SS33
  typing name, SS32
  using multiple, SS200–SS211
Workbook window, SS11, SS13–SS20
  arranging, SS200–SS203

features, SS16–SS18
resizing, SS203–SS206
switching between, SS200
Worksheet, SS4, SS13
  adding lines, SS112–SS114
  adjusting number format, SS75–SS82
  aligning data, SS72–SS75
  changing color, SS111
  changing font, SS107–SS111
  creating, SS34–0043
  editing, SS51–SS56
  entering constant values and formulas, SS36–SS40
  moving around, SS13
  printing, SS48–SS51
  resetting defaults, SS95–SS100
  selecting, SS244
Worksheet data, transforming into chart display, SS149
Workspace, SS13
WYSIWYG, SS4

YEAR, SS283